The Althouse Press

Majhanovich / *Re-Forming Teacher Education*

Re-Forming Teacher Education:
Problems and Prospects

Edited by
Suzanne Majhanovich

THE ALTHOUSE PRESS

First published in Canada in 1995 by
THE ALTHOUSE PRESS
Dean: A. Pearson
Director of Publications: J.T. Sanders
Faculty of Education, The University of Western Ontario
1137 Western Road, London, Ontario, Canada N6G 1G7

Editorial Assistants: K. Butson, T. Johnston
Cover Design: The Aylmer Express

Canadian Cataloguing in Publication Data

Re-forming teacher education

Selection of rev. papers presented at the conference entitled Continuity and
change in teacher education, held at the Faculty of Education, University of
Western Ontario, Oct. 30-No. 1, 1991.
Includes bibliographical references.
ISBN 0-920354-37-8

1. Teachers - Traning of - Congresses.
I. Majhanovich, Suzanne, 1943-

LB1707.R44 1995   370'.71   C95-932223-X

Printed and bound in Canada by The Aylmer Express Limited, 390 Talbot Street
East, Aylmer, Ontario, Canada N5H 1J5

CONTENTS

Introduction

Recently, the Faculty of Education at the University of Western Ontario hosted a conference on teacher education. The conference, entitled "Continuity and Change in Teacher Education" was the culmination of a two-year project on teacher development that the Faculty had undertaken with the support of a grant from the Ontario Ministry of Colleges and Universities. Presenters were invited to address four broad themes related to current issues in teacher education: its curriculum, its history and politics, research perspectives, and alternative models of delivery. Speakers included some of the foremost teacher educators from across Canada and the United States. The Ontario Ministry of Education, teacher federations, and local teachers joined University of Western Ontario faculty members as presenters and participants.

The papers in this volume represent a selection drawn from the plenary and concurrent session addresses edited and adapted for this collection. They have been grouped into four areas: traditions and conceptions of teacher education, and their implications for current or proposed programmes; policies that affect teacher education; alternative approaches to teacher education research; and, innovative approaches to teacher education involving collaboration between the university and the field.

The first four chapters focus on the history and curriculum of teacher education programmes. Kenneth Zeichner's article, "Traditions of Practice in U.S. Preservice Teacher Education Programmes," outlines and analyses four traditions of practice in U.S. teacher education: the academic tradition, the social efficiency tradition, the developmentalist tradition, and the social reconstructionist tradition. He argues that individual preservice teacher education programmes in the United States cannot be seen to represent a single tradition but will reflect with varying degrees of emphasis all four, probably favouring one or two. He offers as an example the model of elementary teacher education at the University of Wisconsin wherein the developmentalist and social reconstructionist conceptions provide a major focus for the programme, but academic and social efficiency elements are included where required. Although drawn from American teacher education traditions and experience, his analysis of the issues is highly relevant for teacher educators in Canada and elsewhere as they grapple with constructing and reforming their own programmes.

In "Teachers as Models of Educated Persons," Nel Noddings reviews traditional justifications for the inclusion of various elements in the secondary school curriculum, and finds all of them insufficient to some degree. Her vision of a meaningful high school curriculum involves a combination of traditional subjects and disciplines central to the students' interests combined with a study of universal, integrated areas organized around "themes of care." She is not referring to integration in a superficial sense, but rather interdisciplinary studies that require a depth of understanding of a variety of content areas. In addressing the type of education prospective teachers should undergo to prepare them for the challenge that this curriculum change would bring, she argues that they, as educated persons, should be reasonably well versed in any subject that high school students might be required to take. They would also need to possess a great deal of general knowledge on significant issues and be open-minded and flexible enough to be able to weigh and debate them. In effect, the educated person (teacher) begins with a depth of knowledge and understanding in an area and then expands its boundaries to explore how it connects with and overflows into other areas of concern. Her vision of the new curriculum and the teacher education needed to prepare those who will be involved in it recognizes that change will not come about by disparaging what is contained currently in the curriculum even if one finds it unsatisfactory. Rather, change can come by valuing and understanding what is there and enlarging it to encompass broader human concerns and realities.

David Labaree offers a sobering view of teacher education in "An Unlovely Legacy: The Disabling Impact of the Market on American Teacher Education." Conventional wisdom regarding teacher education, he says, has found it to be lacking in academic rigour and ineffectual from a pedagogical point of view. Without trying to deny these problems, he nevertheless traces their origins to the market influence which limits the purpose of schooling to social efficiency and social mobility. Teacher education, he argues, has been subject to the same pressures. Unfortunately, the result has been a conflict between teacher education organized on the basis of quantity, quality, and efficiency, with quantity and efficiency predominating, and pressure to make teacher education institutions providers of liberal education for upwardly mobile groups at the expense of pedagogical learning and content.

A recent attempt promoted by the Holmes Group to professionalize teacher education may counteract some of the nefarious influence the marketplace has had on teacher education. Nevertheless, Labaree argues that this incentive stems mainly from a need to redress status problems that teacher educators have always felt in the university community. In his opinion, teacher education should strive for a more political and crucial goal, namely, preparing teachers to support democratic schooling and help students to function effectively and independently in a democratic society. Perhaps the programme described by Zeichner would meet some of his concerns.

The fourth article of this collection, "Crafting the Curriculum of Teacher Education" by Peter Grimmett, argues for the inclusion of craft knowledge as part of a teacher education programme. He contends that in this age of cost-cutting, governments for economic and political reasons might move to replace university-based teacher education with an exclusively field-based model, and he provides several examples where this has already happened. Echoing David Labaree's concern about the low esteem in which teacher education programmes are generally held, Grimmett feels that they are vulnerable unless a strong argument could be made to link the vital role he feels faculties of education must play in articulating teachers' craft knowledge. This he believes can best be accomplished in collaboration with the field.

He follows with different perceptions of "craft knowledge" held by educators who identify with conservative or progressive and radical patterns of thinking, and then moves to his own definition of craft know-how in teaching. Clearly, he is convinced of the power, educational and political, that teachers versed in craft knowledge can wield. He concludes with examples from the teacher education programme he is involved in to illustrate just how craft knowledge can be integrated into the teacher education curriculum.

The next two chapters deal with government policies and how they impact on teacher education. Donald Maudsley in his article "The Role of Teacher Education in the Restructuring of Education in Ontario" outlines the Government of Ontario's restructuring initiatives, first announced in the Throne Speech of April 1989. He reviews events and studies that led up to the enunciation of a policy designed to reform schooling and teacher education, and traces the subsequent developments with special emphasis on the implications for teacher education. He identifies six principles regarding implementation of changes to teacher education and five barriers that act to undermine or retard change. He describes his view of the role of teacher education in the general restructuring and suggests some strategies for implementation. It is noteworthy that in the interim period since the 1991 conference when Maudsley pointed out elements that acted as obstacles to restructuring, only the problem of multiple governance of schooling and teacher education has been addressed somewhat by a streamlining of agencies, probably more as a result of economic considerations than any real attempt to facilitate mandated change.

In "The Politics of Teacher Education in British Columbia," Nancy Sheehan provides another perspective of a similar issue. It is instructive to follow her review of the procedures and events that led in British Columbia to the development of the British Columbia College of Teachers (BCCT), since some of the restructuring initiatives in Ontario were modeled on policies that had already been implemented in British Columbia. This was especially true, however, with regard to changes in the school curriculum in, for example, the Ontario Transition Years document which parallels the British Columbia Curriculum 2000 document in several ways. In May of 1993, the Ontario Government by an order in council set up the Royal Commission on Learning to examine all aspects of education in Ontario. The four-volume report, *For the Love of Learning*, was completed by December, 1994 and released to the public early in 1995. An entire volume is devoted to teachers and teacher education. As expected, the commissioners recommended the creation of an Ontario College of Teachers as the certification body. No doubt those responsible for the implementation of the recommendations relating to teacher education will look to the case of British Columbia. Nancy Sheehan describes the problems the BCCT has faced during its evolution very succinctly as well as its positive and negative features. Ultimately, she is optimistic about the future of teacher education in British Columbia. Let us hope for positive outcomes in Ontario teacher education as well.

The third section provides some insights into innovative approaches to research on teacher education and teachers themselves. Two of the papers argue for a more collaborative approach to research involving teachers and teaching practice; the third, while operating from a more traditional scientific type of inquiry, nevertheless resonates with the other two in its authors' concern for providing preservice teachers with a safe holding environment in which they can experiment and develop strategies to deal with the large human and social problems teachers have to face routinely.

In the first paper, "The Devil's Bargain: Educational Research and the Teacher," Ivor Goodson asks the provocative question: "Why is it that so much educational research has tended to be manifestly irrelevant to the teacher?" His response is that schools of education entered into a "devil's bargain" when they entered the university milieu; once there, they had to embrace more traditional forms of university scholarship at the expense of what should be their real concern, namely, the practice of schooling. The fact that even the emphasis on research methods more in line with traditional university social science approaches still did not bring the schools of education esteem in the eyes of their university colleagues, he contends, places education faculties at risk—isolated from their true centre of study (schools and school practice), and lacking respect in their university environment. In this regard, Goodson echoes warnings voiced by Labaree and Grimmett in their papers.

Goodson wishes to reconceptualize educational research and refocus it on practitioners and practice. He speaks to the importance of action research, but is wary of advocating that university researchers might simply go out to examine practice and impose their agendas on unwilling practitioners. He believes that research should be more collaborative, and a sound starting point, he argues, would be to study teachers' lives. He buttresses his arguments for this approach to educational research both by anecdotal accounts and with seven arguments for employing data on teachers' lives. From that perspective, researchers can best have access to what teachers do—their practice, and they will be able to gain information about it in a collaborative way.

The following article by Ardra Cole and Gary Knowles explores further how the researcher can enter into truly collaborative research. Their paper, "Teacher Development Partnership Research: A Focus on Methods and Issues," addresses this alternative research approach and offers some examples from their own work to illustrate how they have come to engage in collaborative research. Their paper tries to come to grips with a sensitive issue in much classroom research: its hierarchical nature, and the relative positions of power of the players which often results in a situation where the researcher can pursue a chosen agenda while the subject, the classroom teacher, although providing consent, actually has little or no control over the process and ultimate interpretations of the results.

Particularly helpful is their clarification of the difference between cooperative and collaborative research, the former exemplified by informed consent of the subjects but no real voice in the research agenda, and the latter as a process of ongoing negotiation. To assist in the explication of this very delicate, negotiated approach to research, they provide examples of their own research with teachers, a matrix revealing the phases of research activities and another representing the phases and scope of the issues in teacher development partnership research including technical, personnel, procedural, ethical, political, and educational issues. Their concern with the power structure and with the relationships between the researcher and the researched is expressed in other papers in this collection, particularly those dealing with alternative approaches to teacher education (Chapters 10, 11, and 12), and so this article is particularly helpful in setting the context of others that address the issue.

In the last paper in this section, "Teacher Education Problem Solving Within a 'Holding Environment'," Anne Cummings and Ernest T. Hallberg present a research study designed to explore how student teachers go about solving typical problems they might encounter during their preservice teacher education. They view teacher education ideally as a "holding" environment—a safe, supportive space in which preservice teachers can experiment with different ways of solving problems. Starting from this premise, they encouraged students to use a "think aloud" methodology to illuminate different strategies they might use at different points in their preparation to deal with four typical problems: an instructional problem, a discipline problem, a personality conflict with an associate, and the problem of balancing time demands of the job with needs in their personal life. Their analysis uncovered several cognitive strategies employed by students. They also traced the development of the strategies over the period of the year. They found encouraging signs that as the self-confidence of the students grew in the safe "holding environment," they typically began to develop more efficient approaches to problem solving. Only in the case of the problem relationship with the associate teacher did they tend to rely on indirect strategies. This speaks to the unequal power relationship between the student teacher and the associate. In the next section, dealing with alternative approaches to teacher education, all three papers address this issue by exploring ways to make the process of induction into the profession more collaborative for all parties concerned.

The final three chapters are research studies which address the conference theme of alternative and innovative approaches to teacher education.

Interestingly, although the papers take different perspectives, each represents research that views collaboration and cooperation among all the players (student teacher, the cooperating or associate teacher, and the university teacher educator) as central to the ultimate success of the endeavour. Each study describes how the central players come to terms with their role in the process.

Jean Clandinin's paper, "Learning to Live New Stories of Teacher Education," addresses the unexpected difficulties encountered when she and her colleagues attempted to make teacher education truly collaborative. This was to be accomplished through an alternative teacher education programme that involved student teachers in ongoing experience in the field while participating in university seminar classes on alternating days. Connections were made in small response groups on campus where all participants tried to make meaning of the process of becoming a teacher through telling and discussing their own stories. Well aware of the "rhetoric of collaboration" in which much is promised but in effect, the power structure remains in place and the relationship between the university and field remains one of "mandated collaboration" with the university researchers calling the shots, she sought to overcome this by truly giving the other players equal voice to tell their stories of their perception of what was occurring. Despite mutual trust among the participants, the university members still found that the others looked to them for guidance to set the agenda. She found it took time for all participants to learn to listen to each other, and for the student teachers and associates to gain enough confidence not to expect the university members to "lay down the plot lines." Eventually a middle ground was found where all parties could learn from each other. She sees this approach as only a beginning, but one that holds possibilities for constructing new stories of teacher education that will move beyond the traditional hierarchy where the university dictates the scenario and controls the answers.

Chris Fliesser and Ivor Goodson's paper, "Negotiating Fair Trade: Towards Collaborative Relationships Between Researchers and Teachers," takes up many of the issues raised in Clandinin's paper and echoes concerns raised by Goodson in his earlier paper and by Ardra Cole and Gary Knowles as well. Fliesser and Goodson are all too aware of the problematical nature of the hierarchical power relationships that exist when research is carried out in the field, even when the goal is to make it collaborative research giving all the players equal voices. This paper is interesting in that it describes the role of a middle person in the research process. Fliesser, who, as a community college professor, is interested in providing an induction programme for new technical vocational teachers in his college, entered into a collaborative project with some university researchers to achieve his goal and assist the new teachers as well. Although all the players were aware of what Clandinin called above the "rhetoric of collaboration," and undertook to negotiate "fair trade" in the project in an attempt to offset the hierarchical power relationships, nevertheless, Fliesser's story which is told in the paper from personal journal entries reveals that the journey to an equitable partnership was a long and not always smooth one. Ultimately, however, he came to see his role as equal with the university researchers, and he certainly felt that the fair trade had been realized. Since the teachers undergoing the induction programme are not heard from, it is not entirely clear how they perceived their role in the process. The article does close with helpful guidelines for negotiating "fair trade" in such arrangements, and the entire case provides another perception of an alternative way of inducting new teachers into their profession.

The last article, "Forging Partnerships: Faculty and Field Perspectives on French Immersion Teacher Education," also describes a collaborative approach that was used between a faculty of education and a French immersion school to accomplish something that could not have been done without the support of the field: namely, provide preparation for primary French immersion teachers. The historical perspective of teacher education for French Second Language teachers given at the outset of the paper illustrates why, despite a great need for people to teach in French immersion situations, Ontario teacher education programmes had never really come to grips with how such preparation might be provided. The only possible solution was to work closely with the field while devising a course that could run simultaneously during the faculty preservice programme. In the article, various participants voice their opinions of what an appropriate teacher education programme for prospective French immersion teachers would entail, and offer their perspectives on how the experiment worked and the benefits they saw in the partnership approach.

The Teacher Development Project at the University of Western Ontario, Faculty of Education had allowed participants in the faculty to explore several specific areas of teacher education that were in the process of evolution. The Continuity and Change Conference at the end of the project brought the investigators from the faculty together with colleagues from the field, Ministry of Education, and other teacher education faculties to share their findings, and consider other aspects of teacher education as presented from the perspectives of the invited speakers. The proceedings of this conference, represented in this volume, address issues of major interest: teacher education traditions and curriculum, implications of government policies on teacher education, findings of educational research and alternative approaches to it, and finally, reports of new developments in the delivery of teacher education. These issues provide foci around which much informed deliberation on teacher education revolves.

*Traditions and Conceptions
of Teacher Education*

Chapter One

Traditions of Practice in U.S. Preservice Teacher Education Programmes*

Kenneth Zeichner

~~~~~~

This chapter is concerned with the issue of identifying alternative approaches to teacher education. I will describe some work that I have been engaged in for the past several years in which I have attempted to understand the different traditions of practice which have existed in U.S. teacher education during this century. Then, I will discuss how I think the traditions framework that I have outlined can help us understand the ideas and commitments which drive individual teacher education programmes. In doing so, I will also describe some of the things I think do not represent alternative approaches to teacher education such as the use of the term "reflection" and the use of particular instructional strategies. I want to emphasize from the onset, that the reform traditions which I will describe, have been derived from my analysis of the development of teacher education in the U.S. during the 20th century (Liston & Zeichner, 1991) and on my colleague Herb Kliebard's study of the development of curriculum in U.S. elementary and secondary schools (Kliebard, 1986).[1] Whether or not this particular framework is relevant to the Canadian context or to other countries and, hence, represents a more general view of alternative approaches to teacher education is still an open question.

My attempt to try to understand different traditions of practice in teacher education is a reaction against the historical amnesia which has characterized the current reform movements in teacher education in both the U.S. and Canada. Very little attention has been given in the current literature in teacher education to the historical roots of contemporary reform proposals. From reading the literature (with very few exceptions such as Clifford and Guthrie's *Ed School*, 1988), one could conclude that nobody has ever tried anything or learned anything in teacher education over the last 50 years.[2]

One consequence of this lack of historical consciousness in teacher education is a lack of clarity with regard to the theoretical and political commitments underlying specific reform proposals. Currently popular terms like "reflective teaching," "action research," "subject matter," "development," and "empowerment" are bandied about the teacher education community with a great deal of confusion about the underlying commitments and assumptions which distinguish one proposal from another. In some cases (e.g., reflective teaching), the use of particular terms has become almost meaningless because of the way in which teacher educators, holding very diverse perspectives, have often expressed allegiance to the same slogans. Also, in my opinion, very little of what has been proposed today in the most recent version of the great debate on teacher education is new despite the new labels which have been attached to familiar practices. One of the benefits of focussing on traditions of practice in teacher education is that it can help clarify some of the important differences among contemporary reforms in teacher education which appear on the surface to be similar. It can also help us see more clearly the particular ways in which our work and the work of our colleagues build upon and/or challenge the labours of those who came before us. It is my contention that efforts to reform teacher education in the 20th century have always reflected, often implicitly, varying degrees of commitment and affiliation to several distinct traditions of practice. Dan Liston and I (Liston & Zeichner, 1991) have recently described four traditions of practice in our *Teacher Education and the Social Conditions of Schooling*: (1) an academic tradition, (2) a social efficiency tradition, (3) a developmentalist tradition, (4) a social reconstructionist tradition.[3] In briefly describing these four traditions here, I'll try to convey some sense of the tensions and contradictions which exist within each tradition (none of them is uniform and free of internal conflict), and of the overlaps between them. My description of the traditions themselves will be relatively brief because I want to take time to discuss the important point of how I think the traditions can help us think more clearly about different approaches to teacher education within our own institutions and in the field as a whole.

The Academic Tradition

Prior to the existence of formal programmes of teacher education in the U.S., a classical liberal arts education was equivalent to being prepared to teach (Borrowman, 1965). During the twentieth century, as programmes for the preparation of elementary and secondary teachers became established in colleges and universities, the point of view persisted that a sound liberal arts education, complemented by an apprenticeship experience in a school, is the most sensible way to prepare teachers for their work. Throughout this period, the contributions of schools, colleges, and departments of education to an education for teaching (with the exception of the practicum) have been severely criticized for their alleged inferior intellectual quality and for interfering with the liberal education of teachers. The academic orientation to teacher education emphasizes the teacher's role as a scholar and subject-matter specialist and has taken many different forms depending upon the particular view of the disciplines and of subject matter knowledge underlying specific reform proposals.

One of the earliest critics of professional education courses for prospective teachers in the U.S. was Abraham Flexner, who was also noted for his role in the reform of medical education. In his widely cited study of European and U.S. universities in 1930, Flexner lodged a number of criticisms of teacher education which have been raised repeatedly by advocates of the academic tradition ever since. He argued, for example, that the mastery of subject matter is the most important thing in the education of a teacher and that education courses interfere with this fundamental goal. Flexner, like many who were to follow him, criticized education courses for their intellectual superficiality, education professors and their students for their meager intellectual resources, and educational scholarship for its insignificance. Accepting the value of a few legitimate areas of study within education such as educational philosophy and comparative education, Flexner argued that all of the rest of what teachers need to learn, beyond a sound liberal education, could come from an apprenticeship experience in a school.

> Why should not an educated person, broadly and deeply versed in educational philosophy and experience, help himself from that point on? Why should his attention be diverted during these pregnant years to the trivialities and applications with which common sense can deal adequately when the time comes? (Flexner, 1930, pp. 99-100).

Since Flexner's devastating critique of teacher education, a number of highly visible and controversial analyses have articulated these same themes about the adequacy of disciplinary knowledge, and the inferior quality of education courses, faculty, and students. Among these are Lynd's (1953)

Quackery in the Public Schools, Bestor's (1953) *Educational Wastelands.* Koerner's (1963) *The Miseducation of American Teachers,* and more recent examples such as Mitchell's (1981) *Graves of Academe,* and Kramer's (1991) *Ed School Follies.* While there is little doubt that at least some of the charges that have been levelled by these academic reformers have been and continue to be true in some situations, there is some question as to the extent to which these caricatures of teacher education are representative of practice generally or exclusively (Zeichner, 1988). Recently, several scholars such as Lanier and Little (1986), and Clifford and Guthrie (1988) have convincingly argued that these academically oriented criticisms of the field may have less to do with the actual quality of courses, people, and programmes, than with status distinctions based on gender and social class between education faculty and students and those in colleges of arts and sciences. Although even the harshest of these critics such as Bestor admitted that things were not all well within courses in the arts and sciences, the general assumption has seemed to be that courses in the arts and sciences are necessarily liberalizing and that education courses are exclusively technical and vocational in the narrowest sense (Borrowman, 1956).

The programmatic implications of this academic tradition have changed somewhat over time depending upon particular views of a good liberal education and of particular kinds of subject matter knowledge needed by teachers. Following the decline of the Humanist position based firmly in a classical liberal arts education (Kliebard, 1986) and periodic attempts to professionalize subject matter offerings by considering pedagogical implications within academic courses (Borrowman, 1956), most manifestations of this tradition until recently have involved proposals for the preparation of teachers based firmly in the traditional academic disciplines as they are taught to all students regardless of their intended vocations. It has been repeatedly argued that this approach will draw many academically talented students into teaching who would otherwise be repelled by requirements to take many education courses of doubtful intellectual value.

Recently several challenges have been raised concerning the emphasis on the adequacy in a teacher's education of a traditionally defined liberal arts education and of subject matter knowledge based firmly in the academic disciplines. One line of criticism from a feminist perspective, criticizes a traditionally defined liberal arts education for perpetuating in Martin's (1987) words the Platonic emphasis "on mind, not head, thought, not action, production not reproduction, and reason not emotion."

In response to criticisms like these from Martin, and others like Noddings (1986) and Maher (1991), teacher educators in several places have begun to infuse content throughout the entire curriculum which challenge the Platonic dichotomies, and have critiqued the pedagogy and social relations in their programmes through lenses provided by feminist scholarship.

A second challenge to the dominance of conventional perspectives within the academic tradition has emerged in recent work on teachers' subject matter knowledge. Here, stimulated in part by criticisms from those like Shulman (1987), attention has been focussed on the knowledge teachers need to be able to transform subject matter to promote student understanding. Recent work has shown very clearly that knowledge of a discipline alone is insufficient for being able to teach it (e.g., Grossman, 1990).

A third challenge to historically dominant notions of an academic orientation in teacher education has focussed on the Western, white, middle-class bias in the liberal arts curriculum that has led to an absence of non-Western and culturally diverse perspectives in the education of U.S. teachers. There has also been a criticism of the failure of many academically oriented teacher education reforms to attend to the preparation of teachers for schools serving children of the poor (Goodlad, 1990b). Responses to these elitist tendencies in U.S. teacher education have included attempts to incorporate multicultural perspectives into teacher education programmes, and to prepare teachers especially for schools dominated by poor students of colour (Grant & Secada, 1990; Zeichner, 1992).

Despite these various challenges to historically dominant notions of a good liberal education and subject matter preparation for prospective teachers, recent policies such as the ones in Texas and several other states placing severe limits on the number of education courses allowed in a teacher education programme (Imig, 1988) and the establishment of alternative routes allowing people to enter teaching with little or no professional education course work (Uhler, 1987) reinforce the unfortunate confusion that courses are necessarily liberalizing if offered by academic faculty and are necessarily technical if offered in a faculty of education. Flexner's views are still alive and well in teacher education today.

The Social Efficiency Tradition

A second major tradition of practice in 20th century U.S. teacher education, the social efficiency tradition, has involved a faith in the power of the scientific study of teaching to provide the basis for building a teacher education curriculum. This tradition, unlike the first, has evolved largely within schools, departments, and colleges of education and has been seen by many as part of a strategy to strengthen "educationists'" claims to legitimacy within the university (Sykes, 1984).

Growing out of a faith in science came innumerable attempts during the 1920s and after to break down and analyze the teaching task into its component parts and to build a teacher education curriculum around these bits and pieces (Cremin, 1953). One of the earliest and most prominent efforts at scientific curriculum making in U.S. teacher education was the Commonwealth Teacher Training Study in 1929. Criticizing existing programmes for lacking a clear definition of objectives and logical plans of procedure, Charters and Waples (1929) sought to demonstrate that a comprehensive description of the duties and traits of teachers would provide the necessary basis for systematically determining what teachers should be taught. Although this study had little direct impact on teacher education programmes, the idea of systematically building a teacher education curriculum on the basis of careful analysis of the work performed by teachers persisted.

One of the subsequent manifestations of this perspective in U.S. teacher education was the emergence of Competency/ Performance Based Teacher Education (C/PBTE) in the 1960s and 1970s. Stimulated in part by applications of behaviouristic psychology to the training of personnel in industry and the military during World War II, and by the U.S. Department of Education's support for the development of model programmes, the idea of C/PBTE received so much attention in the literature that it has been described as the single most influential and controversial trend in U.S. teacher education in this century (Atkin & Raths, 1974).[4]

This general approach to teacher education emphasizes the acquisition of specific and observable skills of teaching which are assumed to be related to student learning. One of the key characteristics of the C/PBTE approach is that the knowledge and skills to be mastered by prospective teachers are specified in advance. Furthermore, the criteria by which successful mastery are to be measured are made explicit. Performance, rather than the completion of specified course work, is assumed to be the most valid measure of teaching competence (Gage & Winne, 1975). Another important element in this approach is the development of instructional management and evaluation systems to monitor the mastery of competencies. A number of significant developments occurred in this area. First microteaching was developed at Stanford University (Allen & Ryan, 1969), as a method for systematically teaching specific teaching skills to students. Microteaching was later incorporated into more comprehensive teacher training packages called "minicourses" at the Far West Laboratory in San Francisco (Borg, 1970). Closely related to these simulation developments was the development of protocol and simulation materials (the antecedent of today's focus on cases) (Cruickshank, 1984), systematic classroom observation systems (Simon & Boyer, 1967), and models for skill training (Joyce, Weil, & Wald, 1970).

Despite the tremendous amount of criticism of these behaviouristically oriented approaches, the social efficiency tradition is alive and well in the current debates on teacher education reform, this time under the label of "research-based teacher education."[5] Many of the current proposals for the reform of teacher education in the U.S. (e.g., Holmes Group, 1986; Goodlad, 1990b) have argued that the past decade of research on teaching has produced a "knowledge base" that can form the foundation for a teacher education curriculum. According to Berliner (1984, p. 94), "we have only recently developed a solid body of knowledge and a fresh set of conceptions about teaching on which to base teacher education. For the first time, teacher education has a scientific foundation."

Although many of the devices for systematically training prospective teachers in the use of specific teaching skills (like microteaching) have disappeared from the literature, newer versions, more compatible with the broader cognitive orientation of current social efficiency perspectives have emerged to take their place such as Cruickshank's (1987) "Reflective Teaching" programme and skill training through microcomputer simulations (Strang et al., 1987). Feiman-Nemser (1990) has made a useful distinction between two major segments of the social efficiency tradition, a technical version in which the emphasis is on skill training to a minimum level of mastery and a deliberative version in which the hope is to foster teachers' capabilities to deliberate about the use of research-based skills along with other factors, within a conception of teacher as decision maker. Despite the variations among social efficiency-based approaches throughout the century, the common thread that ties them together is their reliance on the scientific study of teaching (by those other than teachers) and the application of the results of that study as the basis for determining the teacher education curriculum.

The Developmentalist Tradition

The third tradition of practice in 20th century U.S. teacher education, the developmentalist tradition, has its roots in the child study movement initiated by G. Stanley Hall and others near the turn of the century.

According to Kliebard (1986), the most distinguishing characteristic of this tradition is the assumption that the natural order of the development of the learner provides the basis for determining what should be taught to both pupils in the public schools and to their teachers. This natural order of development was to be determined by research involving the careful observation and description of learner behaviour at various stages of development. In the early part of the century, this tradition was most visible in the efforts of the "Bohemian progressives" to prepare teachers to teach in the new child-oriented progressive schools that were springing up all over the country. One critical element in these early developmentalist efforts which has remained today is that it was felt that teachers for progressive schools must be educated in the same kind of supportive and stimulating environment that they were expected to provide for their students. Advocates of this new "student-centred" teacher education were often very critical of the mechanical methods that they felt were used in most teacher education institutions because they felt that mechanical teacher preparation led to mechanical and passionless teaching. According to Perrone (1989), three central metaphors were associated with early manifestations of this progressive/developmentalist tradition in teacher education: (1) the teacher as naturalist, (2) the teacher as artist, and (3) the teacher as researcher. The teacher as naturalist dimension of the tradition stressed skill in the observation of students' behaviour and capability in building a curriculum and classroom environment consistent with patterns of student development and students' interests. Here it was thought that classroom practice should be grounded in the close observation and study of students in natural settings or in a literature based on such study. Educating prospective teachers to be good observers of their students and to be able to learn from and plan classroom activities on the basis of their observations were key features of developmentalist proposals for teacher education reform.

The teacher-as-artist aspect of the developmentalist tradition had two dimensions. On the one hand, the artist teacher, who has a deep understanding of the psychology of development, is able to excite students about learning by providing them with carefully guided activities in a rich and stimulating learning environment. To do this however, the teacher needs to be a wide awake and fully functioning person in touch with his or her own learning. A common developmentalist proposal was to provide prospective teachers with a variety of experiences in dance, creative dramatics, writing, painting, and storytelling, so that they would be able to exemplify for their students an inquiring, creative, and open-minded attitude (Mitchell, 1931).

The third guiding metaphor in the developmentalist tradition in teacher education is the teacher as researcher. Here the focus was on fostering an experimental attitude toward practice on the part of the teacher. Child study was to become the basis for these teacher inquiries, and teacher educators were to provide instruction to prospective teachers about how to initiate and sustain ongoing studies in their own classrooms about the learning of specific students.

During the 1960s and 1970s, when student-centered pedagogy and "open education" once again received widespread attention in the U.S., a number of teacher education programmes were initiated that resembled those of the child-centred progressives of earlier years (see Crook, 1974). About this same time several other versions of the developmentalist tradition emerged such as Comb's (1972) "Humanistic" teacher education programme at the University of Florida and Fuller's (1974) "Personalized" teacher education programme at the University of Texas. Today along with the recent cognitive revolution in education, we have also seen the emergence of many current examples of this tradition based on a variety of constructivist orientations (e.g., see Amarel, 1988; Fosnot, 1989; Diamond, 1991; Knowles & Holt-Reynolds, 1991; and, Feiman-Nemser & Featherstone, 1992).

The Social Reconstructionist Tradition

The fourth and final tradition in U.S. teacher education, the social reconstructionist tradition, defines both schooling and teacher education as crucial elements in the movement toward a more just and humane society. According to Kliebard (1986), this tradition derived its central thrust from discontent about the U.S. economic and social system in the 1920s and 1930s. Schooling was seen as the vehicle by which social injustice would be redressed and the evils of capitalism corrected.

A critical mass of influential social reconstructionists was located in New York City at Teachers College, Columbia in the 1930s. Following the forceful articulation of the reconstructionist position by Counts (1932) in *Dare the Schools Build a New Social Order*, in which teachers were challenged to reach for political power and lead the nation to socialism, this reform perspective continued to be expressed and debated in the John Dewey Society for the Study of Education and in the pages of *The Social Frontier* and its successor *The Frontiers of Democracy*. This tradition which was given strength by an economic depression and by widespread social unrest, stressed the role of the school, allied with other progressive forces, in planning for an intelligent reconstruction of U.S. society where there would be a more just and equitable distribution of the nation's wealth and where the "common good" would take precedence over individual gain.

Although collective ownership of the means of production was not essential for all reconstructionists, most felt that at least the private economy must be regulated to help ensure full employment, economic opportunity, and an adequate income for all (Stanley, 1985). Given the vast number of changes wrought by science and technology, these "frontier educators" argued that it was the task of education

> to prepare individuals to take part intelligently in the management of conditions under which they will live, to bring them to an understanding of the forces which are moving, and to equip them with the intellectual and practical tools by which they can themselves enter into the direction of these forces (Kilpatrick , 1933, p. 71).

One of the major issues of debate among social reconstructionists was the degree to which teachers and teacher educators should consciously indoctrinate their students with socialist and collectivist values or rely on the methods of experimentalism and reflective inquiry. Counts (1932) was representative of those who argued for deliberate indoctrination of socialist values and ideas. Holmes (1932) of Harvard was among those who rejected the notion that the school should be used to promote a previously determined social programme. Holmes and many other reconstructionists placed the emphasis on cultivating students' abilities to think critically about the social order.

Because the teaching profession was being asked by the "frontier educators" to assume a leadership role in the reconstruction of U.S. society, teacher education was viewed as playing a key role in the process. It was argued in *The Social Frontier* that:

> The duty of the teachers colleges is clear. They must furnish over a period of years a staff of workers for the public schools who thoroughly understand the social, economic, and political problems with which this country is faced, who are zealous in the improvement of present conditions, and who are capable of educating citizens disposed to study social problems earnestly, think critically about them, and act in accord with their noblest impulses (Brown, 1938, p. 328).

Two prominent early examples of efforts to apply the proposals of these radical progressives to teacher education were New College, an experimental teacher education programme at Teachers College, Columbia from 1932-39 (New College, 1936) and the emergence of an integrated social foundations component in teacher education programmes (Cohen, 1976). The newly developed social foundations components of teacher education programmes and the "educationists" who taught them became the main targets for reformers in the academic tradition like Bestor and Koerner who charged that the interdisciplinary focus of the foundations approach destroyed the integrity of the disciplines.

Another aspect of the social reconstructionist tradition in U.S. teacher education has been the commitment evident in several national teacher education programmes such as the National Teacher Corps and Trainers for Teacher Trainers (TTT) to alter social inequalities by focussing on the improvement of educational conditions for children of the poor. There are many contemporary examples of this tradition in U.S. teacher education including some which are inspired by feminist theory and/or multicultural educational concerns. At various times, the focus has been on the curricular content of programmes, the skills of critical analysis and curriculum development, the nature of relationships between teachers and their pupils and between teacher educators and their students, or on the connections between teacher education and other political projects which seek to address the many instances of suffering and injustice in the society. What ties all of these efforts together, despite differences in emphasis and focus, is a common concern to help prospective teachers to see the social and political implications of their actions and the contexts in which they work, to see how their everyday choices as teachers are necessarily joined to issues of social continuity and change.

These, then, are the four traditions of practice in U.S. teacher education: (1) an academic tradition which emphasizes teachers' knowledge of subject matter and general education, (2) a social efficiency tradition which emphasizes teachers' abilities to apply a "knowledge base" about teaching that has been generated through research on teaching, (3) a developmentalist tradition which stresses teachers' abilities to base their instruction on their direct knowledge of their students' current understandings of the content under study, and their developmental readiness for and/or interest in particular activities, and (4) a social reconstructionist tradition which emphasizes teachers' abilities to see the social and political implications of their actions and to assess their actions and the social contexts in which they are carried out for their contribution to greater justice, equality, and more humane conditions in schooling and society.

Using the Traditions to Understand Teacher Education Programmes

How then are these traditions to be used in helping us understand the alternative approaches to educating teachers represented in individual teacher education programmes? The most common approach over the years has been to come up with a set of categories such as I have just done and then try to match individual programmes with specific categories. Feiman-Nemser (1990), in her recent chapter on structural and conceptual alternatives in teacher education, gives specific examples of teacher education programmes which illustrate each of the conceptual alternatives she identifies. For example, the Academic Learning programme at Michigan State is cited as an example of an academic approach and the elementary student teaching programme at my own university, the University of Wisconsin-Madison, is cited as an example of a critical/social programme (her term for social reconstructionism). Although she follows the dominant pattern in the field in labeling programmes according to their dominant themes, Feiman-Nemser is well-aware of the problems of classifying programmes in terms of a single orientation. Several times in her analysis she makes comments which indicate that she believes that specific programmes in reality, embrace multiple commitments. This position regarding the multiple commitments embedded in programmes is supported by the observations of many who have actually studied specific teacher education programmes with the purpose of understanding the ideas which drive them (e.g., Atkin & Raths, 1974; Howey & Zimpher, 1989; Goodlad, 1990b).

In our recent discussions of the four traditions of practice in U.S. teacher education (e.g., Liston & Zeichner, 1991), Dan Liston and I have argued that all teacher education programmes reflect particular patterns of resonance with all four of the various reform traditions. No teacher education programme can be understood in relation to any one tradition. The four traditions focus our attention on different aspects of teaching expertise. All teacher educators are concerned about the particular issues that are emphasized in each of the traditions. It is the degree of emphasis and particular meaning given to these various factors within particular teacher education programmes which give programmes their identities.

Some (Tom, 1991) have agreed with us about the multiple commitments in programmes but have proposed a synthesis of the various traditions which treats each one equally. While I accept the view that individual teacher education programmes need to address the conceptions of teaching expertise embedded in all of the traditions, I reject the ideological evenhandedness that Tom and others have called for because it denies the inevitable reality that individual programmes will have particular identities that reflect the priorities of educational and social philosophies of specific groups of teacher educators, and the reality that the meaning of each tradition in a programme will be different depending upon the guiding programme philosophy. For example, the meaning of the social efficiency focus on the development of technical skills of teaching will be very different in a programme which makes the development of generic teaching skills its major goal than it will be in a programme that situates these skills within particular subject areas, or in relation to particular conceptions of development, or in relation to the achievement of educational equity. The guiding tradition in a particular programme will help define the way in which all of the others are dealt with by teacher educators. There can never be a grand synthesis that washes away ideological differences. The best way for me to illustrate how the traditions of practice can be used to help us more clearly understand the ideas and commitments involved in particular teacher education programmes is to take a specific teacher education programme and briefly show how the traditions framework can help us to understand it.

Elementary Teacher Education at the University of Wisconsin-Madison

The conception of teaching expertise underlying our efforts in elementary teacher education at the University of Wisconsin-Madison can be described in relation to all four of the reform traditions. Although individual faculties within the programme emphasize somewhat different elements in their courses and practicums, the programme as a whole can be characterized as emphasizing two of the reform traditions in particular, the developmentalist tradition and the social reconstructionist tradition. It is these two traditions which give the programme its identity.

We also give substantial attention, however, to the academic and social efficiency dimensions of teaching expertise in ways that reflect the developmentalist/social reconstructionist orientations of the faculty. For example, all of the methods courses in our programme assume that students bring many misconceptions about content to their courses and focus a great deal on helping students to examine their own understandings of content, the range of understandings about particular topics (e.g., photosynthesis) that typically exist among different groups of pupils, and on the general idea of curriculum knowledge as representing socially constructed and value-governed selections from a larger universe of possibilities.

The faculty who teach these courses typically assume that students do not know a lot of history, mathematics, health, science, etc. and see as part of their mission the teaching of content as well as pedagogical content knowledge and general pedagogical knowledge. The emphasis here though, consistent with our focus on knowledge as a social construction within particular social and historical contexts, is to expose students to a range of perspectives about particular topics which represent different theoretical and political positions, positions which are often different from the ones our students were exposed to in their own schooling. We think that this exposure to multiple perspectives and the subsequent analysis causes students to reexamine their own understandings and makes it more likely that they experience conceptual change in their own learning and teaching, and teach in a manner that honours the various cultural traditions and diverse perspectives which exist in our society.

For example, in the social studies methods course, students read accounts of history such as Zinn's (1980) *A People's History of the United States* and analyses of various contemporary social and political issues written from the perspectives of different political and cultural groups. In the health education course, students consider different views of health and sickness in relation to historical and social contexts and examine the embeddedness of knowledge of various topics. In the area of puberty and sexuality education, for example, students' initial understandings are often challenged when they consider various arguments about the misuses of biology in describing changes in adolescence to be a result of certain hormonal changes. Here, and in the other methods courses, students consider how knowledge is produced by those who practise the various disciplines and the disciplines, themselves, are considered as investigative and model-building activities rather than as objective and static knowledge to be transmitted and learned.

The social efficiency tradition also receives attention in our programme in a way that reflects the overall programme emphases. There are two important aspects in our approach to this aspect of teaching expertise. First, most of the attention to research on teaching in the programme is domain-specific. Unlike other teacher education programmes which give much emphasis to generic research on teaching (e.g., Ross & Krogh, 1988), our programme considers most of the issues addressed in the generic research (e.g., teaching strategies, classroom organization and management) within the subject-specific methods courses. Second, our approach to research on teaching emphasizes our desire to help our students become both critical consumers of this research and able to participate in its creation. This approach to research does not lend itself to the distribution of recipes for teaching, but to a set of ideas and skills that feed into a process of deliberation about teaching.[6] Our focus on teachers as knowledge producers is emphasized in two ways: (1) classroom action research studies which are conducted by student teachers (Noffke & Brennan, 1991; Gore & Zeichner, 1991); and, (2) a concerted effort on our part to include the writing of elementary and secondary teachers in our course reading material.[7] An example of the way in which we attempt to help our students become critical consumers of research is the attention that is given in our courses to the critical analysis of various instructional and classroom management programmes which are allegedly based on research such as Hunter's "Instructional Theory into Practice" (Gentile, 1988) and "Assertive Discipline" (Canter & Canter, 1976).

One of the most striking characteristics of our teacher education curriculum is its developmentalist impulse—the commitment in a number of the required courses to developing students' abilities to conduct their teaching in a way that incorporates and builds upon their pupils' cultures, language backgrounds, interests, and current understandings of particular subject matter under study. In this view of instruction, the role of the teacher is to help her pupils construct knowledge (e.g., solutions to mathematical problems) rather than to merely attempt to transmit knowledge to pupils. There are three prominent examples of this developmentalist emphasis in our curriculum, all of which are related to research of our faculty: (1) cognitively guided instruction in mathematics (Fennema, Carpenter, & Peterson, 1989), (2) conceptual change teaching in science (Hewson, Zeichner, & Tabachnick, 1990), and, (3) culturally relevant teaching in the language arts and social studies methods courses (Gomez, 1991).

Of these three constructivist views of teaching, culturally relevant teaching most clearly illustrates the connections between the developmentalist and social reconstructionist impulses in our programme. In the language arts methods class, for example, much attention is given to the teaching of learners whose backgrounds and cultures are different from the white, middle-class norms which dominate our student cohort groups. One thing that this course focusses on is helping students to reexamine the deficit view of cultural differences that many of them bring to the course.

Students are required to read various accounts of schooling experiences from the perspectives of people of colour (e.g., Taylor & Dorsey-Gaines, 1988). Through discussions of these readings and various class assignments (e.g., interviewing parents of backgrounds different than their own), students develop greater sensitivity to and respect for a variety of cultural traditions. Through other class assignments which are implemented in the concurrent practicum experience (e.g., observations of children), students are helped to become more sensitive to the cultures and lives of their own pupils and to learn effective strategies for teaching skills of literacy to all of the diverse learners in their classrooms. The goal is to help student teachers link the teaching of literacy skills to the cultures, backgrounds, and interests of their pupils.

This emphasis on cross-cultural communication and on bridging the gap between home and school with regard to the teaching of literacy skills is one example of how we address the connections between the daily classroom realities of teaching and social continuity and change—how teachers' actions can help maintain and/or disrupt the status quo in schooling and society.[8]

Although we give attention to the personal and academic implications of classroom events for individual pupils (Pollard & Tann, 1987), we also extend the analysis to consider the social and political implications as well. Recognizing that there are political implications in all teaching actions, we want our students to consider the ways in which various alternatives for action in particular situations reflect political choices. We also want our students to become committed to acting in ways which lessen the harmful effects of the inequities which pervade our schools and society. This includes both increasing the commitment of students to work in those schools where these inequities are most visible (e.g., see Kozol, 1991), and a commitment wherever they teach, to demonstrate an active respect for the diverse cultural traditions in the society.

Underlying this concern with the development of social responsibility, are efforts to help our students develop the skills of curriculum development, school and community leadership, and self-monitoring, which will enable them to be active participants in the making of more democratic school environments. In many of our core courses, including student teaching, we have attempted to accomplish these goals by focussing on the development of our students capabilities to be "reflective" about their teaching and the contexts in which their teaching is carried out.

Because all teachers are reflective in some sense about their work, it is insufficient to state merely that reflectiveness, in general, is a goal of a teacher education programme. We do not accept the view implicit in much of the contemporary literature on reflective practice in teaching and teacher education that teaching is necessarily better merely because teachers are more deliberate and intentional about their actions. In some cases, greater intentionality may further solidify and justify teaching practices that are harmful to students. The important issues are concerned with the particular kinds of reflection that we want to encourage in our teacher education programmes, among ourselves, between ourselves and our students, and among our students.

Over the years, we have attempted to become more explicit about the content and quality of the reflection that we hope to encourage in our teacher education programme. Our use of the term "reflection" emphasizes the developmentalist and social reconstructionist dimensions of teaching expertise which I have just been discussing. This perspective means:

1. That the student teacher's attention is focussed both inwardly on his own practices *and* outwardly on their students and the social conditions in which their practices are situated.

2. That there is a democratic and emancipatory impulse in the reflection which leads to the consideration of the social and political dimensions of teaching along with its other dimensions.

3. That reflection is treated as a social practice rather than merely as a private activity.

Over the last decade, we have experimented with a number of instructional strategies to attempt to accomplish our goals. These have included such things as ethnographic studies read and conducted by students, journal writing, classroom action research, the use of case studies of student teacher learning to help focus our students on their own learning, and an emphasis on multicultural teaching practices and curricula. We have also experimented with a variety of structural changes such as the use of school-based supervisors instead of university teaching assistants, and the use of student cohort groups which stay together for many of their classes.

None of these strategies, by itself, signifies anything in particular. Many teacher education programmes emphasizing different traditions of practice use these same strategies and programme structures. The important issues are the purposes toward which they are directed and the specific quality of their use. It is the ways in which the different traditions of practice are served by the instructional strategies and programme structures which needs to be the focus in our discussions, not the strategies or structures, themselves.

Conclusion

This brief analysis of some of the ideas and commitments underlying elementary teacher education at the University of Wisconsin-Madison is one example of how the framework of traditions of practice can help us better understanding the specific approaches to teacher education represented in various programmes, without oversimplifying the complex reality of those programmes. It also helps us see particular programmes of work and/or proposals for reform within a broader socio-historical context. Whatever you think of the relevance of this particular framework of reform traditions for Canada or other countries, or of the specific commitments which guide our work in elementary teacher education at the University of Wisconsin-Madison, I hope that you will at least accept my general argument that currently dominant ways of talking about alternative approaches to teacher education (which are largely ahistorical, decontextualized, and overly simplistic) need to be replaced. I hope that you will reject the idea that individual teacher education programmes can be understood as reflecting any single tradition of practice. Finally, there is one other point which was implicit in much of what I have discussed here. This is, that in understanding the approach to teacher education in a particular programme, one must look at more than the content of the teacher education curriculum. One must also look at the pedagogy and social relations in the programme to understand its orientation. What is it that teacher educators do and how do they do it? The *approach* to teacher education is represented by all of those factors, not just the content of the formal curriculum.

Notes

* Reprinted with permission from *Teaching & Teacher Education*, 1993, Vol. 9, No. 1, pp. 1-13.

1. This framework also benefitted from several other efforts to describe alternative approaches to teacher education such as Joyce (1975), Zeichner (1983); Kirk (1986), and, Feiman-Nemser (1990).

2. A very interesting Canadian exception to the lack of historical consciousness is a study of teacher education in Alberta by Patterson (1991).

3. See Zeichner and Liston (1991) and Zeichner and Tabachnick (1991) for more detailed discussions of these traditions.

4. In actuality, teacher education practice was affected only minimally by this movement (Sandefur & Nicklas, 1981).

5. The use of this term outside of the U.S. often refers to preparing teachers who have the disposition and skill to conduct research in their own schools rather than as, in the U.S., teachers who are enthusiastic consumers of research produced by university academics (see Lucas, 1988).

6. Zumwalt's (1982) distinction between teaching as a technology and teaching as a deliberative activity is relevant here. Our view of teaching skills is similar to the latter.

7. We especially try to include in our courses the writings of those progressive teachers who "teach against the grain" (Cochran-Smith, 1991). Sources for these writings include publications like *Rethinking Schools*.

8. For more detailed information about the programme see Zeichner and Liston (1987), Gomez (1991), Maas (1991), and Zeichner (1991).

Chapter Two

Teachers as Models of Educated Persons

Nel Noddings

Suppose a high school student were to ask her English teacher for help with algebra or her mathematics teacher for assistance in interpreting a passage from *Moby Dick*. What are the odds that adequate help would be forthcoming? Or suppose a high school boy stops in to visit his fifth grade teacher and asks for help with a geometry problem. Will the fifth grade teacher respond with mathematical behaviour (as Skinner used to call it) or with an apologetic explanation that she "never was very good at math"?

For many students, teachers are their only, or at least their main, models of educated persons. Here are people who have been through high school and college—sometimes even graduate school. By definition, they are educated people. For heuristic reasons, I suggest we leave the definition in that naive state for now. To most precollege students, college graduates are educated people. How is it, then, that teachers know so little of the high school curriculum outside their own specialty and, worse, often so little even within it? It should not shock us if students were to react to this obvious lack by asking, *What's the point of learning all this stuff if "educated" people don't remember it?* In this article, I want to explore possible answers to this reasonable question. If there is no satisfactory answer, we should consider a total restructuring of the curriculum.

Possible Answers

One answer, given swiftly by many critics of education, is that *educated* people do know "this stuff"; teachers are just stupid. They lack intellectual curiosity, come from the bottom of their college classes, and are content to follow a textbook as they stay a few pages ahead of their unfortunate students. Thus, it only seems that educated people don't remember what is taught in schools. *Teachers* don't remember.

Now, I do not believe this. The empirical evidence today shows that, by and large, students preparing to teach do as well or better in their majors as students preparing for other fields. Further, there is little evidence that other educated people remember their high school lessons any better than teachers do. Some educated people—indeed some highly successful people—simply brush off most of their high school education as irrelevant. A statement, attributed to Fran Lebowitz, goes something like this: "Stay firm in your resolve to remain unconscious in algebra class. In real life, I assure you, there is no such thing as algebra." She has a point. In real life, for most of us, there might as well be no such thing as algebra. As a former math teacher—a highly enthusiastic, competent one—I freely admit this. Why should we expect English teachers to know algebra? But that's not the question right now. The immediate question is, given that they have studied algebra, how is it that so few know anything about it? A second question follows: If we know they will forget it, why do we force prospective English majors to study algebra?

A recommendation made by the critics who charge teachers with academic dullness is to recruit brighter students to teaching. We have lost the almost automatic enlistment of academically talented women in teaching, so the recommendation is not on its face a silly or empty one. But it is doubtful that teachers in general were ever "brighter" than they are today.

What do critics have in mind when they call for recruitment of "brighter" teachers? Almost always they are looking for people with higher GPAs and test scores. Such people have proved themselves competent in academic work and should serve as fine models of educated people for their own students. But many of these successful teacher-students, like all students, have pursued grades—not intellectual interests. They have gritted their teeth and got through required courses, concentrating more and more narrowly on their particular interest. Sometimes they even lack a passionate interest in their major and merely chase grades there, too. There may be a slightly higher probability that our high school student looking for math help from her English teacher will get it if the English teacher was valedictorian of her high school class, but I wouldn't count on it. Further, if the basic high school subjects are so important and central to success in life, why should we not expect that all college graduates should demonstrate mastery of them? Why should every professional field have to recruit heavily from among the "brightest and best"? Unless it can be convincingly demonstrated that engineers are better at interpreting *Romeo and Juliet* than math teachers and that journalists are better than English teachers at algebra, I think we have to reject any answer that locates the problem in teachers themselves.

By the way—and this is foreshadowing a later idea—I think that many talented women who became fine teachers were highly successful academically because they knew they would wind up teaching. Therefore, everything they studied took on a pedagogical colour. I know that the test of my own knowledge all through school was whether I could explain to friends the material I was supposed to know. What I learned best was that set of material clearly related to my own goals and interests. For me, that was practically everything because I knew I wanted to teach. A second possible answer is that students—even excellent ones—are not expected to retain the material they learn in high school. Wrestling mentally with these carefully chosen subjects trains the mind and facilitates future learning. This is the old faculty psychology rationale, and I do not think it has ever been absolutely debunked, although it has certainly fallen out of favour. Most of us would agree that using our minds is instrumental in keeping them in working order, but must they be used on particular subjects? It seems obvious that a person with a passionate interest in cooking and cookbooks can stay as mentally alive and sharp as someone involved with logic puzzles. Thus, although it seems generally true that we must exercise our faculties in order to maintain and develop them, it is not clear that we have to study particular subjects to do this.

Today we are more likely to talk about capacities, talents, or intelligences than about faculties. Howard Gardner (1983) has posited seven "intelligences," and this seems to me a great improvement over the two that apparently underlie most of the school curriculum. But questions arise immediately. Should all seven capacities be cultivated in everyone? Is the cultivation of one more important than that of another? Why? Might the scattering of effort required to develop seven capacities reduce the vitality available in one's greatest capacity? Further, if we really believe in such capacities, why not provide curricula and instruction that deal directly with the capacities? What are we trying to develop when we require all students to study history or biology?

Most of us do not believe that the standard school subjects "develop minds." Some of us do not even believe in minds! Asked how schools could develop children's minds without Latin or mathematics, A.S. Neill answered, "I don't know what 'mind' is. If the experts in mathematics and Latin have great minds, I have never been aware of it" (1960, p. 378). Many of us, however, might accept a modification of the old faculty notion along cognitive lines. On this account, the subjects we study leave traces or a form of skeletal structure on which we can hang new information if the opportunity arises. As teachers, we would not expect students to remember the details of the subjects we teach. Rather, we hope that these skeletal outlines will be formed and that future learning will thus be facilitated.

This seems more reasonable, but questions arise again. Suppose it is highly unlikely that a student will need a skeletal structure for mathematics. Why attempt to construct it then— often at great pain to both student and teacher? Well, one might argue, students do not always know what they will need, so to be on the safe side, we'd better provide the skeletal structures most often needed. Here, I'm with Neill. When people recognize the need for knowledge of a particular kind, they are amazingly fast in acquiring it. That's the time to teach, to facilitate, to build skeletons if we must. Otherwise, the skeletons are likely to be rickety and, eventually, overcome by intellectual osteoporosis. If these structures exist (and I think there's a good chance that they do), they are not created by external force anyway, but by internal motivation and effort.

I am suggesting a fairly cautious position here. I admit that the study of music by someone who loves music and has a talent for it may indeed increase that person's capacity to do musical things. But study can also destroy or impede development, so if we believe in the development of specific capacities, we have to find a way to evaluate that development and be sure that we are not working against it. That implies that, far from expecting everyone to know much of what they have been force fed in school, we would not force feed them. Curricula and instruction would be designed with capacities—or, better, interests—in mind. When students have an interest, they will learn much that is related clearly to that interest.

There's still another reason given for putting students through the traditional academic rigors. The object, again, is not to "learn all that stuff" but to become sufficiently acquainted with it to make intelligent choices. This is the exposure argument, and it, too, has been around for a long time. From this perspective, future English teachers study algebra not so much to learn it as to make an intelligent decision to study something else. The idea of exposure, like the idea of training faculties, is not a silly one. Most good parents spend considerable resources on experiences to which they think their children should be exposed. Wise parents, however, stop short of coercion. Opportunities are provided. The experiences are meant to be fun, and their results and effects are evaluated openly by both parents and children. To force all children to study particular subjects on the grounds of giving them later choices seems contradictory.

Further, our significant life choices do not centre on English, algebra, or history. We are, rather, in need of material that will help us decide what kind of person to be, how to relate to other beings, how to live, how to choose a satisfying occupation. Recognizing these needs, we should provide experience or problem-centred curricula, not pre-cut subjects. We would still teach mathematics, of course, but to people who have already made a significant choice—even if that choice is negated at some later stage of experience.

Another answer to the wise student question, "Why should I learn this stuff if hardly anyone will remember it?" goes like this: By demonstrating that you've learned "this stuff" even temporarily, you've earned an important credential. You've shown your society that you can do what it values. Further, you've acquired the discipline to apply yourself in future endeavours.

It's hard to deny the first part of this response, and it's an answer sufficient for many docile students. They've joined the club and know how to stay in it. The second part of the answer is much more problematic, first, because there are other—perhaps more healthy—ways to acquire discipline and, second, because it may not be true. It may be that students acquire a set of strategies that bear little resemblance to what educators call "discipline." Again, discipline is the result of yielding to the demands of subject matter, and people do this when they are interested. Interest precedes true discipline.

At any rate, if all we claim to accomplish from the study of high school subjects is a form of credential, why insist on *these* subjects? Why not devise a curriculum that has genuine worth and attach credentials to that? Obviously, I think we have to reject the credentialing answer along with the others, although I might still use it, sympathetically and apologetically, with particular students whose futures are in jeopardy. In this case, it would be a political answer, not an educational one.

There is at least one other answer worth considering. A teacher might say, "You should learn this stuff because I love you and I think it might be good for you." This is the kind of thing parents often say to their children. I advised several of my own children to major in math because they seemed to have the inclination, because I enjoyed sharing my interest with them, and because—knowing them well—I felt there was a high probability that they would choose a field requiring mathematics. However, I could never figure out a justification for their *having* to study all "this other stuff" or for the nonmathematical children to study math.

The main reason that the argument based on love is important is that kids often construct it for themselves. They study math or history because they love their math or history teacher. That great English teacher, Wayne Booth (1988), confesses to struggling with a choice between English and chemistry because he so admired a teacher of each. Goethe, too, insisted that we learn from those we love. Thus, children will slog through the standard curriculum because they trust and love the parents who tell them, "It will be good for you." We overlook this reason at the peril of our children. It suggests, among other things, that teachers should remain with students long enough to develop relations of love and trust. It is the only reasonably dependable way to get kids through a curriculum that they would otherwise reject. But, then, if we really love them, we ought to design a curriculum—a whole new structure of schooling—that would make genuine learning possible. Kids will, out of love, learn the stuff we force on them and even accept the fact that they will quickly forget it all, but surely such an experience must lead them to suspect that academic life—and maybe life itself—is absurd.

Is There a Better Way?

Many of us think that the high school curriculum should be totally redesigned. In *The Challenge to Care in Schools* (1992), I have argued for a curriculum organized around centres of care: care for self, for intimate others, for global others, for nonhuman life and the environment, for the human-made world, and for ideas. The last is ostensibly the present concern of the curriculum, but, of course, its separation from the deepest concerns of human life, its concentration on isolated segments all bent on maintaining themselves in pseudo-integrity, and our unfortunate determination to force everyone through it—all these factors ensure that there will be little caring for the ideas so presented.

The notion—curriculum organized around centres of care—sounds wild and impractical at first hearing, especially to those well-acquainted with school bureaucracies. But, actually, practical educators can get a start in this direction. I have suggested that the high school day could be divided into two parts. In one part, students would study subjects central to their interests—subjects that would have familiar names, such as math, physics, art. In the other, universal part, students would explore topics organized around themes of care. Magnet schools could easily be converted to a scheme of this sort, and a heartening number of schools are now introducing related practices such as core courses and home room counselling. So the idea is not totally impractical.

Feminism and minority movements give us another reason to hope that real change might occur. Women looking critically at the current curriculum might well ask: Why do we insist on teaching Shakespeare and quadratic equations to so many of our students and totally ignore teaching them anything about the great human task of raising children? For most of us, parenting is among the most significant tasks we will ever undertake. Yet it has long been supposed that we are automatically equipped to do this simply by having grown up with parents! This supposition has always been questionable, but today, when so many children are obviously poorly parented, it is downright dangerous.

Similarly, minorities have drawn our attention to a central (if often hidden) purpose of curriculum—to give students a sense of time, place, and pride of identity. To provide such benefits for all children will require drastic changes in content. Students must be able to relate content to their own interests. To help them, teachers need to know what these interests are.

Thinking openly and deeply on these matters does not imply that no familiar, traditional questions will be asked. Schools should, of course, teach certain skills required in our society. Reading, writing, and basic mathematics are important, but they can be taught through themes of care as well as through, say, British literature and general mathematics. Indeed, John Dewey long ago argued that such skills would be better taught in settings of genuine engagement. Even on this topic—the identification of skills required by all people—we should be more imaginative and critical. I would supplement reading, writing, and arithmetic skills with speaking, negotiating, listening, relating, and analyzing oral and written texts.

A word of caution is necessary here. In identifying skills that may be of universal importance, I do not mean to suggest that the curriculum should be organized around those skills. Brave and sophisticated attempts have been made to do this. They have all miscarried and will always do so because people do not learn skills in the abstract, but when they are fully engaged in *content* that matters to them. Therefore, content is crucial. However, there may be no particular content that has the power to engage everyone. For this reason, there must be a reasonable number of options within each centre of care. I think it is safe to say that all people do or should care about themselves, but not all will be interested at a given time in health care, or spiritual development, or life stages, or physical safety. Teachers and students have to work together to locate topics that will spur students into action.

Before I talk about teacher education, try to envision the kind of school I'm talking about. It is sympathetic to organization around centres of care, but it is practical. It has not given up the traditional subjects because colleges might not accept its students and it does not yet have the resources or knowledge to make such a radical change succeed. It is trying out plans that allow teachers and students to stay together for several years so that teachers can counsel intelligently—to give love a chance to exert its educational powers. It has some classes organized around themes of care for all students. It continually challenges the idea of disciplinary requirements. It encourages interdisciplinary work. It praises teachers who push back the boundaries of their subjects and engage students in discussion of existential, social, and emotional questions. Now, how do we prepare teachers for such a school?

Preparing Teachers

What exactly should we prepare teachers to do? First, I have argued that, logically, teachers should know reasonably well any subject we require all students, or all college preparatory students, to study. If we persist in requiring all college preparatory students to study three years of mathematics, then all teachers should be reasonably proficient in three years of high school mathematics. Of course, a sensible alternative, and it is the one I really am advocating, is that we stop requiring three years of mathematics and promote such study only for those who want or need it. Second, I have suggested that all teachers should be prepared to discuss matters of great human importance even though none of us can properly be said to "know" these matters in any conclusive way. Teachers should have the attitude, if not the wisdom, of Socrates.

How do we prepare teachers for this work? I will start this part of the discussion by saying what we should *not* do. In working with inservice teachers, we should not force them into new patterns of curriculum and instruction. We should share our ideas, invite suggestions from them, support and provide resources for them. What should we do if teachers' practices run counter to the direction we are discussing here? What if the practices seem to us miseducative? The problems still must be submitted to a public forum. Suggestions and counter-suggestions must be discussed. People who work in the new mode should do so voluntarily. Just as we recommend intelligent choice for students, so we must allow it for teachers.

In the early 1970s, I was a curriculum supervisor for a K-12 district. These were the days when supervisors and administrators were expected to be "change agents." Starting with fourth to sixth grades, we were to move the whole district in the direction of open education. Wisely, we started where many teachers were agreeable. Even so, we lost several teachers whose educational philosophies differed from ours and who could no longer feel respected in the new environment. Worse, teachers in the junior and senior high schools watched all this with foreboding and prepared mechanisms of resistance. I'm convinced now that educational change cannot be accomplished in a heavy-handed, top-down manner. Inservice teachers who want to move in this direction will, however, need much of what I'll recommend for preservice teachers.

The recommendations for preservice teachers run counter to those made by several national groups in the U.S. Whereas the Carnegie Forum (1986) and the Holmes Group (1986) both recommend deferring most work in professional education to the graduate years, I think we must concentrate on a radical revision of undergraduate education.

Our object should be to provide a curriculum that will prepare teachers to be models of educated persons. There are two large components of this preparation. First, teachers should know most of what high school students are expected to learn (we may, of course, change our minds about what they should learn, and this change will alter our conception of "educated persons"); second, teachers should have broad repertoires in themes of care and an attitude like that of Socrates—that is, a willingness to explore, question, and debate issues of human significance even if they "do not know." Thus, part of their preparation would involve the acquisition of thorough knowledge in all the *required* secondary school subjects; another part would involve the development of attitudes and skills to handle the great questions of life—questions whose answers no one *knows*, but upon which all of us should think.

How do we teach preservice teachers so that they will know most of the high school curriculum? I'll use mathematics teaching as an example because I know it best. People preparing to teach high school mathematics should study high school mathematics from a higher standpoint. They do not need the courses that prepare other students for graduate work in pure mathematics. Indeed, unless students actually go on to graduate work in mathematics, they are as likely as high school students to forget what they have learned. The aim should be to consolidate and deepen knowledge, not to add bits and pieces that will fall away.

Preservice mathematics teachers should study abstract algebra in the context of the algebra they will teach; they should have at least one course in geometry from a higher standpoint (most college students get no geometry at all); number theory should begin with and extend the arithmetic they will teach; and, their courses in analysis should focus on the calculus taught in high school. Not only would such a curriculum be more appropriate for high school teachers than the present one, but it might even turn out that people so educated would actually know more mathematics at the end of their studies than other students.

What should their other courses look like? Their history courses should include history of mathematics (and science, art, music, language, and whatever else is taught in high school). Their literature classes should include the great works of science fiction and fantasy focussing on mathematics or written by mathematicians (*Alice in Wonderland*; *Flatland*; *Godel, Escher, Bach: An Eternal Golden Braid*). Mathematics, literature, and history classes should include the biographies of mathematicians, and attention should be given to their nonmathematical interests—especially when these interests focus on themes of care. The religious interests of Newton, Descartes, Pascal, and Euler should be thoughtfully explored; so should the scientific and political interests of Leibniz. Philosophy should be a central part of such a curriculum, but it should concentrate on questions of importance in every human life: What kind of person should I be? How should I relate to others? How did the universe start? How did life begin? Are there gods? Even here, the questions need not be—should not be— treated in a technically philosophical way. When discussing how life began, teachers should be able to refer to many stories, crossing disciplines, religions, and ethnic origins.

Teachers should have similar preparation in every required subject. Starting with the particular subject they will teach, preparation should centre on the high school curriculum and then extend more deeply into that subject and more broadly into its connections with all other subjects.

As long as the disciplines are in place as organizers of the curriculum, we will have to be content with pushing back their boundaries. A well-prepared mathematics teacher should be ready to discuss a wide range of topics generated by the mathematical subject at hand. For example, suppose Ms. A. is teaching rectangular coordinates to an algebra class. She should be prepared to tell her students something about their inventor, Rene Descartes. She need not remember everything she has read or heard about Descartes, but she should be aware of several sources to consult in preparing material that will have the appearance of spontaneity. She might talk about Descartes' flashy style of dress and his swordsmanship. She should be able to run through his proof of the existence of God and solicit comments on its adequacy. She might talk about the times in which Descartes lived and how careful he had to be in suggesting anything unorthodox in religion. Certainly, she should be prepared to discuss Descartes' contribution to a whole new era—one of emphasis on method and a scientific quest for certainty. She might send students to a map to locate France and the Scandinavian countries Descartes visited. She might encourage students to report on living conditions during Descartes' lifetime. What was happening in Europe? in America? in Africa? What great music was composed? What great art was produced? What might Descartes have read?

In addition to the material suggested by biographical interests, she should point students to everyday uses of rectangular coordinates on road maps and be ready to discuss other coordinate systems. If we were scheduled to meet Descartes at $2°$ E. Longitude and $48°$ N. Latitude, what else would we need to know in order to keep our appointment? What coordinate systems are used by radar operators on ships? by air traffic controllers? These are topics regularly mentioned when mathematics and science educators talk about interdisciplinary study. I mention them here because I, too, believe they are important, but they should be supplemented by interdisciplinary topics in the humanities.

At least as important as the knowledge I've been describing is a willingness to explore existential questions and interests as they arise. In such explorations, teachers and students are more nearly equals. Both tell and listen to stories. The stories we tell convey in their very telling the love and trust we have for each other. Further we may come to realize that stories are often more powerful than arguments in getting people to appreciate the positions we take.

An education of the sort I am describing for teachers assumes that the material they will teach—the material their students will be expected to learn—is important. They should be so thoroughly in command of it that they will represent for their students proud and convincing models of educated persons. I have argued here that the present high school curriculum does not comprise material so important that every educated person should know it. I would prefer to see it radically transformed. But whatever we do with it, the college education of teachers should concentrate on the material contained in that curriculum. After all, mastery of that material will be a living symbol that some people—some educated people—have found the high school curriculum significant and useful.

Chapter Three

An Unlovely Legacy:
The Disabling Impact of the Market
on American Teacher Education*

David Labaree

American teacher education is back in the news, but unfortunately the news is not good. This, however, is far from being a novel situation. From my reading of the history of American education, it seems that it has always been open season on teacher education. Now, as in the past, everyone seems to have something bad to say about the way we prepare our teachers. If you believe what you read and what you hear, a lot of what is wrong with American education these days can be traced to the failings of teachers and to shortcomings in the processes by which we train them for their tasks. We are told that students are not learning, that productivity is not growing, that economic competitiveness is declining—all to some extent because teachers don't know how to teach.

As a result, politicians and policy makers at all levels have been talking about a number of possible remedies: testing students as they enter and leave teacher education programmes, extending and upgrading the content of these programmes, and even bypassing the programmes altogether through alternative certification. The latter option means pushing people with subject-matter expertise or practical occupational experience directly into the classroom, thus protecting them from the corrupting influence of schools of education. Meanwhile, academics in the more prestigious colleges within American universities ridicule the curriculum of the school of education for what they consider its mindlessness and uselessness. Ordinary citizens also get into the act. For example, there is a recent book written by a journalist, Rita Kramer, who spent some time sitting in teacher education classrooms and interviewing professors. Her title quite nicely captures the general lack of restraint with which critics have tended to approach teacher education: *Ed School Follies: The Miseducation of America's Teachers* (1991).

As I said, none of this criticism of teacher education is particularly new. The training of teachers has never been revered by the academy or terribly popular with the public. If one could sum up the usual complaints about teacher education in one sentence, it would be something like this: Schools of education have failed to provide an education for teachers that is either academically elevated or pedagogically effective. Instead of rallying to the defense of the teacher education establishment, of which I am a part, I would like to explore why this enterprise has earned such a bad reputation.

Yes, teacher education in the U.S. has been and in many ways continues to be an intellectually undemanding and frequently ineffectual form of professional training. Where I disagree with the current pattern of criticism, however, is in the diagnosis of the roots of the problem. The most popular current diagnosis of what ails American teacher education follows directly from the reigning view of what the problem is with schooling in general. In the conservative climate of the past decade, that understanding is simple to state. The problem with schools, we are told, is that they have been ruined by too much politics; the solution, we hear, is to inject a little discipline from the marketplace. This interpretation has become part of the fabric of contemporary thought about schools, but the most prominent ideological weavers currently working in this tradition are John Chubb and Terry Moe, authors of *Politics, Markets, and America's Schools* (1990).

My own interpretation is precisely the opposite of theirs. I argue that both K-12 education and teacher education have been ruined by too much market influence and not enough democratic politics. A generous democratic rhetoric has surrounded teacher education from the days of the first normal schools, but the fact of the matter is that the dominant influence on the form and content of teacher education has come not from politics but from the market.

This market influence has resulted in the widespread belief that education has two purposes: one, I call "social efficiency"; the other, "social mobility." These two objectives have had some contradictory effects on teacher education. But they have a great deal in common, since both represent ways that teacher education has been required to respond to demands from the market—the job market in the case of social efficiency and the credentials market in the case of social mobility. The net result has been to undermine efforts to enrich the quality, duration, rigour, and political aims of teacher education. The history of teacher education has not been very elevated, either academically or politically—thanks directly, I suggest, to market influence.

In pursuing this theme, I will explore the following issues. First, I will say a little about the nature of these market-oriented purposes and their impact on American education in general. Then I will examine the historical role that each has played in shaping teacher education. This in turn will lead to a discussion of the kinds of problems that these objectives have brought about for the form and content of teacher education. And finally, I will explore one current reform initiative, known as the teacher professionalization movement, which represents an effort to buffer teacher education from the influence of the market. Will this effort move teacher education in a desirable direction or just replace one undesirable influence with another?

Alternative Purposes in American Education

Both social efficiency and social mobility are purposes that have shaped American schooling in significant ways over the last 150 years. Let me say a little about the nature of each purpose and the character of its impact on schools.[1]

From the perspective of social efficiency, the purpose of schooling is to train students as future workers. This means providing them with the particular skills and attitudes required to fill the full range of positions in a stratified occupational structure. In short, according to this view, schools should give the job market what it wants. Social efficiency is an expression of the educational visions of the employer, the government officials, and the taxpayers. These constituencies share a concern about filling job slots with skilled workers so society will function efficiently, and they want schools to provide this service in a cost-effective manner.

From the perspective of social mobility, the purpose of schooling is to provide individuals with an equal opportunity to attain the more desirable social positions. This goal expresses the educational visions of the parent with a school-age child. Such a parent is concerned less with meeting society's needs and keeping down costs than with using schools to help his or her child get ahead. From this angle, the essence of schooling is to provide not vocational skills but educational credentials, which can be used as currency in the zero-sum competition for social status.

Note that both social efficiency and social mobility are purposes that link education directly to the job market. The key difference is that a person promoting the first goal views this link from the top down, taking the perspective of the educational provider, while a person promoting the second goal views the link from the bottom up, taking the perspective of the educational consumer.

In addition to these two market goals, however, there is also a third type of goal—arising from democratic politics—that has offered a more generous vision for American education. This is the goal that primarily motivated the founders of the common schools. The leaders of the common school movement saw universal public education as a mechanism for protecting the democratic polity from the growing class divisions and possessive individualism of an emerging market society. The common schools, they felt, could help establish a republican community on the basis of a shared educational experience cutting across class and ethnic differences. These schools could also help prepare people to function independently as citizens in a democratic society. This goal is at its heart an inclusive one, grounded in political rather than economic concerns.

In spite of the power of the market, this democratic goal has found expression in American education in a number of ways over the years. There was the common school, itself—which drew students from the whole community, presented them with a common curriculum, and generally chose to ignore the problem of articulating schooling with the structure of the job market. Then at the turn of the century came the comprehensive high school, which brought a heterogeneous array of students and programmes together under one roof, even though students experienced quite different forms of education under that roof. More recently we have seen expressions of this goal in efforts at inclusive education, as reformers have sought to reduce inequalities associated with race, class, gender, and handicapping conditions of the students.

These three goals have frequently collided in the history of American education, resulting in an institution driven by contradictory impulses coexisting in a state of uneasy balance. However, the history of American teacher education has demonstrated a narrower range of purposes than this. There has been very little sign within teacher education of the effects of the democratic purposes that helped to shape schooling more generally—except, perhaps, a thin strand of democratic rhetoric running through the teacher education literature. In practice, teacher education has shown primarily the politically and socially narrowing effects of the market. Let's consider what effect each of these market purposes has had on American teacher education over the years.[2]

Social Efficiency

While social efficiency goals for the teaching of students arose around 1900 (with the emergence of the high school and the advent of vocationalism), this emphasis came much earlier for the teaching of teachers. From the perspective of social efficiency, the central problem for teacher education was the chronic undersupply of teachers that developed in the mid-19th century and continued on into the early 20th century. The initial source of this problem was the development of universal public education, which produced a powerful demand for a large number of certified elementary teachers. In answer to this demand, the larger urban school systems opened their own normal schools, parallel to or incorporated within city high schools, for the purpose of staffing their elementary classrooms. At the same time, state governments around the country created state normal schools to meet the needs of those districts that could not support normal schools of their own.

Then, after elementary education had filled up, there came the rapid expansion of high school enrollments at the turn of the century. (High school attendance doubled every decade from 1890 to 1940.) This in turn created a strong demand for high school teachers, and the answer to that demand was found in the creation of state teachers' colleges.

The essence of the social efficiency impulse was to create a form of teacher education that was organized around three basic principles—quantity, quality, and efficiency. The issue of quantity was the most obvious. The large number of slots to be filled created a need for a form of teacher education that could effectively mass-produce teachers. The issue of quality was a bit more complicated. The problem here was the need for a publicly credible system for certifying that the new teachers met some minimum standard of quality—a form of assurance that was necessary in order to maintain public support for the investment in schooling. This meant that teacher education needed to be established under public administration and around state certification requirements. The concern for quality, however, was undermined substantially by the concerns for quantity and efficiency.

By efficiency I mean simply that teacher education was under great pressure to prepare teachers at both low cost and high speed. The fiscal burden of expanding enrollments at the elementary level was enormous, and it only increased with the expansion of the high school. One answer to the efficiency problem was to feminize teaching, which school systems did in great haste starting in the mid-19th century. By paying women one-half of what they paid men, school systems found an effective way of getting two teachers for the price of one. The side effect, however, was to create a profession characterized by very high turnover, since, as a general rule, women tended to teach only during the half dozen or so years between the completion of their own education and marriage. As a result, teacher education found itself forced to turn out teachers even faster and more cheaply in order to compensate for the brief duration of teachers' service.

The consequence of the goal of social efficiency was that it put emphasis on the creation of a form of teacher education that could produce the most teachers, in the shortest time, at the lowest cost, and at the minumum level of ability that the public would allow. All in all, this hardly constituted an elevating influence.

Social Mobility

Much to the chagrin of the founders and funders of the various teacher education enterprises, these institutions quickly became subverted by another powerful market force: the demand by individuals for access to high school and college degrees and, through them, to social mobility. Teacher education was designed to be accessible and easy in the name of social efficiency. But ironically it found itself the most accessible and easiest route to middle-class status for a large number of ambitious students and their parents. Jurgen Herbst (1989) has described this problem quite nicely in his book on the history of teacher education. There quickly emerged a strong form of consumer pressure on teacher education institutions to provide general liberal arts education for students who, in fact, had little or no intention of teaching.

The result was that normal schools underwent a gradual transition into general-purpose high schools. A case in point is the history of Philadelphia's Girls High School. Created in 1848, this school went through a series of name changes over the rest of the century—from Girls High School to Girls Normal School to Girls High and Normal School and finally back to Girls High School again. The problem in Philadelphia as elsewhere was that the purpose of the institution, though initially to train elementary teachers, was in fact up for grabs. Policy makers and fiscal authorities wanted these schools to retain their social efficiency aims and train teachers, but the parents of the school-age girls, wanted them to provide a broad secondary education for their daughters.

We discover the same sorts of tensions playing out in the history of state teachers' colleges after the turn of century. These institutions were under considerable pressure from students to transform themselves into liberal arts colleges. And, given the extreme sensitivity of American higher education to consumer pressures, they eventually did just that in the 1920s and 30s. By the 1960s and 1970s they moved one more step in that direction by becoming general-purpose universities. What was once the Michigan State Normal School in Ypsilanti is now Eastern Michigan University.

Consider the implications for teacher education of this pressure to provide social mobility. The fact that many teacher education students did not want to become teachers put the emphasis on a form of teacher education that was unobtrusive in character and minimal in scope for the convenience of students seeking a general education. These students were focussed more on credentials and status than on learning and content, which meant that teacher education was expected to make only the most modest of demands so as not to block a student's access to the desired degree.

Now let's examine some problems with teacher education that can be traced to this pressure from the job market and the credentials market.

Market-Based Problems in Teacher Education

Some of the problems that markets create for teacher education derive from the conflict between the goals of social efficiency and social mobility. One such difficulty was simple inefficiency. The consumer pressure for mobility through teacher education promoted considerable inefficiency, since it led to the expansion of the system of teacher education that was producing a large number of nonteaching graduates. In effect, this amounted to a collective subsidy of individual ambition. As a result of this situation, teacher education grew accustomed to functioning as a system of mass production with a low net yield. It was under constant pressure to produce ever more graduates and to keep ever more rigid control of the unit costs of this production, simply because the ultimate number of teachers produced was so small relative to the number of students processed.

In addition, teacher education developed a serious identity crisis because of the confusion over which market it was supposed to serve. Trying to run a teacher education programme is quite difficult when you cannot agree on its purpose. Is the primary focus on general or vocational education? Should the programme concentrate on liberal arts or teaching methods? Is the aim to provide an individual benefit for the consumer of higher education or a collective benefit for citizens needing qualified teachers? This uncertainty about purpose has afflicted teacher education from the very beginning and has continued right up to the recent past.

Some of the problems that teacher education has experienced derive from market-based commonalities between the goals of social efficiency and social mobility. After all, both of these tendencies arose from the perceived need to adapt teacher education to market demand. In the case of social efficiency, this was expressed as a need for more bodies in the classroom; in the case of social mobility, it was expressed as a need for credentials to equip students to compete for social positions. Neither of these, I suggest, was a terribly noble goal for an educational institution. Neither provided any political vision for teacher education—any vision of exactly what education and teacher education should be, what kind of teachers we needed, what kind of learning we wanted them to foster, or what political/moral/social outcomes we wanted to produce.

In addition, both approaches to teacher preparation tended to undercut the creation of a strong educational content in teacher education programmes. Social efficiency undercut content in the rush by policy makers to mass-produce teachers of minimum competence. Social mobility undercut content in the rush by ambitious individuals to use teachers' colleges as a means for climbing the social ladder. There is nothing in either goal that would press teacher education to provide an intensive and extensive educational experience for prospective teachers, nothing in either to promote academic rigour or prolonged application. In fact, everything urges toward superficiality (providing thin coverage of both subject matter and pedagogy), brevity (keeping the programme short and unintrusive), accessibility (allowing entry to nearly anyone), low level of difficulty (making the process easy and graduation certain), and parsimony (doing all of this on the cheap).

This, I submit, is the market-based legacy of limited vision and ineffectual process that afflicted teacher education in the past and continues to do so today.

An Alternative Vision: Teacher Professionalization

One recent effort to remedy some of these historical problems that are embedded in teacher education has come from within the community of teacher educators via the Holmes Group (1986, 1990). This group is made up of approximately 100 deans from colleges of education at research-oriented universities. Their answer is a reform proposal that focusses on the goal of teacher professionalization.

The Holmes Group argues that teachers need to receive an extensive and intensive professional education much like that accorded to doctors and lawyers. Such an education, they assert, would help to free teachers from the subordination within schools and, more importantly, would enable them to provide students with the kind of empowered learning that would allow them full participation in a democratic society. This approach tries to buffer teacher education from the corrupting influence of the marketplace by wrapping it in the armour of professionalism (and the rhetoric of democracy). However, as I have argued elsewhere, this movement is likely in practice to submit teachers and students to another kind of power—the intellectual and social power of the university within which teacher education has become imprisoned (Labaree, 1992a, 1992b).

The problem, I suggest, is that the movement to professionalize teaching has arisen from the status needs of teacher educators within the university. When it comes to academic prestige, teacher educators have always been at the bottom of the ladder. Arriving in the university relatively late and bearing the stigma of the normal school, they found themselves ill-equipped to compete for professional standing within the university. Yet the rules of academic status are well-defined. To gain prestige within the university, professors need to pursue a vigorous agenda of research activities, especially those framed in the methodology of science. Starting in the 1960s, teacher educators drew on the behavioural scientific model pioneered by educational psychologists and set off a landslide of research publications. The quantity of output since then has been so great that it has taken three large handbooks just to summarize the recent research on teaching and another to summarize the research on teacher education (Gage, 1963; Travers, 1973; Wittrock, 1986; Houston, 1990).

The result for teacher education has been to push it to adopt a curriculum for training teachers that is based on its own scientific research. While this move may represent a partial reduction in the extent to which teacher education is a simple expression of the market, it serves to transform teacher education, at least in part, into an expression of the power and knowledge of the university—particularly reflecting the status concerns and scientific world view of the educational professoriate. Like its market-based predecessors, driven by the goals of social efficiency and social mobility, this approach to teacher preparation undermines the kind of emphasis that would support democratic schooling. What it promises to do is to add the rationalized authority of the university researcher to social efficiency and social mobility as driving forces behind teacher training.

Sadly, a truly democratic politics remains one goal that has never been implemented within the mainstream practice of teacher education. This more generous vision, which has intermittently influenced thinking about schools, also needs to become a factor in the way we think about the teachers within those schools and in the way they are prepared. Instead of structuring teacher education around the base concerns of efficient production and personal ambition, I suggest that we need to think about organizing it in a way that reflects what I hope are our more elevated concerns about the quality of education our teachers and students will receive and the political and social consequences that will emerge from that education.

Notes

* Reprinted with permission of the *Phi Delta Kappan*, 1994, Vol. 75, No. 8, pp. 591-595.

1. I have developed this analysis of the impact of the market on American schools at greater length in the following works: *The making of an American high school: The credentials market and the Central High School of Philadelphia, 1838-1939* (New Haven, CT: Yale University Press, 1988); and "From comprehensive high school to community college: Politics, markets, and the evolution of educational opportunity." In Ronald G. Corwin, (Ed.), *Research in sociology of education and socialization*, 9 pp. 203-240. Greenwich, CT: JAI Press.

2. The best general history of American teacher education is Jurgen Herbst, *And sadly teach: Teacher education and professionalization in American culture* (Madison: University of Wisconsin Press, 1989). See also John I. Goodlad, *Places where teachers are taught* (San Francisco: Jossey-Bass, 1990).

Chapter Four

Crafting the Curriculum of Teacher Education*

Peter Grimmett

~~~~~~

The Context of Teacher Education in the 1990s

Goodlad, Soder and Sirotnik (1990) suggest that there has been an erosion of the foundational disciplines (e.g., sociology) in university-based teacher education programmes. Fullan (1991) notes that preservice teacher preparation still lacks a serious focus on issues arising from the current social context of teaching, i.e., multiculturalism, English as a Second Language (ESL), and the education of students with special needs.

At the same time, university-based teacher education is coming under close scrutiny in Canada not from right-wing governments of an anti-intellectual stance but from left-of-centre governments intent on staying in power during tough economic times. Such governments have suddenly realized that, to counter the "socialist hordes" label that could potentially bring about the demise of their new-found power, they have to become fiscally conservative. Conservative fiscal policies in a time of economic recession lead inevitably to cost-cutting measures. Cost-cutting measures usually hit those areas of the public sector deemed to be most expendable. University-based teacher education could thus be seen to be quite vulnerable. Relative to other professional schools in the university setting, faculties of education appear to be unsupported either by the field or by other faculties on the university campus. Consequently, university-based teacher education could be perceived as an easy target for cut-back measures.

The current trend towards collaboration with practising teachers in the field raises an important issue. Given the emphasis in teacher education on valuing and respecting the life, work, and knowledge of practising teachers, what constitutes the vital role of faculty members, both individually and collectively? Is this the beginning of a "selling out" of university involvement in teacher education, thus making the enterprise that much more susceptible to possible draconian economic measures, or do the faculty members have a vital and viable role to play?

Two points need to be made at the outset. First, there is a distinct need to articulate the vital role that can (and must) be played by faculty in collaborative approaches to teacher education.[1] Second, as Goodson (1991) has pointed out, there is a need to re-inscribe the foundations into the curriculum of teacher education in a manner which permits a focus on problems and dilemmas inherent in the social context of teaching. This chapter attempts to show one way in which this can be undertaken. Based on the premise that such problems and dilemmas become more accessible and meaningful to teachers when their own conceptions of teaching and learning are taken seriously, I shall argue that a propitious beginning for such re-inscription of foundational knowledge can most efficaciously be achieved through an emphasis on integrating teachers' craft knowledge into the teacher education programme.

Introducing the Concept of Craft

There is a table which adorns the library of the Coastal Ridge Research and Educational Center[2] in Point Arena, California. It was made by a Japanese craftsperson. It is beautifully carved and finished and projects an aura of completeness, which, to the naive Western eye, appears to epitomize what is best about accomplished carpentry. But the roving hand of an inquisitive visitor unsuspectingly finds a blemish; underneath one of its ledges; the carpenter has left a hollow knot in the wood that appears to take away from the smoothness and polish of its finish. Preliminary credulity gives way to doubt; doubt sparks inquiry; and, inquiry reveals that it is the custom to leave one piece of the "sacred" wood in its original form. Such custom marks the craft of the Japanese carpenter. The so-called "blemish" is part of the finished product. Without it, the table would be inauthentic and incomplete. What the Western eye sees as a blemish, the Japanese eye sees as something special. In similar vein, teaching as craft does not purvey the packaged effectiveness that scientistic mindscapes would desire but reveals the vicissitudes of learning (both visible blemishes and hard-earned insights) that accompany teachers who are impassioned in their endeavour to develop students' minds and to help them grow as human beings (Kohl, personal communication, 1991).

That craft knowledge exists as a powerful determinant of teachers' practice is neither new nor controversial. What *is* new is the possibility that such knowledge could become an integral part of teacher education; what is controversial is the debate over whether this would be a productive direction to take. I argue here that, in addition to codified knowledge bases framed around university-based research, teacher education could benefit from the contribution that craft knowledge can make to the formation of skilful, reflective, and empowered teachers.[3] In this chapter, I define what craft knowledge is, grapple with its validity and morality as a form of knowing, and develop a framework for understanding the essential contribution it could make to the development of inquiring minds in teachers. Finally, I attempt to grapple with the thorny question of how it might be of value in the education of teachers.

Ways of Thinking About Craft Knowledge

Liston and Zeichner (1991) note that "our understanding of the role of the teacher and the activity of teaching is conceptually dependent on particular communities" (p. 43). Their purpose is to grapple with the ways in which the role of teacher and the activity of teaching is differentially understood according to three patterns of educational thought, namely, "the conservative, progressive, and radical traditions" (p. 6).[4] I regard an understanding of craft knowledge as being analogous to the case of the role of teacher and the activity of teaching. Craft knowledge is also understood differentially by those who subscribe to each of these respective traditions.

The Conservative Pattern of Thinking

The conservative pattern essentially views the educational process as a means of cultural transmission (Liston & Zeichner, 1991). The teacher's role is either to initiate students into predetermined and distinct forms of public knowledge (Hirst, 1965) or to re-establish a common cultural heritage that is shared by all Americans (Hirsch, 1988). Whenever the term "craft" is associated with classroom practice emanating from this tradition of educational thought, it is frequently used in a pejorative sense. Broudy (1956), Gage (1985), and Scheffler (1960) view craft knowledge in this tradition as having an inherently anti-scientific bent and rue its effects on the professional status (or lack thereof) of teaching. It is equated by some British writers to the mindless imitation of practice (Hartnett and Naish, 1980; Stones, 1990; Turner, 1990). Consequently, the growing evidence that some teachers learn considerably by reflecting on their practice (see Grimmett & Erickson, 1988; Clift, Houston, & Pugach, 1990) in a manner which is belief-challenging, instructive, and theoretically sensitive is a manifestation of these different educational beliefs at work. When this occurs, teaching as craft essentially represents transformed experience. It is this latter view of craft, based as it is in the progressive and radical patterns of educational thought, which provides the focus for this chapter.

The Progressive and Radical Patterns of Thinking

The central aim of the progressive pattern is "for students to become competent inquirers, capable of reflecting on and critically examining their everyday world and involved in a continual reconstruction of their experience" (Liston & Zeichner, 1991, p. 48). Unlike the conservative pattern with its emphasis on teacher-centred didacticism, the progressive tradition assumes that a process of inquiry revolving around students' interests gives rise to mastery of subject matter.

The radical pattern assumes that men and women "are capable of being free and equal members of a just, democratic, and caring society...[it starts] from a position of critique arguing that our public schools do not support or develop these capacities equally for all children" (Liston & Zeichner, 1991, p. 49). Consequently, the central aim of the radical tradition is to change the current nature of schools as a means of bringing about equity and social justice.

Craft as a metaphor for teaching (in the progressive and radical, non-conservative sense) has recently received more serious and non-pejorative attention. Tom (1980, 1984) and Tom and Valli (1990) characterize teaching as a moral craft. Blumberg (1989) attempts to change the language used to describe administration from one of science to one of progressive craft. His intent is to focus attention on the implicit, tacit, and intuitive aspects of administration—the ways in which school principals develop a certain "know-how." Cohen (1977) argues that understanding educational phenomena in a manner consistent with a progressive and radical craft orientation will increase the likelihood of reforming practice in schools, and Perrone (1989, 1991), a progressive educator, states clearly that teachers need to learn from practice in order to refine their craft. Major works by Kohl (1988, 1986), by Greene (1984), and by Lieberman (1984) have the craft metaphor as a central feature. Further, the way teachers learn their craft would seem to be consistent with Resnick's (1991) and Liston and Zeichner's (1991) theory of situated practice,[5] because it leads to "action-based situated knowledge of teaching" (Leinhardt, 1990, p. 23). How, then, can craft knowledge be understood?

Toward a Definition

Blumberg (1989) builds his definition of craft around the work of Collingwood (1938) and Howard (1982). He draws on Collingwood (1938) to suggest that "craft always involves a distinction between means and end, each clearly conceived as something distinct from the other but related to it...the end is always thought out first, and afterwards the means are thought out" (pp. 15-16; cited in Blumberg, 1989, p. 24). Craft, according to Blumberg, is inherent in a knowledge and mastery of the means that are appropriate for realizing a given end. He asks, "[But] how does a man get a 'nose' for something? And how can this nose be used?" (Howard, 1982; Wittgenstein, 1958). This essentially raises the idea of "know-how" that Blumberg sees as central to an understanding of craft. Kohl (1988) is much more definitive about what constitutes such "know-how" as it relates to the craft of teaching:

> The craft of teaching has a number of aspects. It relates to the organization of content and the structuring of space and time so that student learning will be fostered. It requires an understanding of students' levels of sophistication and the modes of learning they are accustomed to using. But most centrally, the craft of teaching requires what can be called teaching sensibility. This sensibility develops over a career of teaching and has to do with knowing how to help students focus their energy on learning and growth. (p. 57)

According to Kohl (1986), craft involves the proficient use of some basic skills, including, "balancing teacher-initiated ideas with student-initiated ones,...doing research as a teacher, and observing and responding to what actually succeeded with the students. This is quite different from following a set curriculum or using standard texts, and involves *planning, research, observation, and response...*"(p. 54).

Tom (1984) sets forth a definition by Popkewitz and Wehlage (1973, p. 52) which, though lacking in a moral dimension, encompasses the essential features of craft—"Teaching should be viewed as a craft that includes a reflective approach toward problems, a cultivation of imagination, and a playfulness toward words, relationships, and experiences" (Tom, p. 113). He goes on to show how the addition of a moral dimension essentially helps a craft conception of teaching avoid the trap of representing an unthinking approach to trial-and-error. Zeichner, Tabachnick and Densmore (1987) use craft knowledge broadly as:

a rubric for describing a number of different approaches to studying the psychological context of teaching, from the more conventional studies of teachers' attitudes and beliefs to the more recent attempts to describe the 'implicit theories' of teachers, from the teachers' point of view and in the teachers' own language. (p. 21)

Greene (1984) appeals to the basic definition of craft offered by Kohl to grapple with how educators think about their craft:

To speak of craft is to presume a knowledge of and a certain range of skills and proficiencies. It is to imagine an educated capacity to attain a desired end-in-view or to bring about a desired result.... We may find ourselves reconstructing familiar techniques, honing a set of unused skills, and—significantly—using our imaginations in what turns out to be an effort to improve our craft...[which] is in many ways an example of personal knowledge at work; it is also a reminder that mastering a craft goes far beyond repetitions and routines. (pp. 55, 61)

Teaching as craft, then, assumes certain skills, proficiencies, and dispositions among accomplished teachers—in brief, it suggests an emphasis on a special kind of pedagogical content and learner "know-how," a "teaching sensibility," rather than a knowledge of propositions. Craft knowledge, therefore, concerns itself *both* with teachers' representations of the declarative knowledge contained in subject matter content *and* with teachers' tacit instantiations of procedural ways of dealing rigorously and supportively with learners. As a form of professional expertise, craft knowledge is neither technical skill, the application of theory or general principles to practice, nor critical analysis; rather, it represents the construction of situated, learner-focussed, procedural and content-related pedagogical knowledge through "deliberate action" (Kennedy, 1987).

Validity and Morality of Craft "Know-How"

Schön (1983, 1987, 1988, 1991) argues for the importance of the sort of competence practitioners display in "divergent" settings, i.e., those indeterminate situations that do not conform to the standard "textbook-like" problems of practice. He focusses instead on the "intuitive performance" of the actions of everyday life, and puts forth the construct of "knowledge-in-action." Similarly, in his classic book, *The Concept of Mind,* Ryle (1949) distinguishes between "knowing how" and "knowing that." Schön and Ryle are not arguing for a kind of mindless knowing in action sometimes referred to as "kinesthetic." Rather, they argue that there is nothing in common sense to suggest that knowing how to do something well consists of knowing rules and plans that we entertain in the mind prior to actions.

> What distinguishes sensible from silly operations is not their parentage but their procedure, and this holds no less for intellectual than for practical performance. "Intelligent" cannot be defined in terms of "intellectual" or "know how" in terms of "knowing that"; "thinking about what I am doing" does not connote "both thinking what to do and doing it." When I do something intelligently, I am doing one thing, not two. My performance has a special procedure or manner, not special antecedents. (Ryle, 1949, p. 32)

The assertion that intelligent performance does not necessarily depend upon the consideration of a prior set of procedures is crucial to Schön's analysis, too. However, this is not to say that thinking in advance of a situation has no bearing on how one subsequently executes action. As Ryle elaborated:

> Certainly, we often do not only reflect before we act but reflect in order to act properly. The chess-player may require some time in which to plan his moves before he makes them. Yet the general assertion that all intelligent performance requires to be prefaced by the consideration of appropriate propositions rings unplausibly, even when it is apologetically conceded that the required consideration is often very swift and may go quite unmarked by the agent. I shall argue that the intellectualist legend is false and that when we describe a performance as intelligent, this does not entail the double operation of considering and executing. (pp. 29-30)

Ryle's example of the "wit" provides a good illustration:

> The wit, when challenged to cite the maxims, or canons by which he constructs and appreciates jokes, is unable to answer. He knows how to make good jokes and how to detect bad ones, but he cannot tell us or himself any recipes for them. So the practice of humour is not a client of its theory. (p. 30)

For Ryle, and for Schön, the existence and importance of "knowing how"—what I am calling craft knowledge—is central to the matter of learning a practice. This is not to say that "learning by doing" without analysis is a substitute for "learning by doing" with a theory. Rather, it is to say that "learning by doing" mitigates some of the difficulties that arise when a practitioner is unable to analyze competent performance and articulate its features. Certainly, intuitive actions are subject to thoughtful consideration and further articulation and understanding. The point is, however, that the reverse is not the case; intelligent performance does not follow automatically from knowing a set of procedures and maxims. As Ryle puts it:

> Efficient practice precedes the theory of it; methodologies presuppose the application of the methods, of the critical investigation of which they are the products. It was because Aristotle found himself and others reasoning now intelligently and now stupidly and it was because Izaak Walton found himself angling sometimes effectively and sometimes ineffectively that both were able to give their pupils the maxims and prescriptions of the arts. It is therefore plausible for people intelligently to perform some sorts of operations when they are not yet able to consider propositions enjoining how they should be performed. Some intelligent performances are not controlled by any anterior acknowledgements of the principles applied in them. (p. 30)

So far I have argued that craft knowledge represents *intelligent and sensible* "know-how" in the action setting. But I would also argue that it is more than this. Craft knowledge contains within it certain criteria that comment on the "rightness" of such intelligent and sensible action. I find Gutman's (1987) elaboration of what constitutes democratic education to be persuasive and useful in establishing guidelines for *morally* appropriate intelligent and sensible action. Gutman maintains that a democratic education honour three basic principles: first, it must develop a deliberative, democratic character in students; second, it cannot repress rational deliberation; and, third, it cannot discriminate against any group of children. Her reasoning is that, within a democracy, we are collectively committed to recreating the society we share:

> As citizens, we aspire to a set of educational practices and authorities [a core commitment to conscious social reproduction] of which the following can be said: these are the practices and

authority of which we, acting collectively as a society, have consciously agreed. It follows that a society that supports conscious social reproduction must educate all educable children to be capable of participating in collectively shaping their society. (Gutman, 1987, p. 39)

A society thus committed to conscious social reproduction through the broad educational aim of critical deliberation, however, requires some limits to preserve the rights of all its democratic members. Gutman (1987) suggests two such limits: 1) non-repression, which "prevents the state, and any group within it, from using education to restrict rational deliberation of competing conceptions of the good life and the good society" (p. 44); and 2) nondiscrimination, which prevents the State and families from "excluding entire groups of children from schooling or denying them an education conducive to deliberation among conceptions of the good life and the good society" (p. 45). Following Gutman, then, I would claim that intelligent and sensible action is morally appropriate when it is nonrepressive and nondiscriminatory in its attempts at developing critical deliberation in students.

Thus, craft knowledge of teaching is not substantive, subject-matter knowledge; nor is it syntactical knowledge (that knowledge which derives from the disciplines and enables people to know how to acquire further disciplinary knowledge); rather, it is a particular form of morally appropriate intelligent and sensible "know-how" which is constructed by teachers, holding progressive and radical educational beliefs, in the context of their lived experiences and work around issues of content-related and learner-focussed pedagogy.

A Brief Overview of the Substance of Craft Knowledge

Grimmett and MacKinnon (1992, pp. 13-53) provide a thorough review of research and writings bearing on the craft knowledge of teachers. They suggest that the substance of craft knowledge is made up of first- and second-order abstractions of pedagogical content and learner knowledge. By first-order abstraction, they mean research and writing that is undertaken by practising teachers in the action setting. By second-order abstraction, they mean studies that are undertaken by university researchers who are themselves highly sensitive to and rigorously curious about teachers' pedagogical content and learner knowledge. They do not, however, present the review along clearly differentiated first- and second-order lines of investigation. Their purpose is to bring first-order abstractions into the teacher education curriculum equation, not to downplay university research; thus, their focus is on the substance of craft knowledge and its potential use in the education of teachers, not on its derivation.[6]

The review consists of two broad sections. The first section presents five interrelated (and rather loosely categorized) genres of research representing pedagogical content and learner knowledge that have furthered our understanding of craft knowledge in teaching. This part of the review examines studies conducted in the genres of pedagogical content knowledge, reflective practice, narrative/storytelling (and the cinema), teachers' lives, and teacher research.

The second section examines the writings of major practitioners whose work has made important contributions to an understanding of craft knowledge. Three authors are selected on the basis of each being a recognized successful and experienced scholarly-oriented practitioner. They also represent differences in gender and race and exemplify the progressive and radical ways of thinking about craft. Their writings represent exemplary cases in which the wisdom of practice is documented. They are Herbert Kohl (1986, 1988), Vivian Gussin Paley (1981, 1989), and Eliot Wigginton (1985, 1989, 1991).[7] Wigginton represents a progressive scholarly practitioner whose writings embody wisdom gained over the last 25 years or so. Paley is a female progressive educator whose work deals extensively with radical-like issues of social justice and cultural differences. Kohl is a radical scholarly practitioner, who moves with apparent ease between the academic world of universities and the challenging rigours of classroom practice.

Framing Craft Knowledge

Craft knowledge is essentially the accumulated wisdom derived from teachers' and practice-oriented researchers' understandings of the meanings ascribed to the many dilemmas inherent in teaching. As such, craft knowledge emphasizes judgment—often in aesthetic terms—rather than following the maxims of research generated knowledge. It relies heavily on intuition, care, and empathy for pupils. It is steeped in morality and ever critical in its search for meaningful schooling and benefit for pupils.[8] Understandings derived from craft knowledge would appear to revolve around the purposes of teaching, the context of work within which learning takes place, teachers' sentiments about their role as facilitators of learning, and their need to be heard during a tumultuous time of restructuring.

A primary purpose of the craft of teaching is to understand and engage the minds of all learners. Teaching is not telling, talking, cajoling, or coercing; nor is it a case of teachers merely teaching and students merely learning. Crafty (in the dexterous, ingenious sense) teachers seek to know their students, to listen and reach out to them with care and understanding. Such understanding provides the basis for teacher-student engagement. This engagement, in turn, enables teachers to create opportunities and capacities for students to reach beyond what they currently know toward what is yet to be known.

Crafty teachers set out to foster an insatiable desire for learning, a zestful curiosity about events, encounters, and experiences. This purpose is based on the assumption that all students have legitimate ways of making sense of phenomena and experiences, and that curriculum content can be organized in ways that "validate" students' ideas. Such reorganization is often thematic and interdisciplinary. Together with students, teachers frame the essential questions of inquiry and focus directly on what it takes to make learning memorable to students.

Learning becomes memorable when all students become active explorers and teachers themselves. To promote this purpose, however, it is not always possible to cover every aspect of the curriculum content. As Whitehead (1957) points out:

> Let the main ideas which are introduced into a child's education be few and important, and let them be thrown into every combination possible. The child should make them his own, and should understand their application here and now in the circumstances of his own life. (p. 14)

Understanding, not speed, is the essential aim of crafty teachers; for students who learn to understand their world also acquire the skills necessary for searching out new information when it is needed. Thus, a main purpose associated with craft knowledge is that of becoming an advocate for all students and their learning. This typically means refusing to believe that any student cannot learn and striving with colleagues to ensure that no student is disadvantaged by unfair diagnosis, labeling, or institutional pressure. Crafty teachers set out to transform classrooms—and ultimately schools into places in which all students become celebrated learners controlling their own uniqueness.

An important aspect of craft knowledge in teaching is that the work context of inquiry and student learning is collaborative in the sense that teachers and students negotiate meaning and work activities together. Further, the work context in the classroom is intimately related to the "real world" outside, as crafty teachers see connecting points everywhere. To function in the work context in a manner consistent with the accumulated wisdom of craft knowledge, teachers have to prepare assiduously by anticipating some of the situations that could arise in classroom teaching. They gather materials, they note down ideas and activities, they hunt out different kinds of teaching resources, and generally prepare much more than they could ever use in any given lesson, unit, or year. This preparation gives them a repertoire upon which they can draw as they attempt to engage the minds of all students and negotiate with them potential work activities.

It also permits teachers to act flexibly within the work context, as they engage in "rolling" planning. Anticipatory preparation happens before classroom teaching begins. It equates to Jackson's (1968) notion of preactive teaching. "Rolling" planning occurs when the teacher is actively involved in the engagement process with students in the classroom— Jackson's (1968) notion of interactive teaching. In other words, anticipatory preparation before teaching is the foundation for "rolling" planning during classroom interaction. Such preparation is not a prescription for action (like a lesson plan) that determines what the students can and cannot do; rather, its function is to prepare the teacher (not student work) for what could happen in the classroom. Once instruction is under way, the anticipatory preparation becomes a safety net of ideas and activities that the teacher can fall back on as he or she "rolls with the punches," as it were, in negotiating work activities with the students. "Rolling" planning, therefore, involves teachers in observing, analyzing, hypothesizing, and responding as they attempt to create curriculum-on-the-spot with their students. It consists of balancing teacher-initiated ideas with student-initiated ones so that the work context of inquiry becomes one that truly facilitates student learning.

Exceptional teachers assume that all students have within them an inherent desire to learn. Of utmost importance to them is finding ways of channeling that desire within the classroom. Consequently, it becomes sacrosanct for crafty teachers to ensure that all classroom work is infused by student choice, student volition, and student action. This perspective attempts to treat students not as potentially wayward children but as able members of society.

Teaching is not just a job for crafty teachers; it is a vocation for which they have developed a passion. They are obsessed by the urge to help others learn and grow. Caring for students and nurturing them as persons is a theme that runs through much of the writings on teaching as a craft. Kohl crystallizes this in his phrase, "loving students as learners." Unlike an undifferentiated sense of caring and nurturing, such a sentiment is neither unfocussed nor languid; rather, it is the clear communication of teachers' passion for learning.

The purposes of teaching that crafty teachers pursue, the collaborative context within which they do their work, and the sentiments they hold inevitably lead to an emerging moral voice. These teachers speak on behalf of students. Their language is not confined to the expression of educational aims and expectations; its syntax is existential with words like "caring," "loving," "nurturing," "listening," "empathic understanding," and "connecting." They do not write about the technical aspects of teaching; rather, their focus is on ways of relating with all students in a manner which promotes learning. They make promises to students they intend to keep; they reach out to difficult or withdrawn children to include them in the group; they involve students in curriculum-making; they insist that the work be the students' and not an imposition of their own agendas; they are prepared to take risks and face ridicule to contend for student-oriented opportunities to learn. In short, they bring a finely-tuned conscience to bear on all of their actions in the classroom.

This moral voice is not to be confused with professional ethics. The latter is more teacher-centred whereas the former is most definitely student-centred. Thus, it is possible for a crafty teacher to become morally outraged at the talk and actions of a colleague who denigrates students. Such a moral standpoint is closely linked to criticism of taken-for-granted assumptions in the status quo. Traugh et al. (1986) refer to this as "having a voice that is critical and political" (p. 4).

Teachers gain a critical voice when they begin to think about and discuss with others the complex and embedded social, political, and moral frameworks of schooling. They begin to challenge many of the instrumental assumptions embedded in schooling and curriculum guides—they are quick to point out fallacious assumptions about students as learners. They critique the "persistency of individualism, presentism, and privacy" (Little, 1990) among teachers in school and call for a genuine collegiality that permits individuality but not isolation. They rue the conditions of the workplace that militate against teacher reflection, particularly where such lack of reflection condemns teachers to repeat their past inadequacies. They understand the power that resides in the beliefs and values that constitute the normative basis for action in the school culture, and they argue vehemently against those kinds of beliefs and values which do not respect the esteem and learning needs of students. They essentially act in this way because they are committed to changing the way society functions from a meretricious, unforgiving collectivity to an authentic, caring, and responsible community.

The empowering of teachers and development of their moral and critical voice is not, however, unproblematic. Zeichner (1990) has pointed to the contradictions and tensions inherent in the professionalization of teaching and the democratization of schools. Giving teachers more opportunities to shape their work conditions can easily lead to an intensification of the workplace.

> Teacher empowerment does not necessarily have to lead to a situation in which the achievement of the school's academic mission is undermined or teachers are overstressed, but it can, unless efforts are made to incorporate their participation in schoolwide decision making *into* their work instead of adding it *to* their work. (p. 367)

At the same time, an uncritical acceptance of teacher empowerment can "serve under some circumstances to undercut important connections between schools and their communities" (p. 367) leading to teachers using their increased professionalism to further distance parents and communities from attaining a meaningful voice in school affairs. Zeichner (1990) thus maintains that most of the second-wave educational reforms "fail to ac-knowledge the need for...the kinds of economic, social, and political changes outside of schools that will be needed to complement the democratic educational projects advocated for within schools—the social precondi-tions for educational reform" (p. 374). At the same time, he argues that:

> there is little hope of achieving this ideal [of democratic school governance] without linking this project to efforts in other spheres of society that are directed toward the elimination of inequalities based on gender, race, social class, sexual preference, physical condition, and so forth, no matter how noble our intentions. We cannot create democratic school communities in an undemocratic society. We cannot build "tomorrow's schools" in today's unequal society. (p. 374)

Such a direction inevitably involves the cultivation of a political voice for teachers who are committed to a less teacher-centred approach to instruction and to the democratization of schools.

In a time when there appears to be no shortage of advice on how teachers should do their jobs, their political voice stands up to external imposition of others' initiatives, such as standardized testing, national core curriculum, and basic skills in kindergarten. Perrone (1991) succinctly sums up the reasons why teachers need to develop their political voice:

> Children and young people...need our best efforts. But...teachers need to construct for themselves a more powerful voice....I remain convinced that we would not have the same external pressures— for accountability rooted in standardized tests, a regulatory orientation to schools governed by persons or groups who stand far away from particular schools and their students—if teachers themselves were clearer and more articulate about their purposes, speaking and writing about their hopes for children, young people and communities. (p. 133)

Integrating Craft Knowledge Into the Teacher Education Curriculum

Kennedy (1990) posits that there are two broad goals in professional education. One is the goal of providing as much codified knowledge as possible for teachers so that they can be thereby armed with the conceptual, methodological, and curricular instructional knowledge that is foundational to good teaching. The other is the goal of enhancing independent thought and analysis, based on the assumption that best strategies have not yet been discovered or that they are too situation-specific to be prescribed, thus practitioners must learn to create solutions for themselves.

Re-inscribing foundational knowledge in the curriculum of teacher education through an initial focus on teachers' craft knowledge represents the latter goal. Such a focus permits the articulation of those dilemmas and problems, e.g., how to teach in a multicultural context, inherent in the current social context of teaching. It is the responsibility of faculty members engaged in teacher education to bring foundational knowledge to bear on such problems and dilemmas as they attempt to expose teachers to alternative worldviews and challenge the latters' taken-for-granted assumptions about practice.[9] The following ways represent a sketch of how craft knowledge could be used in teacher education.

One obvious way is to include more writing and research (actual studies, not reviews) of teachers in the reading material of teacher education courses. This is something that Ken Zeichner and colleagues at the University of Wisconsin have developed very well. An extension of this is to engage student teachers in a form of active inquiry into their own classroom teaching. Teacher educators can model this process by conducting action research into their own teaching of student teachers, with a particular focus on the role they play in fostering student teacher classroom research. The initial focus at both levels can be on exploring dilemmas of practice, with a subsequent focus on making problematic the classroom, school, and societal context of teaching and learning. In this way student teachers and teacher educators begin to connect their classroom research to issues of equity and social justice and grapple with how such issues constrain student learning.

A different way of incorporating craft knowledge into teacher education would be to follow Clark's (1991) principles of design for self-directed professional development. Briefly, this would involve student teachers in writing their own credo for teaching. They would start with their strengths and proceed to make a long-term plan. They would look in your own backyard, that is, look to other teachers rather than outside experts for useful instructional strategies and information. They would be encouraged to ask for support, go first class in everything they do, and ultimately blow their own horn. These principles would be used to encourage student teachers to begin with themselves (Hunt, 1987) as sources of vital and viable information about the craft of teaching.

A further way of incorporating craft knowledge in teacher education would be to get student teachers to develop their own metaphors of teaching. Lakoff and Johnson (1980) state that "the essence of a metaphor is understanding and experiencing one kind of thing in terms of another" (p. 5). It would, therefore, be possible to frame activities around research strategies found in Russell et al., (1988) and Munby and Russell (1989) as a way of having student teachers develop metaphors which re-frame their classroom experiences. Developing metaphors might, however, appeal only to the more linguistically inclined student teachers. For the more visually-oriented student teacher, it would be possible to have them draw pictures of such ideas as "school," "classroom," "students," "good teaching," and "memorable learning experiences." This is not dissimilar from what Wigginton (1985, 1989, 1991) proposes with students in the Foxfire project courses, except that it is done visually and not orally. A further example of visual expression for incorporating craft knowledge into teacher education can be found in Weade and Ernst (1989). They ask student teachers to take photographs of their field experiences as a kind of visual ethnography.

These photographs then become an instrument for expressing personal meaning. This approach is advantageous for student teachers who are visually inclined but disadvantageous in that this "technical" approach can, if not carefully monitored, lead to the objectification of experience.

I think that three further approaches merit serious consideration. One is using imagination, visualization, and guided fantasy. Allender (1982) uses what she calls the "4th Grade Fantasy Activity" to help student teachers become aware of experiences that inhibit or promote learning.

> I tell everyone to find a comfortable spot, to close their eyes and I then turn off the lights. (This always produces a lot of stirrings and giggling. Remember that most of these students are used to a traditional lecture series.) I then proceed to have them quietly breathe deeply for 2-3 minutes, listening to the air flowing in and out of their bodies, and then 2-3 minutes tensing and untensing each part of their bodies beginning from the feet up to the head. When I feel they are relaxed I begin the activity (pp. 37-38).

In their imagination, Allender takes the students back to their elementary school. They are told they are fourth graders and that it is time for classes to begin. The teachers spend 10 minutes in their imaginary fourth grade classrooms; Allender suggests they look closely at the room arrangement, the wall coverings, the placement of students, the general climate, etc. After 10 minutes, they return to the present and draw a picture or write a story about the classroom they saw in their minds' recollections. In small groups, they exchange their pictures and stories. In the large group, they then share what they discussed in small groups. This activity can then be repeated with a focus on the "ideal" classroom.

The second approach that I think can be used productively for incorporating craft knowledge in teacher education revolves around showing movies, such as the ones reviewed by Grimmett and MacKinnon (1992). A structured task would accompany the showing. Student teachers would be asked to characterize the view of learning embedded within the movie. They would also be asked to respond educationally to some of the dilemmas presented in the film and asked to compare these with their own experiences in classrooms. I have used this approach myself in a recent course. The movie *Dead Poets' Society* was shown and the following represents one student's response:

I remember watching the film and was, I am sure like many, initially captivated by the engaging performance of Robin Williams in his portrayal of the charismatic, seemingly unconventional English teacher who touches the souls of his students. For some reason, however, the movie gave us [a group of students] feelings of discomfort....

What kind of teacher is portrayed in this film? In what sense is he unconventional? The word which leaps to mind in trying to characterize the man is charismatic. The teacher appeals to us because he is humourous, personally engaging, and does strange, unorthodox things like stand on desks and speak in odd accents. I think, however, if we remove the gloss that what we are left with is a teacher who, like many of his more "conservative" counterparts, is the centre of instruction, the fount of knowledge and inspiration for his students, one who uses the classroom to play out his own psychodramas. It is interesting that in the film the metaphor commonly employed by the young men is that of the "captain," the leader, the officer of highest rank, not the craftsman. My interpretation, albeit somewhat harsh, helps me to explain why the young man, at the end of the movie, unable to cope with his problems, commits suicide. How can we expect him to cope? He has been presented with an alternative vision but has never been given the tools with which to construct it; in the end his education has failed him. There is a scene when the star-crossed student approaches his teacher; the streets are snow-covered; the student is obviously distraught; the teacher is in somewhat of a hurry. When he is asked for advice, the teacher responds by telling the student to talk it over with his father; the teacher drives away with his girlfriend while the young man goes home and shoots himself. (Ponsart, 1991)

A third approach to teacher education that would express a view of teaching as craft concerns the design of classes in teaching methodology. Such "methods classes," as they are referred to in many institutions, are often taught in terms of the disciplines of the school curriculum (i.e, science methods, math methods, language arts methods, etc.). Traditionally, these classes in teaching methodology have taken place on campus, in the absence of children. At best, they have engaged "microteaching" of peers as a way of introducing the analysis of actual teaching. A craft conception of teaching would justify undertaking some of this work in school settings, where professors of education would join education students in the actual teaching of children. MacKinnon and Grunau (1991) document a school-based teacher education programme in which a group of education students in their student teaching year took most of their coursework in a school setting. They write about the development of a community among these student teachers, the learnings that occurred when student teachers taught alongside their professors and their peers, and when videotapes of that teaching were critiqued. The central argument of this work is that all the participants—beginning and experienced teachers, as well as the professors—learned a great deal about teaching at one anothers' elbows.

Any or all of these approaches could be used to incorporate craft knowledge into the teacher education programme. I have a predilection toward using teacher research reports, active classroom inquiry, the showing of movies, and school-based "methods" courses, but I am convinced that the other methods also provide useful avenues for exploring craft knowledge in teacher education. In the final analysis, finding ways of incorporating craft knowledge about teaching into teacher education is itself a craft that can only be acquired through rigorous and reflective practice on the part of teacher educators.

Concluding Note

Teachers learn the craft of teaching through experience. Analysis and considered response to practical experiences are necessary too. But craft knowledge is vastly different from the packaged and glossy maxims that govern the "science of education"—or, the expectation that rules and "findings" can drive practice. Craft knowledge has a different sort of rigour—one that places more confidence in the *judgments* of teachers, their feel for their work, their love for students and learning, and so on. Ryle and Schön reminded us that there are good reasons for distinguishing between "knowing that" and "knowing how," suggesting that craft is something that is acquired "at the elbows," rather than in books.

Craft knowledge can act as a sensitizing framework for teachers' collaborative explorations with students of how learning occurs. Such a framework, I argue, would constitute a broadly conceived set of principles framed around such themes as: the purposes of teaching; the work context of inquiry in teaching; the sentiments derived by teachers in such a positive work context; and, the moral, critical, and political voices that teachers develop in pursuing the purposes of teaching in a work context of inquiry. These principles would provoke discussion and intellectual ferment; they would stimulate teachers to reflect on why they enact certain classroom practices and resist others. The principles also require a situationally-based, contextually-relevant interpretation. Such discussion and interpretation of problems inherent in the social context of teaching provides a forum for the careful re-inscription of foundational knowledge in teacher education. Craft knowledge, therefore, has a powerful contribution to make to teacher education programmes that are practice-based and whose aim is to instil in teachers a love of learning and a disposition toward student-focussed, reflective inquiry.

Notes

*   I wish to acknowledge the contribution of my esteemed colleague at Simon Fraser University, Allan MacKinnon, to my thinking and writing about craft knowledge and the education of teachers.

1.   See Grimmett, P.P. (1991, October). *Collaborative teacher development: The vital role of faculty.* Paper presented at the first invitational symposium of "Understanding Teacher Development," University of Western Ontario, London, ON.

2.   This Center is next to the home of Herbert and Judith Kohl.

3.   Schneider (1987) notes that historically, the study of pedagogy was considered an integral part of philosophy. When philosophy and psychology divided into two distinct disciplines, educational psychology took up "didactic thinking" and philosophy assumed the moral and ethical aspects of pedagogy. Neither one grappled with questions of "how to teach," leaving teacher education to pick up the technical aspects of pedagogy. This is the reason, so Schneider maintains, why teacher education has been preoccupied with defining "a legitimate substantive knowledge base focused on training" (p. 214). My argument is that craft knowledge can contribute to teacher education's search for what Schneider has termed "a legitimate substantive knowledge base focused on training." Moreover, I agree with the position of Cochran-Smith and Lytle (1990), and Liston & Zeichner (1991) that it would be a mistake to limit the knowledge base for teaching and teacher education to those topics and foci that university-based researchers have chosen to study and write about. I acknowledge that many of the university-based researchers in the progressive and radical traditions make every effort to be responsive to the questions, issues, and dilemmas that practitioners face but would argue that there needs to be a greater appreciation within the established research community of the important contributions that inquiries conducted by practitioners can make to the

process of teacher education.

4. Liston and Zeichner (1991) give a delightful characterization of how representatives of these respective traditions argue the correctness of their own position and complain about students being misled and miseducated by the other traditions. "Conservatives rail against the anti-intellectual orientation of the progressive tradition, and they deride the utopianism and foggy thinking of the radical tradition. Progressives accuse conservatives of seeing only the intellectual powers of children and thereby miscontruing students' engagement in learning, and they criticize radicals for their indoctrinatory practices. Radicals condemn conservatives for their ideological obfuscation and elitist politics, and they chide progressives for their romantic view of the child and liberal view of society" (p. 53).

5   Liston and Zeichner (1991) define teaching as situated practice, as a "view of teachers as social actors engaged in practices within a particular context" (p. 22).

6. Grimmett and MacKinnon (1992) view the task of reviewing the craft knowledge of teachers as being fraught with a dilemma namely, how does one frame it in such a way that it retains the essential features of craft and does not become another prescriptive knowledge base. The tacit character of craft knowledge makes its attempted explication an oxymoron. Tom and Valli (1990) crystallize this very dilemma thus: In what ways can tacit knowledge from the craft tradition be codified? Which forms of codification make this knowledge accessible to other practitioners? Or is the codification of craft knowledge sensitive to various contexts and to contrasting conceptions of good teaching, a knowledge base, appropriate only in the case of positivism, an orientation that presumes that practice can be derived from knowledge? Can craft knowledge ever be viewed as a systematic way of knowing, with its characteristic methods of inquiry, rules of evidence, and forms of knowledge, so that we can talk about an epistemology of craft knowledge? What is the warrant for craft knowledge? (p. 390).

    They also raise further questions. If craft knowledge/teacher research produces the questions that spawn "searchings" (Erickson, 1991) and not "findings" (the usual grist for the "knowledge base" mill), how does one come to a communal understanding of accounts of practice which deliberately make the familiar strange, thereby increasing the alienation and continual uncertainty inherent in teaching? Can "the sweet poison of search," as Erickson (1991) characterizes it, be captured in anything other than a story or a case study? Can one synthesize craft knowledge without colonizing it?

These thorny questions pinpoint the difficulty of their task but do not propose any potential resolution to the dilemma. To attempt to codify the "searchings" of craft knowledge in a manner similar to a positivistic knowledge base would "strip it of its meaning and vitality" (Yinger, 1987, p. 309), because, in the final analysis, teacher education is more a process of moral development than a process of building a knowledge base, skills, and expertise (Sirotnik, 1990). Consequently, they do not present craft knowledge as a knowledge base, as such, but as a framework for helping prospective and experienced teachers develop their "repertoire of responses, understanding, and magical tricks" (Kohl, personal communication, 1991). This course of action precludes the possibility of differentiating this section according to categories, like pedagogical content and pedagogical learner knowledge, that they would see as undermining the essential features of craft in the knowlege that they review.

7. For Grimmett and MacKinnon (1992), the temptation was to include other authors, such as, Maxine Greene, Alan Tom, Ann Lieberman, Lee Shulman, Vito Perrone, Eleanor Duckworth, David Hawkins, William Ayers, and Estelle Fuchs who also write about craft knowledge. They were excluded because, despite their strong practice orientation, not one is a recognized school teacher. Further, the three practitioners chosen were deemed to be representative of the work in craft knowledge.

8. Like Shulman (1987) and Leinhardt (1990), I recognize that craft knowledge can sometimes be faulty and misleading in contexts in which the teacher's subject matter knowledge is less than adequate. However, I see this as further evidence of the tentativeness and uncertainty that, for me, characterizes craft knowledge. I do not hold it up as an example of perfection, but rather as a framework of teacher's searchings and implicit theorizing about the nurturing of students and their learning.

9. See Grimmett (1991) for a characterization of the role played by faculty members in collaborative teacher education.

Policies

Chapter Five

The Role of Teacher Education in the Restructuring of Education in Ontario

Donald B. Maudsley

The role of the Ministry of Education in Ontario, as elsewhere, is not to create new theories, models, and technologies but to recognize them as they are created. It is up to academics to develop innovations and practitioners to test them, and perfect them. Then the government's role is to create policies and programmes to facilitate their use across the system.

In this chapter, I describe some policy and programme developments that led to the current policy consultation, known as the "restructuring initiatives." I then describe the Teacher Education Work Team and the context it has created for policy development.

In the last section of the chapter, I describe several strategies that might be used and the crucial role that teacher educators, both academics and practitioners, can play to support the restructuring and to transform teacher education.

This last section contains three images of teachers: the teacher as steward, maintaining the traditions of excellence in our system; the teacher as reformer, the key change agent in transforming our education system; and, the teacher as learner, a crucial image. For teachers to play the first two roles, they must be lifelong learners.

The Restructuring Initiatives

The restructuring of education in Ontario has often been traced to the influential study by George Radwanski, *Ontario Study of the Relevance of Education and the Issue of Dropouts* (1987), and the four reports of the Select Committee on Education (Ontario Legislative Assembly, 1988, 1989, 1990a, and 1990b). Radwanski addressed the issue of dropouts and a broad range of related topics including streaming, evaluation, and the impact on their studies of secondary school students' part-time employment. The

Select Committee looked at the goals of education, the school day and the school year, education finance, and early childhood education. In fact, these studies documented trends that had already been visible for several years prior. The restructuring initiatives announced in the Throne Speech of April 1989 were, rather, the logical outcome of events and influences that predated these studies.

There are, however, several previous studies which can be considered influential to the restructuring. In the early 1980s, the Secondary Education Review Project (SERP) produced *Ontario Schools: Intermediate and Senior Divisions* (OSIS). Landmark legislation in special education (Bill 82) placed Ontario in the vanguard of school systems in Canada and North America in this area. The Early Primary Education Project (EPEP) of the early 1980s, which popularized the concept of active learning, was the forerunner of the current Formative Years policy discussion.

By the mid 1980s, these programme concerns had been supplanted by issues of educational governance and finance. The French language school system was established with the implementation of French language school boards and sections. The Ontario government extended full funding for the separate schools to the end of the secondary panel, in accordance with constitutional provisions of the previous century. The MacDonald Commission (1985) and the Shapiro Commission (1985) examined, respectively, the financing of education, in general, and the status of private schooling in Ontario. Discussion and analysis of these issues continue but the education agenda had, by the late 1980s, shifted away from governance and finance, and toward a significant examination of programme at all levels.

Several broad trends in society contributed to the restructuring initiatives which were launched in the Throne Speech of 1989. The global economy had arrived in Ontario, with its imperative of worldwide economic competition. The service economy had mushroomed in the province, the country, and the world, replacing the agricultural and industrial economies that had preceded it. The age of the microcomputer and the explosion of information technology had arrived. Too often, the viability and credibility of many of the existing major institutions, such as the church, business, and education were eroded. Rapid change became, and remains today, the only constant in the world at large, and in the world of education.

In the meantime, the Ontario public had begun to express specific concerns about its schools. The dropout rate of approximately 30 percent, although it had declined dramatically from 50 or 60 percent, was no longer considered acceptable in the information society. Parents complained that they simply could not understand the school system, while business and industry, as they have for centuries, emphatically declared that the quality of graduates had decreased. High among these concerns was the rate of functional illiteracy, estimated to be 25 to 35 percent of the adult population.

Secondary school education focussed primarily on the students who had selected the advanced stream, the programme leading to post-secondary studies. Students leaving school for the world of work were not being adequately prepared, and little emphasis was being given to technological literacy. Many students found themselves dead-ended in the basic or vocational stream. In fact, parents had begun *de facto* to de-stream the secondary schools by refusing to enrol their children in the basic stream. These rather negative perceptions of the school system formed the backdrop for the initiatives announced in the Throne Speech of 1989.

The restructuring initiatives were conceived as five interconnected projects spanning the entire school programme from junior kindergarten to graduation. New labels were devised to describe more meaningfully the divisions to which they referred: the Early Years (JK-K), the Formative Years (Grades 1-6), the Transition Years (Grades 7-9) and the Specialization Years (Grades 10 through graduation). Technological education, the fifth, was defined separately, not only because it is a separate category of teacher certification, but also because it applies to the entire spectrum of the programme from junior kindergarten through to graduation. To implement and support changes in all five of these areas, the Ministry recognized the importance and the relevance of teacher education through the provision of the sixth initiative.

Representatives from all segments of the educational community formed the work teams established for each initiative. At any given stage since 1989, approximately 50 people, in total, have been engaged in various facets of the restructuring initiatives. The Ministry of Education devised a matrix management scheme to support the project and, in addition, developed a comprehensive consultation process. These structures are described elsewhere (e.g., Ontario Ministry of Education, *Action Plan 1990-94*).

Each work team's task was to identify and clarify issues, prepare a discussion paper, seek reaction, and develop policy options for senior decision makers in government. At the time of writing, the third annual action plan was ready for publication, four teams had released discussion papers, and the response phase was complete for three of them (the

Formative Years, Technological Education, and the Transition Years).

The Role of the Teacher Education Work Team

I turn now to the role of the Teacher Education Work Team and examine three aspects of the context in which it is developing policy options.

Previous Studies on Teacher Education

The Teacher Education Work Team is conducting the latest in a series of reviews of teacher education. Since 1950, the topic of teacher education has never been far from the thoughts of educational reformers. No fewer than 10 reports in Ontario, although focussing primarily on other aspects of education, have made explicit references to teacher education. The earliest, the Hope Commission (1950), proposed that the universities assume the responsibility for teacher education, which was, at that time, conducted by the Ministry-run teachers' colleges. This became a reality in 1975. The Hope Commission further advocated field-based preservice programmes which have only begun to appear in the 1980s.[1]

The most recent report on teacher education, the 1988 *Report of the Teacher Education Review Steering Committee* (TERC) produced 33 recommendations, only two of which were immediately implemented. These led to the establishment of the Teacher Education Council, Ontario (TECO), whose role is to generate policy advice, and the changes to the role of the Ministries of Education and of Colleges and Universities, which led to the formation of the Centre for Teacher Education (CTE). The Centre has as its main function to implement policy and programmes. The other 31 recommendations in this report were referred to TECO for study. In the interim, the government, in a process most kindly described as "austerity driven," disbanded TECO and reduced the size of the Centre for Teacher Education to a unit within another branch. This change in government has had little impact on the ideas presented with the obvious exception of governance.

This preoccupation with teacher education is currently widespread in both Canada and the U.S. (Fullan, Connelly, & Watson, 1990; Association of Teacher Educators, 1991; British Columbia, 1988; Sikula, 1990). However, the explicit connection of teacher education with the restructuring of education systems is relatively recent. In a recent review of the literature, Thiessen et al. have described the trends of intensification and restructuring in education, and have traced the role of teacher education "as an aid to reform, then as a problem to solve, and more recently, as one of the focal points of [the] calls to restructure the educational system" (1991, p. 11). Later, I will return to their ideas.

Present Arrangements for Teacher Education

The 1988 Teacher Education Review Committee's (TERC) recommendations led to a division of responsibilities for teacher education into four spheres. The faculties of 10 Ontario universities continued to deliver teacher education programmes through nine English and two French faculties (the University of Ottawa delivers both English and French programmes). The Ministry of Colleges and Universities (MCU) retained the mandate of funding teacher education as part of its overall funding of post-secondary education. MCU continued to provide programme development funding as well, a function which has created a degree of ambiguity about the role of both the Ministry of Colleges and Universities, and the Ministry of Education. The Teacher Education Council, Ontario (TECO), was established, comprising representatives of the four constituencies: school boards, the teachers' federation, the universities, and the government. TECO is an advisory council of the Ontario government which reports to both ministries through the Deputy Minister of Education. It will develop policy advice based on the 33 TERC recommendations and respond to referrals from either ministry on policy questions. At the present time, TECO's agenda includes admissions, faculty renewal, programme review, preservice education, and inservice education. Through its task forces and research programme, TECO has involved representatives from its four constituencies.

Government responsibility for teacher education was for a long time located in the Ministry of Education. After a brief period in MCU, the Centre for Teacher Education was created out of some of the functions of the University Relations Branch and of the Professional Development Branch of the Ministry of Education, and located once again in the Ministry of Education, to provide a locus for policy development and programme implementation. The Centre contains the registrar's function for teacher certification as well as responsibility for Regulation 269 and for the sections of Regulation 262 that spell out how teachers may be appointed. Regulation 269 specifies the components of preservice and inservice teacher education programmes, and defines the various types of certification that teachers may hold. These regulations have since been renamed 297 and 298 respectively; and the Ministries of Education and Colleges and Universities were recently collapsed into one Ministry of Education and then renamed the Ministry of Education and Training.

To these four entities, the Ministry of Education, as part of the restructuring initiatives, added the Teacher Education Work Team, whose role is to define issues and develop policy and programme options to support and implement the recommendations of the other five teams within the restructuring initiatives.

All of the players described earlier have crucial roles to play: TECO and the work team in outlining policies and strategies, the Centre and the faculties in implementing them. The work team has focussed on changes that support the restructuring while TECO is dealing with the broader issues of long-term policies. Inevitably, the strategies and vehicles they propose will be similar or even identical.

Context of Policy Development: The Principles and Barriers

The Teacher Education Work Team has developed two assumptions underlying its task. First, the education of teachers is the key to all change in education. Teachers must have opportunities to define their needs as learners, and to acquire new skills and knowledge, all with the aim of eventually feeling comfortable in bringing both new methods and new content into their classrooms. This image of the teacher as a learner is an important part of the role of teacher education.

Second, the restructuring of education requires the restructuring of teacher education. Change and improvement in teacher education also can drive broader change in the system. Consider for a moment that there are approximately 120,000 active teachers in Ontario. Over the next decade, at least half of them will leave the profession for one reason or another. Most of their replacements will come from the faculties of education. Therefore, strategically re-designed preservice and inservice programmes can be at the cutting edge of reform. The opportunities to influence the system have never been greater.

Out of these two assumptions, the team has developed a statement of six principles which are commonplaces of teacher education, but serve as reminders to the team as they examine issues and propose policies and implementation strategies. These principles are:

1. *Programmes must be Teacher-Centred*

Teachers are professionals engaged in a career-long process of learning and changing. At their most effective, they will be self-directed, reflective, critical, and inquiring. Thus, teachers can embrace the need to change and take responsibility, as individuals and as groups, for fostering change. This is not to suggest that policy makers need not introduce issues and concepts to teachers; however, teachers will have to develop their own needs and priorities for change, if change is to occur. The restructuring of education requires teachers to generate and manage much of their own change.

2. The School is the Locus of Change

At least half of the teachers who will implement the restructuring are already in the profession. Therefore, the school is the most appropriate place in which to develop innovation and to improve learning conditions. Furthermore, school improvement and teacher development are inextricably linked. Individuals who wish to bring about change have great difficulty changing themselves in an environment that is not changing along with them. With support from other educational partners, such as the faculties and the teachers' federation, school-based inservice programmes will foster improved teacher performance, improved school organization, a more professional workplace, and, hence, more effective instruction for the children who are the students. The schools are the places where the changes that really matter must occur, and for this to occur, both teachers and students must be learners.

3. Teacher Education is an Integrated Continuum

The development of teachers begins before preservice teacher education and continues throughout their careers. The various phases of pre-preservice education, preservice education, induction, and inservice education, both for the classroom and for leadership roles, must be connected and interrelated in order to create a meaningful career growth pattern for each teacher.

4. Teacher Education is a Collaborative Venture

The continuum can only become a reality if those who are responsible for each distinct part of teacher education share responsibility for the whole. School boards, universities, the teachers' federation, and the government must work collaboratively wherever possible to achieve this goal. Partnerships of various sorts will prove to be important vehicles of change.

5. Teacher Education integrates Theory and Practice

The essence of excellence in teacher education is the integration of theory and practice. It involves all the components of knowledge, skills, and attitudes. Currently, teacher educators in the faculties of education seem to be rewarded more for pure research and publication than for applied research and outstanding teaching. Although the development and extension of theory in education is a valued priority, many graduates of the preservice programme regard the theoretical component of their education as less relevant than the practicum. These two aspects must be melded, through the collaboration of faculty- and school-based educators, in a judicious blending of theory and practice.

6. *Quality of Programmes must be Demonstrated*

The best candidates for teaching will be attracted and held by high quality, results-oriented teacher education programmes, both preservice and inservice. To attain that quality, the evaluation of programmes in teacher education is a significant priority that should involve all stakeholders. Faculties of education, student teachers, practising teachers, and the general educational community all have their own criteria by which to judge the quality of programmes. Collaboration on the assessment models and evaluation criteria will enhance the profile and status of teacher education. This, in turn, will benefit the profession as a whole.

Barriers to Change in Teacher Education

It must be acknowledged that several barriers to effective change in teacher education currently exist. The Teacher Education Work Team believes these must be addressed if the restructuring initiatives are to succeed. Five of these barriers are described briefly below.

1. *Overloaded Preservice Curriculum*

Recently, urgent societal needs confronting youngsters have been translated into curriculum issues. Recent additions to the school programme, such as AIDS, sex education, family violence, global education, drug education, and race relations have outstripped the ability of faculties of education to prepare teachers to deal with them. Although the Ministry of Education has supported inservice programmes in these areas, preservice and induction programmes should be modified and developed in order to prepare all teachers to deal with them. Until programme components in the preservice programme have been examined and time re-allocated, there is little room in the current set-up for these issues to receive adequate treatment.

2. *Resistance to Change*

Change is difficult and often quite stressful, but change is required at all levels of the system: teachers, teacher educators, administration, and so on. In order for faculties of education to provide leadership in this change, they must first display the ability to change themselves. Second, since teacher educators often possess an understanding of the change process, they can provide support and leadership to school system change projects.

Fullan (1991) describes three levels of change that are appropriate to teachers and teaching, i.e., materials/structures, second, skills/practices/behaviours, and third, beliefs/understandings. He suggests that too often reformers fail to address all three. The implementation of restructuring and reforms in teacher education must be both sufficiently sophisticated to address all these levels and to provide support at each of them. Faculties of education have the opportunity to model change processes by addressing their own renewal and restructuring, using the tools of research and the knowledge they already possess about change.

3. Low Status of Teaching in Universities

Goodlad (1990a) has documented graphically the woes of teacher education in American universities, identifying the apparently inverse relationship between the prestige of the institutions and their interest in educating teachers. The high prestige accorded to research and publication in the university culture in the United States, noted by Goodlad, pertains to Canada as well. Similarly, the low status of teaching in American universities and the low prestige experienced by the faculties and schools of education within that setting have parallels in the Canadian and Ontario university settings as well. Unless this issue is addressed, the delivery of preservice education in the faculties of education will continue to suffer.

4. Insufficient Resources

There are never sufficient resources to effect all the changes the education system demands. We can be thankful in Ontario for two things: first, that our financial problems have never, to date, become as great as in many parts of the U.S.; second, that substantial political will, dollars, and human resources have been, and continue to be available.

The essence of the resource problem is careful planning to make the best use of existing resources in collaborative ways. Many of the pilot projects funded through the Transition Years initiative attracted additional resources from the partners involved. A recent symposium on technological education made very effective use of a frugal budget and the skills of faculty members, ministry officials, teachers and staff from the colleges of applied arts and technology. A prime example to North America of the potency of resource sharing is The Learning Consortium, composed of the Faculty of

Education at the University of Toronto and four Greater Toronto area school boards. The Consortium has organized summer institutes for teachers and has provided opportunities for its member boards to participate much more directly in teacher education.

5. Lack of Clarity in Governance of Teacher Education

The role of government in teacher education varies quite significantly within Canada, and within the United States and the United Kingdom as well. In British Columbia, the government recently created a College of Teachers which has been given most of the responsibilities for teacher education policy and certification while leaving delivery of preservice education in the hands of the faculties of education. The College is still relatively new and its eventual success remains to be seen. It appears that the teachers who control the college may be opening the door to broader participation of other constituencies.

In Scotland, a council of constituents performs a similar role. I am told it is the model for TECO, although the size of the two councils (49 as opposed to 16 at TECO) is drastically different. Of all the provinces of Canada, Ontario seems to be the most heavily regulated and the hardest to change with any speed. This may be seen both as an advantage and a disadvantage. Although change cannot be made without due deliberation in a process that requires regulative and legislative change, it is often a year or more before the simplest revisions can take effect.

The presence in 1991, however, of four sets of players, not to mention the funding ministry, the Ministry of Colleges and Universities, suggested the need to address the governance issues. Educators both in the faculties of education and in school boards were very confused by the roles of the Centre for Teacher Education and of TECO. New programmes had to receive approvals from two ministries and TECO's part in that process was poorly defined. The overlap between TECO and the work team was confusing, especially when the life span of each of them was not known. No one could be sure, even when policy changes were decided, who would provide leadership in implementing them. As mentioned above, TECO has been disbanded and the Ministry of Education and Training has replaced the former Ministry of Colleges and Universities and the Ministry of Education. Most of the players concerned believe that programme review should be resumed and that admissions procedures require changes, but there is little agreement about who should ensure that these things happen.

It is very clear, however, that most of the players share an impatience to get on with change. The faculties are already deeply engaged; they require assistance and support from their partners in channelling this energy, and in extending these changes. The lack of clarity about who is providing the direction is diffusing much of the energy required.

The Role of Teacher Education in the Restructuring

Modes and Images

Having described the restructuring initiatives and the context that the Teacher Education Work Team has developed for its work, I would like to turn to the role of teacher education in supporting and implementing the policy options generated by the five projects.

Thiessen et al. described two modes of educational reform: intensification and restructuring. The pattern of intensification is "reform through centralization, standardization, structured direction, and strategic intervention" (p. 12). This mode essentially means working harder and smarter through existing mechanisms. Thiessen described several waves of reform through intensification that have included supplying more beginning teachers, updating the education of experienced teachers, and the application of legislated reforms (p. 15). However, these changes did not involve stepping back, looking at, questioning and clarifying the existing structures, policies and procedures, to see whether and how restructuring could be a much more effective form of change.

Restructuring, on the other hand, is "reform through decentralization, adaptation, and personal and professional responsibility for the conduct of schooling" (p. 14). Restructuring, as the word itself implies, involves a significant change in how teachers work together and how schools are organized and operated. For the restructuring of education to be effective, teacher education must also be restructured. "Restructuring affords teacher educators the possibility of working in a different 'place' in partnership with reforms in schooling" (p. 15). Thiessen's two images of the teacher as "steward" or "reformer" define a vision of what teaching has been and can become in the restructured system. In fact, these contrasting images are the ends of a continuum in which the tensions of maintaining tradition and exploring new possibilities are worked out. The role of teachers can be dramatically different, both in their relationships to one another in schools and in the professional responsibilities they assume in restructured schools. For each of these changes and for others, there is a corresponding place for teacher educators in helping to define these changes and in creating models to guide their development. This "place" should involve, on the one hand, an extension of both theory building and research, and, on the other hand, the refinement of practice, i.e., teaching.

To these images I added a third image, that of the teacher as lifelong learner, learning "how to teach and how to be and become a teacher" (Thiessen et al., 1991, p. 71). For this image to become real, restructuring must take a particular direction: schools must become learning environments not only for students, but also for teachers, as proposed by Seymour Sarason (1990).

We must recognize that education will change only if teachers are able to take responsibility for their own change and to change themselves. The rest of us, the government, the faculties, TECO, must all become supporting players in this drama—to provide support in our various roles, to enable teachers to learn, to change, and to continue to grow as professionals.

In order for teacher educators to play a significant role in the restructuring, faculties of education must maintain an orientation outward from the university to their professional colleagues. Professional schools of all types have been successful by doing so. The University of Western Ontario Business School and the McMaster Medical School seem to be two professional schools that have; I could also cite some egregious failures which have not observed this simple necessity.

Teacher educators, not only in faculties of education, but also in boards of education, and elsewhere, must share a vision of the teacher as learner. But simply to perpetuate the old mode of a limited inservice programme used to implement mandated reforms will not serve restructuring. That is an intensification strategy. The teacher educators will, in my estimation, succeed by becoming co-learners and transforming their own structures, while enabling teachers to transform theirs.

Strategies for Reform

I would like to turn now to some teacher education strategies which respond to the principles described earlier and represent efforts to remove some of the barriers described. They are opportunities to provide stronger links between the faculties of education and the teaching profession so that all partners are fully prepared to grapple with programme and organizational issues. These changes require not only subject and pedagogical expertise but also knowledge of the change process and the ability to assist teachers to bring about reform in themselves, in their schools, and in their systems.

The list of strategies is not exhaustive but it is an agenda of some complexity. In presenting selected strategies, I have distinguished individual/school/level strategies from within or across organizations strategies as proposed by Thiessen. To these I have added two systems strategies.

Individual/School Strategies

If real change is to occur, the old mode of simple inservice programmes, while still needed, will be insufficient. Therefore, some systematic teacher institutes or summer short courses must be developed with three goals: to train the teachers who will return to their schools and lead change projects, to support them with an understanding of the change process, and to support them with succinct, carefully prepared resource materials geared to very specific and narrow topics such as active learning, techniques for mixed ability groups, technology for early years, etc. Such programmes will be teacher-centred, will create expertise that can be used at the school level, and will integrate practice with theory. By their narrow focus, such programmes can equip teachers to adapt rapidly to specific needs they have identified for themselves and their students. They will make effective use of scarce resources while providing growth opportunities and leadership experience for those selected as trainers.

School improvement projects have already emerged in the Early Childhood Education Project and in Transition Years pilot projects. They are an excellent example of the kind of professional development that moves beyond the implementation of mandated changes to deal with questions such as the relationships within school staffs and the ways in which schools are organized and can become learning environments. Induction programmes may often be the entry point for this type of strategy.

Within/Across Organizations Strategies

The strategy here is really a single strategy with two related components: the professional practice school including demonstration schools and centres for instructional development. Goodlad's description of professional practice schools (1990b) offers a model not only for demonstration projects, in-school research, and the cross-fertilization of school staffs and faculties, but also the innovation in faculties of centres for instructional development. Faculties of education can and will eventually earn the respect of their university colleagues by raising the status and value assigned to teaching. This can be accomplished not only by attending to research and publication about teaching, but also by application in school settings and in university settings as well.

For the restructuring to be fully realized, demonstration schools must be developed where new ideas can be tested, evaluated, and refined. They will become laboratories in which teachers, prospective teachers, and faculty members can all be learners. These projects need not be expensive, but should come from the re-allocation and re-direction of current resources.

Systems Strategies

The strategies I cite here are systematic changes to the structure of preservice and induction programmes at the faculties and in schools, and the development of long range school system plans. Elsewhere, I have argued that only half of the teachers who will implement the restructuring are yet in the classroom. Therefore, preservice programmes must play a significant role in these changes. Preservice programmes are already in transition, but much more diversity can be realized in content, structure, and time frames.

A large proportion of the 6,000 teachers who are educated each year finish their undergraduate programme in May of one year and become classroom teachers 16 months later. Ten months afterward, they finish their first year of teaching. In that 26 months they get seven months of preparation, usually including a woefully short practicum, and ten months of grueling on-the-job training. Surely there are more effective ways to organize that period into more valuable and better designed components of preservice programme, induction, and reflection. More involvement by school boards and school staffs in the preservice year, and more linkages with faculty in the induction year could integrate theory and practice, and develop the school as a learning environment for teachers and for faculty members.

Finally, school systems must be encouraged or required to develop five-year plans that will create focussed inservice programmes, develop demonstration projects and demonstration schools, and encourage linkages with faculties of education, the teachers' federation, and with individual researchers and consultants. The need for participation of all stakeholders in collaboratively developing such plans is crucial.

Conclusion

I have reviewed the history and progress of the restructuring initiatives which are now more than half way through their predicted development period. The role of the Teacher Education Work Team within the restructuring was described with particular emphasis on its focus upon principles of teacher education and barriers to change. Finally, using several images of the teacher as a point of departure, I have outlined six strategies for implementing the restructuring in which teacher educators can play a significant role. The vision of change in teacher education I have presented is an image of the teacher as learner, learning to balance the roles of steward and reformer. Teacher education can take a leading role in this period of reform. In doing so, teacher educators can use their expertise and knowledge to restructure and strengthen their own role.

Note
1. Previous inquiries into teacher education in Ontario include chronologically:

Report of the Royal Commission on education in Ontario. Toronto, ON: Author, 1950.

Report of the Minister's Committee on the training of secondary school teachers, 1962. Toronto, ON: Ontario Department of Education, 1966.

Report of the Minister's Committee on the training of elementary school teachers, 1966. Toronto, ON: Ontario Department of Education, Ontario, 1966.

Report of the Committee on the aims and objectives of education in Ontario, Living and Learning. Toronto, ON: Department of Education, Ontario, 1968.

Fleming, W.G. (1971). *Ontario's education ssociety IV: Supporting institutions and services.* University of Toronto.

Committee on the cost of education, interim report number one, report on the education of elementary and secondary teachers in Ontario: Facilities, organization, administration. Toronto, ON: Ontario Department of Education, 1972.

The final report of the Commission on declining school enrolments in Ontario. Toronto, ON: Ontario Ministry of Education, 1978.

Issues and directions: The response to the final report on the Commission on declining school enrolments in Ontario. Toronto, ON: Ontario Ministry of Education, 1980.

Update '84: Results of issues identified in issues and directions. Toronto, ON: Ontario Ministry of Education, 1984.

Chapter Six

The Politics of Teacher Education in British Columbia

Nancy Sheehan

~~~~~~

Introduction

In 1987, by an Act of the Provincial Legislature in British Columbia, the British Columbia College of Teachers was created. The enabling legislation, the Teaching Profession Act, established the College as the professional body of teachers with jurisdiction over membership. The legislation provided for a College Council of 20 individuals as the governing body. Membership of the Council was to be composed of 15 teacher members, each elected by teachers in one of the 15 zones in the province; two members appointed by Cabinet; two appointed by the Minister of Education; and the last, a representative of the Deans of the Faculties of Education in the province, appointed by the Minister but selected by the Deans. The Teaching Profession Act was proclaimed in August 1987. Elections were held in the fall and the College and the Council began operations in January 1988. Control over certification, discipline, and professional development was in the hands of the teaching profession. To teach in the public schools of British Columbia, membership in the College was mandatory.

As the representative of the Deans on the Council of the College, I have been involved in the establishment of the College from an idea created by legislation to a body of more than 42,000 members with policies, by-laws, offices, staff, a budget, and numerous committees. I have both participated in and been a keen observer of the growth of a bureaucratic enterprise. Here, I wish to address the history of the development of teacher profession-alism in this province from the goals of the British Columbia Teachers' Federation (BCTF) for control over teacher certification, to the develop-ment of present legislation, from the first years as the College struggled to determine what powers it had, to the present stage of understanding the limitations of the legislation and its authority. I conclude by speculating on the future of the British Columbia College of Teachers.

History: Teacher Certification

In 1956, the normal schools in British Columbia were closed and all teacher education was transferred to the University of British Columbia. The university had for some time offered programmes in secondary education, but in 1956 the establishment of the Faculty of Education moved all elementary teacher education to the university as well. The move to the university marked the first important step in elevating the status of the teaching profession.

An amendment to the Universities Act created a Joint Board on Teacher Education to advise the Minister and the university on matters respecting teacher education. It was comprised of representatives from the BCTF, the British Columbia School Trustees' Association (BCSTA), the university, and the Department of Education. Over time, particularly after Victoria College became autonomous as the University of Victoria, and Simon Fraser University was established, both with Faculties of Education, some felt that the university representation dominated the Joint Board. The BCSTA, in a study done in 1973, made their position clear, saying "...no single group should have, or appear to have, authority over several aspects of teacher training" (p. 20).

With university status for teacher education well-established, other issues of professional status were pursued. Several reports through the 1970s and 1980s addressed the issues of professional autonomy and of university/field collaboration. One of the first of these was *Teacher Education in British Columbia— Final Report* of the British Columbia Commission on Education (known as the Bremer Commission). The *Final Report*, following a conference on teacher education, was produced in 1974. The recommendations included:

1. That those making use of educational institutions must participate in their management and policy.
2. Teacher education must be democratized.
3. We should be pluralistic in our vision of teacher education.
4. Teachers must be consumers of lifelong learning.
5. There is a need for research and for adequate systems of dissemination.

In 1974, the British Columbia Teachers' Federation produced a paper for the Ministry called "A Proposed Teaching Profession Act." The proposal was based on the assumption that the teaching profession should be assigned a major role in guaranteeing the quality of teaching service within the profession (pp. 1-2). Under the proposed act, the BCTF would retain autonomy in its internal operations. The BCTF wanted an Act which would not require conformity to a single organizational model of schools, establish a teacher certification board independent of the Ministry with major representation from the BCTF; and,provide that this board be funded on the same basis as the registrar's office of the Department of Education. It wanted the teacher certification board and the Teaching Profession Act to have control over teacher certification and teacher education, as well as other areas. The board would have seven members, a majority to be selected by the BCTF. The public at large, the Minister, and institutions concerned with preparation and certification of teachers would make up the other three members. In consultation with the Joint Board, the teacher certification board would establish standards and criteria for accreditation of teacher education institutions and programmes and have the power to make rules and regulations governing certification of teachers (pp. 5-6).

The BCSTA report, the Bremer report, and the report from the BCTF were all submitted to the short-lived New Democratic Party government in office in the mid-1970s, but no action was taken by it. With the Social Credit party back in power, these recommendations were shelved. Then in 1979, the Minister of Education, Science and Technology commissioned the Joint Board of Teacher Education to do a study on the preparation of teachers for the public schools of British Columbia. That document was produced in 1981. In its preamble, it says "Teaching should be viewed and declared as a profession. The Joint Board looks forward to the development of a teaching profession act which will accord teachers more responsibility for decision-making at all levels" (p. 22). One of the recommendations of this document had to do with the governance of teacher education and required changes in the statutes. It recommended that a collaborative board be given legislative responsibility for the accreditation of teacher preparation programmes and that, in addition, it advise the Minister, or Ministers, and all other appropriate constituencies on all other matters related to teacher education, pre- and post-certification. The Report recommended that the Board be established for five years and evaluated in the fourth year. It recommended that it have a 16-member composition as follows:

- 5 to be selected by the BCTF;
- 3 Deans of Education, by Statute;
- 3 to be selected by the BCSTA;
- 2 selected by the Deputy Minister of Education;
- 2 lay members appointed by the Minister of Education; and,
- 1 member selected by the BCSSA.

The report recommended that there should be a certification advisory committee with statutory recognition, its composition consisting of three teachers, one superintendent and the Chair of the Joint Board, as voting members; that the Director of Teacher Services be a non-voting chairperson; and, that one representative from each faculty be non-voting members. This certification committee would be advisory to both the Minister and the collaborative board (pp. 32-33).

Several issues stand out from these reports: the BCSTA's report, the Bremer report and the report of the Joint Board on Teacher Education all recommended that there should be a change in the governance of teacher education in British Columbia and that no one group should dominate. The BCTF agreed with the need for a change in governance; however, it clearly felt that it should have control on any board or certification authority which was established. The other issue was that of finance. The BCTF felt that the cost for a certification authority should be borne by the government. Although the Joint Board recommendation is not specific, it would appear that it assumed that the collaborative board would be funded by the Ministry and by the Joint Board on Teacher Education.

Throughout the last three decades, as the universities consolidated their responsibility for all teacher education, the BCTF, with compulsory membership, was becoming a powerful organization for teachers in British Columbia. The BCTF established an agenda which many have argued has been at odds with the agenda of the Social Credit government. Charles Ungerleider (1991), in a perceptive study of the ideology of both the BCTF and the government, indicates that each approached education with a very different ideology. What this has meant is that over the last three decades there has been growing antagonism between the BCTF and the government of British Columbia. The BCTF continually took issue with the Social Credit government, supported the New Democratic Party, and took some credit for its victory in 1972.

Legislation: The Teaching Profession Act (1987)

During the 1980s, rapport between the BCTF and the government continued to deteriorate. There was retrenchment at all levels of education, accompanied by a fair amount of education-bashing. Then in 1987, the government introduced new legislation, Bills 19 and 20. Bill 19 was labour legislation which gave teachers the authority to strike, bargain collectively for wages and working conditions, removed the principals and vice-principals from the BCTF making them managers with signed contracts and terms of service, and indicated that teachers could either form local teacher associations or become unions within the BCTF (Industrial Relations Act, 1987). Bill 20 was the Teaching Profession Act which created the British Columbia College of Teachers (BCCT). The legislation was developed without consultation with teachers, the universities, or other members of the education community.

There are several issues arising from the lack of consultation. The first is that control of neither the collective bargaining structures nor the College of Teachers was given to the BCTF. Second, on this Council of 20 individuals, there was only one person who is a teacher-educator, despite the College's authority to accredit teacher education programmes and to control certification. Third, the legislation did not include revenue from the province. The College, therefore, had to be self-supporting. The Council was forced to establish both membership and service fees which means that a service formerly controlled by the government and free to teachers is now controlled by but also paid for by the teachers.

Bills 19 and 20 were fought by both the labour movement and the teachers in the province. There were one-day strikes and work-to-rule campaigns in the spring of 1987. In the end, the government legislation was successful, the College of Teachers was introduced as the professional body of teachers and teachers throughout the province gave the BCTF a union mandate. Once it became clear that the Teaching Profession Act would pass, the BCTF believed that it could control the College by having the teachers elect BCTF members. All 15 members first elected in the fall of 1987 had been supported, and supported willingly, by the BCTF. The 15 members in all cases had at one time or another held executive positions in either a local or the provincial association. The chairperson of the Council, elected at the first meeting, was Bill Broadley, a former president of the BCTF. The BCTF announced that it had control over the Council of the College and believed it had circumvented the legislation which had created a second body of teachers.

A variety of factors produced significant difficulties for the Council in its first term. Legislated authority was not coupled with established mechanisms or expertise. Specifically, while the Council had control over discipline in the teaching profession, it was without disciplinary by-laws and had no established system to deal with new cases not to mention those left over from the Ministry. The Council was to oversee the certification of all teachers in the province but was without officers, a registrar, or a certification system. The Council was responsible for approving the programmes of the three universities in teacher education, but was without standards to appeal to when deciding upon accreditation. An additional problem resulted from the Council's responsibility for professional development, a responsibility that had for some time been carried out by the BCTF and its Provincial Specialists' Associations. The need to establish procedures and systems from the ground up and to avoid conflicts over turf with the BCTF was made more challenging by the fact that the 20 members of the Council were new to these responsibilities. In addition, the College of Teachers was the first-ever attempt, certainly in North America but I think world-wide, to put control of teacher certification, discipline, and professional development in the hands of the professions. Therefore, it had no precedent upon which to base its decisions. The only other jurisdiction to give substantial control over who should be admitted to the register of teachers and, therefore, entitled to teach, was Scotland where the General Teaching Council for Scotland was established in 1965. This Council has a much broader membership and, although teachers are in the majority, there is substantial representation from the teacher education institutions. The Council and the institutions are also subject to decisions by the Scottish Education Department in such areas as policy, course approval, and degree stipulations (Kirk, 1988).

In spite of the above mentioned difficulties, the College managed to become operational within six months. During this initial time period, committees were established to produce by-laws, a budget was developed, membership and service fees were designed, space was rented, and a registrar hired. To avoid disruption of teacher education in the province while the Council developed standards for certification and programme approval, the College of Teachers gave interim approval to the three universities' teacher education programmes.

British Columbia College Of Teachers: Issues

While the Teaching Profession Act gave the College control over professional development in the province, the College decided not to exercise this mandate. Since its founding, the British Columbia Federation of Teachers, along with its numerous Provincial Specialist Associations, had been responsible for the professional development of teachers. Rather than create an antagonistic relationship between itself and the Teachers' Federation, the College requested a legislative amendment deleting its responsibility for professional development.

A second issue connected with the BCTF is the matter of membership. The BCTF has been unhappy from the beginning with the legislation that created the BCCT and in particular with the election of the 15 teacher members by teachers in each of the 15 regional zones, and not by the Representative Assembly of the BCTF. Although the 15 elected members have all had BCTF support they are elected as individuals and not as BCTF representatives. In some matters of jurisdiction and policy, the College has not followed BCTF practice, and this has caused conflict with the BCTF. It has also caused some internal and personal conflict for councillors who have been vocal and active BCTF members in the past. The BCTF is lobbying hard to have the legislation changed to give it control over membership.

The College's mandate in the area of discipline has been difficult. The meaning of the term "conduct unbecoming a teacher" is vague and one with which both the College and the courts have struggled. Unfortunately, the majority of the discipline cases handled by the College have been cases of sexual abuse. Since this is a broad term and incidents of sexual abuse vary in severity, penalties have also varied from decertification to indefinite suspension to suspension for limited terms. Both members of the public and the Ministry view such variation in penalty as unacceptable and argue that those convicted of sexual abuse should never be able to return to the classroom. The College must weigh the seriousness of the offense, the probability of repetition, the damage to the reputation of the profession as well as the concept of rehabilitation for the individual. Human rights legislation, legal advice, and court decisions guide College councillors in attempting to make fair decisions.

As mentioned above, in the initial months of its operation, the College gave interim approval to the three universities' teacher education programmes and adopted the Ministry's certification practices on a temporary basis. It has since developed certification policy, by-laws, and appeals procedures. One of the particularly challenging aspects of the certification process has concerned the assessment of qualifications of out-of-province teachers who have many successful years of classroom experience but fail to meet British Columbia's academic requirements. Issues of equity have also emerged since in-province candidates are required to meet more stringent requirements. Is it just to certify out-of-province candidates with qualifications that are less than their in-province counterparts? Interpretation of certification criteria is also an issue. The College has tended towards more literal interpretation of criteria causing problems for the admissions process in the faculties who believe they should have some autonomy to exercise judgment in the admissions process based on professional expertise.

A second issue affecting the universities has to do with a decision by the government to begin to move toward degree-granting status for three of the colleges in the province—Cariboo, Okanagan, and Malaspina. It was agreed that for a five- to ten-year period, a college, in cooperation with one of the universities, would offer a university degree at the college, with the eventual plan that each college would become autonomous and give its own degrees after a period of time. The University of British Columbia has been offering its two-year elementary programme at Cariboo College and the University of Victoria has been offering its teacher education programmes at both Okanagan College and Malaspina College (in Nanaimo). The students are students at the colleges where they register, pay their fees, and receive student numbers; the courses they take are the university courses. The universities have control over the course content, course instructors, the evaluation of the instructors, course examinations, and graduation decisions. The students receive a college transcript "in association with a university." In each case, the universities have coordinators both on-site and on campus to provide liaison. They work very closely with the colleges to ensure that the programmes are the equivalent in quality to programmes on campus.

At issue is that only the programmes at the universities have been approved for certification by the College of Teachers and a university transcript is required as evidence. The students at the university colleges are registered as college students and receive a college transcript noting a degree in affiliation with a British Columbia university. The question of how to grant British Columbia certification to these students and not violate the policy that only the universities have received approval for programmes has been a difficult one to resolve. In the meantime, the teacher shortage, the belief of the College of Teachers in decentralized programmes, and the provincial move to establish university colleges supported by the three universities are very much factors that cannot be overlooked as the College of Teachers struggles with a solution that maintains its authority but allows flexibility in the Provincial post-secondary system.

British Columbia College of Teachers: Review of Teacher Education

To establish standards for programme approval, the College undertook a review of the pre-certification programmes of the three faculties of education. To facilitate this review, faculties of education were asked to produce self studies and interested parties in the province were asked to submit briefs to the College. This major effort by the College involved a survey of practising teachers, practicum supervisors, faculty advisors, and students as well as two forums on teacher education and on-site visits to the faculties by a three member team. This team consisted of one teacher educator, one teacher selected by the BCTF, and the Chair of the College of Teachers. Jim Bowman, a consultant and a former teacher and BCTF executive member, coordinated this review and produced a report (Bowman, 1991). A third forum was held to discuss the report, *Teacher Education in British Columbia*. Criteria for the approval of both existing and new teacher education programmes were developed by the College on the basis of this effort.

There were 32 recommendations in the Bowman report, covering positively such topics as teacher education as a collaborative endeavour, the important role of sponsor teachers, the benefits of off-campus and Native Indian programmes, and the need to respond to the principles rather than the details of reform. The report emphasizes the organization of teacher education without proposing a clear vision of what knowledge, abilities, skills, and attitudes an educated teacher ought to have. In so doing, it made no distinction between the substance and the organization of teacher education, and the logical boundaries of College and university responsibilities were blurred.

Needless to say, this blurring of the boundaries has been problematic. Although the review process and the Bowman Report have been educative for all involved, considerable debate around a number of issues has occurred. In particular, concerns have been raised with respect to university autonomy in the face of College prescriptions and with respect to the status of teacher education programmes and faculties of education within the broader educational community. The College's relative newness has been evidenced in its struggle to establish approaches and methodologies. Some of its suggestions have been overly idealistic rather than practical and this has caused concern among established teacher educators.

Important both to faculties of education and to the teaching profession as well in its search for status are concerns about the place of faculties of education within the university community and the need to achieve a balance between graduate and teacher education programmes within faculties. It is crucial that the College both develop and benefit from, collaborative relationships between itself and the faculties and within the teaching profession as a whole in developing an effective accreditation process.

A final issue which has been the subject of much discussion and debate is the perceived distinction between preservice and ongoing teacher education. While the College's decision to forego its mandate to oversee professional development, leaving it in the hands of the BCTF and its specialty associations, made both political and practical sense, there is concern about suggestions that seem to run counter to the notion (and reality) of a full continuum of teacher education. It is obvious that preservice and professional development programmes must be linked by high levels of communication and collaboration between providers.

Conclusion

We look forward to working with the College. From the very beginning I have said that we must make this work. I think it will do wonders for the profession of teaching if, in fact, there is a self-governing body which ensures the highest respect for its members. By creating a body that is devoted exclusively to the profession and not to the self-interest of the individuals in it, I believe that the College has been given a mandate which is extremely important, and that it has a unique opportunity to enhance teaching as a career. At the same time, I think it would be a disaster if the College failed. What would that be saying about teaching and the teaching profession if teachers were unable to manage their own business? The College has been given a very important role to focus quite explicitly on the development of teaching as a profession. I think it is in everyone's interest that this be successfully done. To do this, the College must rise above the politics of education in British Columbia. It must educate its own members about the complexity of the process, allow the universities some latitude to exercise their own judgment in following the criteria established and not be swayed by the biases of those who base their assessment of teacher education on little and outdated knowledge.

The new NDP Government has promised the BCTF a review of Bill 20, particularly with regard to membership on the governing council. The BCTF passed a motion at its Representative Assembly (RA) on October 26, 1991 that all 15 teachers be elected by secret ballot by the RA. College Council members are not happy with this. They believe there should be a full BCTF membership discussion of the pros and cons of the 1987 legislation at an annual general meeting. To date, no substantive changes have been made to the legislation. Should changes in membership be entertained, then the token representation from the universities and the lack of a school official with senior administrative experience should be discussed and broader representation considered.

The discussion and debate, and the focus on teacher education in the province itself, engendered by the creation of the BC College of Teachers through the enactment of the Teaching Profession Act, has been highly beneficial. In particular, the review process, through its surveys, site visits, and forums, has brought together representatives from a number of constituents of the educational community in the province. The dialogue and debate has been characterized by genuine interest and growing respect, and has increased the possibilities for further meaningful exchanges and collaboration between teachers, administrators, Ministry personnel, trustees, and faculty members. The BCTF has elevated the attention given to teacher education and produced a revised position for approval by its membership. This position paper was discussed with representatives of the three faculties and the College. This level of interest in the education community is healthy and one which, if nourished appropriately, should provide a basis for continuing dialogue and the improvement of professional practice and the education system. As a dean of a faculty of education in British Columbia, a member of the Council of the College of Teachers, and a teacher of many years standing, I am optimistic for the future of teacher education and of education in the province.

*Alternative Approaches to
Teacher Education Research*

Chapter Seven

The Devil's Bargain: Educational Research and the Teacher*

Ivor Goodson

~~~~~~

The concern of this chapter is to explore why it is that so much educational research has tended to be manifestly irrelevant to the teacher. A secondary question is how that irrelevance has been structured and maintained over the years. There are I think three particularly acute problems: first, the role of the older foundational disciplines in studying education; second, the role of faculties of education, generally; third, the dangers implicit in too hasty an embrace of the panacea of more *practical* study of education, related to the decline of foundational disciplines and the crisis in the faculties of education.

The decline of modernism makes this an interesting time because of the associated decline and, in some cases, collapse of the disciplinary canons on which much of educational research has been built. The disciplinary study of education—i.e., history of education, philosophy of education, sociology of education and so on—has always had a shaky purview within the realm of practitional lore. Long before postmodernism, there was a common-sense view among practitioners that the disciplinary study of education was irrelevant to their concerns. This problem of the older disciplines arises in many cases because the scholars working in disciplinary modes often develop their first allegiance to their home discipline—say, history or philosophy. Whilst this is not intrinsically or inevitably a problem, it has the effect over time of divorcing such scholars from the world of schooling. This problem is often exacerbated by the fact that foundational disciplines adopt a hands-off posture with regard to schools; added to which, all too often, these scholars have no previous experience within schools. None of this adds up to a conclusive proof of irrelevance, but one can see, I think, why practitioners in the schools would over time come to view this group as irrelevant.

Here I am at one with what Schwab (1978) said about curriculum research and I think it applies to educational research generally. He said the field of curriculum was "moribund." "It is unable, by its present methods and principles, to continue its work and contribute significantly to the advancement of education. It requires new principles which will generate a new view of the character and variety of its problems. It requires new methods appropriate to the new budget of problems" (p. 287).

There are just too many points at which credibility is strained—the manifest allegiance to the host discipline and not to the educational endeavour; the distance, occasionally disdain, in relationship to school and teachers; the absence of any experience of teaching school. None of these is itself an insurmountable obstacle to communication, but put together it amounts to a collapse of credibility. This is a tragedy for the faculties of education not least because so many able proponents of the theoretical mission are located within foundational disciplines. I should note that in my own faculty the potentially invigorating and rejuvenating project of reconceptualization is well under way with the support of many foundational members. It may not be widely known in the province, but this same faculty has made very substantial strides in the last years towards some of the reconceptualizing and restructuring I want to discuss.

Schwab's diagnosis of the problems with curriculum research should be read alongside Veblen's and Clifford and Guthries' strictures about the relationships between university schools of education and schooling. Veblen (1962) said, "the difference between the modern university and the lower schools is broad and simple; not so much a difference of degree as of kind" (p. 15).

> This distinctiveness of purpose and mission unavoidably leads them to court a specious appearance of scholarship and so to invest their technological discipline with a degree of pedantry and sophistication whereby it is hoped to give these schools and their work some scientific and scholarly prestige. (p. 23)

The resonance of Veblen's strictures has been confirmed in Clifford and Guthries' (1988) recent characterization of faculties of education in their book *Ed School*:

> Our thesis is that schools of education, particularly those located on the campuses of prestigious research universities, have become ensnared improvidently in the academic and political cultures of

their institutions and have neglected their professional allegiances. They are like marginal men, aliens in their own worlds. They have seldom succeeded in satisfying the scholarly norms of their campus letters and science colleagues, and they are simultaneously estranged from their practicing professional peers. The more forcefully they have rowed toward the shores of scholarly research, the more distant they have become from the public schools they are duty bound to serve. Conversely, systematic efforts at addressing the applied problems of public schools have placed schools of education at risk on their own campuses. (pp. 3-4)

In short, the schools of education entered into a devil's bargain when they entered the university milieu. The result was their mission changed from being primarily concerned with matters central to the practice of schooling towards issues of status passage through more conventional university scholarship. The resulting dominance of conventional "disciplinary" modes has had a disastrous impact on educational research.

The devil's bargain on the part of education was an especially pernicious form of a more general displacement of discourse and debate which surrounded the evolution of university knowledge production. University knowledge evolved as separate and distinct from public knowledge, for as Mills (1979) noted:

Men of knowledge do not orient themselves exclusively toward the total society, but to special segments of that society with special demands, criteria of validity, of significant knowledge, of pertinent problems, etc. It is through integration of these demands and expectations of particular audiences which can be effectively located in the social structure, that men of knowledge organize their own work, define their data, seize upon their problems. (p. 613)

In Mill's view, such a structural location of "men of knowledge" (sic) in the university could have profound implications for public discourse and debate. Mills believed this would happen if the knowledge produced in this way did not have public relevance, particularly if it was not related to public and practical concerns:

Only where publics and leaders are responsive and responsible, are human affairs in democratic order, and only when knowledge has public relevance is this order possible. Only when mind has an autonomous basis, independent of power, but powerfully related to it, can it exert its force in the shaping of human affairs. Such a position is democratically possible only when there exists a free and knowledgeable public, to which men of knowledge may address themselves, and to which men of power are truly responsible. Such a public and such men—either of power or of knowledge, do not now prevail, and accordingly, knowledge does not now have democratic relevance in America. (p. 613)

The dilemma facing "men of knowledge" which Mills describes is acute when that knowledge relates to schooling. In the schools, knowledge is transmitted to future generations. If our knowledge of such knowledge transmission is flawed, we are doubly imperilled: schooling is so intimately related to the social order that if either our knowledge of schooling is inadequate or it has no public relevance, then major aspects of social and political life are obscured. In a real way, the future of democracy in any meaningful sense is called in to question.

Hence the question "whither educational research" is one of great importance. Mills, I think, comes close to the nature of our dilemma and spells out the implications of the devil's bargain when he talks of the way "men of knowledge" orient themselves to "special segments of society." This has been the fate of much educational and curriculum theory and the effect has been that, as Mills put it, different groups "talk past each other." With few exceptions I would argue this is precisely the relationship between educational researchers and school practitioners: they constitute a model of how to "talk past each other."

The problems of faculties of education are particularly worrisome because of the political climate in which we currently operate. Hence, I should make it clear that my mission in seeking to reconceptualize educational research is to revive and reconstitute one of the important missions, so often neglected, inside faculties of education. Hence, what I am seeking is a relationship between faculties of education and practitioners which is meaningful, vivid, and vital. It is my view that unless this relationship is rapidly explored and reinforced, new agendas will begin to work. Many governments are actively reconstituting educational patterns throughout the Western world. In particular, they are moving towards more practical "classroom-based work," funding direct training of teachers, and generally marginalizing faculties of education or restructuring their mission toward exclusively practical and professional development concerns. Just to substantiate these points, let me quote from a recent article by Paul Hirst (1989), that established advocate of foundational disciplines:

> Are the curricula of teacher education programmes being sufficiently informed by research conducted under the new policies and practices? The answer is "certainly not." Initial teacher education programmes are now subject to a set of criteria promulgated by the Secretary of State for Education and require considerable *practical* preparation. There has, therefore, been an *inevitable decrease in the attention to theoretical matters* in these programmes... (p. 272)

He adds,

> Inservice teacher education is now concentrating severely on the *practical* demands of new legislation...research has had little influence. Advanced study of systematic kind is now much reduced. (p. 272)

Amongst his conclusions and relevant to the argument deployed here is this statement: "it is only in the closest collaboration with teachers and acting on their initiatives, that we can hope to maintain many of the areas of research that interest us, and most of that may have to be done in spare time and without significant resources" (p. 273). Hirst, in short, is saying (and I agree with him) that the old foundational disciplines are no longer politically sustainable and that faculties of education will need to collaborate intimately with teachers. The problem is how to maintain a balance between theory, critique, and practical matters. If we cannot strike such a balance, I think the main mission and the over-arching rationale for faculties of education will begin to erode.

The particular problem that I want to focus on now is how to maintain, revive, and establish a collaborative and theoretical mission within this new terrain and in so doing bring new strength and vigour to faculties of education in their work with teachers. I believe this means looking closely at the potential collaboration between teachers and externally located researchers in faculties of education. I think the best mechanism for improving practice is if teachers, in an ongoing way, research and reflect upon their own practice. This may not seem as self-evident as I have stated it: many great teachers would say "Why the hell should I need research, I can teach already?" They are right at one level, but let me deconstruct this statement because I suspect many teachers would go along with it.

First, when they say research is irrelevant in this statement, they mean the kind of irrelevant gobbledegook written by one professor for another, which has been regrettably all too common. If we had proper collaborative research, teachers would not be able to make this kind of statement. Second, let me look closely at the "great teacher" notion. I have studied a lot of them over the years. They all have one thing in common; whilst they may say they are uninterested in research, in their own lives and in their teaching, they constantly reflect upon and refine their practice. They try new things, work at what is not working well, and generally think through the problems that face them. In a word, they research their own practice. Now you might say that since they do this and are great teachers, obviously there is no place for externally located researchers to aid their ongoing research. And you might well be right. But even if you were, it still leaves the 95 percent of us who are not great teachers looking for help. For us, I believe a collaborative relationship which focusses on researching our own life and work is the most hopeful avenue for enhanced professional development.

What I'm trying to do is to define what the collaborative relationship would look like between teachers and externally located researchers in faculties of education. I want to argue that a narrow focus on "practice" in collaborating on research, a panacea that is politically popular at the moment and very much on the provincial agenda in Ontario, will not take us far. This is for two reasons:

1. Practice is a good deal more than the technical things we do in classrooms—it relates to who we are, to our whole approach to life. Here, I might quote C. Wright Mills talking about scholars, but it is as relevant to any member of the community. He said, "the most admirable thinkers within the scholarly community...do not split their work from their lives. They seem to take both too seriously to allow such disassociation and they want to use each for the enrichment of others." So I would want to argue for a form of research which links the analysis of the teacher's life and work together.

2. The interactive practices of our classrooms are subject to constant change—often in the form of new government guidelines. New initiatives, such as de-streaming in Ontario, (what I call preactive actions) set crucial parameters for interactive classroom practice. Preactive action affects interactive possibilities. In their collaborative research, teachers as researchers and external researchers need to focus on both the preactive and the interactive. What this means, in short, is that

we need to look at the full context in which teachers' practice is negotiated, not just at the technical implementation of certain phenomena within the classroom. If we stay with the latter definition, then our research is inevitably going to involve the mere implementation of initiatives which are generated elsewhere. This reduces the involvement and commitment of everyone involved.

The lens of inquiry I want to sketch out would focus on the teacher's work and practice in the full context of the teacher's life. Some time ago, I became convinced that the study of teachers' lives was central to the study of curriculum and schooling. In reflecting on the development of my conviction, two episodes stand out. Were this merely a reminiscence of personal conversion, it would be of little interest. However, the two episodes do speak to a number of salient issues in the argument for the greatly extended study of teachers' lives.

The first episode took place in the year of post-graduate certification when I was training to be a teacher. I returned to spend the day with a teacher at my secondary school who had been a major inspiration to me, a mentor. He was a radical Welshman. Academically brilliant, he had a B.Sc. in economics and a Ph.D. in history. He was open, humourous, engaging, stimulating—a superb and popular teacher.

But he faced me with a paradox because when the school changed from a grammar school to a comprehensive, it was he who opposed all the curriculum reforms which sought to broaden the educational appeal of the school to wider social groups. He was implacably conservative and traditionalist on this and, so far as I know, only this issue. But he, it should be remembered, was a man who had personally visited the factory to which I had gone after leaving school early at 15. He had implored me to return to school. He had spoken then of his commitment to public schooling as an avenue to working class emancipation. He no doubt saw me, a badly behaved working class pupil, as some sort of test case. I knew personally then that he was very deeply concerned to keep working class pupils in school. So why did he oppose all those curriculum reforms which had that objective?

During the day back visiting my old school, I continually probed him on this issue. At first he stonewalled me, giving a series of essentially noncommittal responses, but at the end of the day, in the pub, over a beer, he opened up. Yes, of course, he was mainly concerned with disadvantaged pupils; yes, of course, that is why he had come to the factory to drag me back to school. Yes, he was politically radical and, yes, he had always voted Labour. But, and here I quote:

> You don't understand my relationship to the school and to teaching. My centre of gravity is not here at all. It's in the community, in the home—that's where I exist, that's where I put my effort now. For me the school is nine to five, I go through the motions.

In short, in the school he sought to minimize his commitment; he opposed any reform which dragged him into more work. His centre of gravity was elsewhere. The point I am making is that to understand teacher development and curriculum development and to tailor it accordingly we need to know a great deal more about teachers' priorities. We need, in short, to know more about teachers' lives.

The second episode began in the late 1970s. I was interested in some work on folk music being conducted at the University of Leeds. At the same time, I was exploring some themes for an ethnography conference that was coming up at the St. Hilda's in Oxford. The work of folklorist Pegg suddenly opened up again the line of argument which I had been pondering since 1970. Pegg says,

> The right to select lies not with the folklorist ("Sorry old chap, can't have that—it's not a folk song"), but with the singer. Today's collector must have no preconceptions. His job is to record a people's music, whether it is a traditional ballad or a hymn or a musical song or last week's pop hit!

With this basic attitude comes another revelation:

> I began to realise that, for me, the people who sang the songs were more important than the songs themselves. The song is only a small part of the singer's life and the life was usually very fascinating. There was no way I felt I could understand the songs without knowing something about the life of the singer, which does not seem to apply in the case of most folklorists. They are quite happy to find material which fits into a preconceived canon and leave it at that. I had to know what people thought about the songs, what part they played in their lives and in the lives of the community. (Pegg quoted in Goodson & Walker, 1991, p. 138)

A similar point is made by the folksong collector Robin Morton:

> The opinion grew in me that it was *in* the singer that the song becomes relevant. Analyzing it in terms of motif, or rhyming structure, or minute variation becomes, in my view, sterile if the one who carries the particular song is forgotten. We have all met the scholar who can talk for hours in a very learned fashion about folksongs and folklore in general, without once mentioning the singer. Bad enough to forget the social context, but to ignore the individual context castrates the song. As I got to know the singers, so I got to know and understand their songs more fully. (Morton quoted in Goodson & Walker, 1991, p. 139)

The preoccupation with "the singer, not the song" needs to be seriously tested in our studies of curriculum and schooling. What Pegg and Morton say about folklorists and implicitly about the way their research is received by those they research, could be said also about most educational research.

The project I am recommending is essentially one of reconceptualizing educational research so as to assure that the teacher's voice is heard, heard loudly, heard articulately. In this respect, the most hopeful way forward is, I think, to build upon notions of the self-monitoring teacher, the teacher as researcher, the teacher as extended professional. For instance, in the early 1970s at The Centre for Applied Research in Education at the University of East Anglia in England, a good deal of work was conducted into how to operationalize this concept. Perhaps the most interesting developments were within the Ford Teaching Project conducted by John Elliott and Clem Adelman in the period 1973-75. They sought to rehabilitate the action research mode pioneered by Kurt Lewin in the post-war period. In the interim period, educational action research had fallen into decline. Carr and Kemmis (1986), who have done a good deal to extend and popularize the concept, give a number of reasons for the resurgence of action research:

> First, there was the demand from within an increasingly profession-alized teacher force for a research role, based on the notion of the extended professional investigating his or her own practice. Second, there was the perceived irrelevance to the concerns of these practitioners of much contemporary educational research. Third, there had been a revival of interest in "the practical" in curriculum, following the work of Schwab and others on "practical deliberation." Fourth, action research was assisted by the rise of the "new

wave" methods in educational research and evaluation with their emphasis on participants' perspectives and categories in shaping educational practices and situations. These methods place the practitioners at centre stage in the educational research process and recognize the crucial significance of actors' understandings in shaping educational action. From the role of critical informant helping an "outsider" researcher, it is but a short step for the practitioner to become a self-critical researcher into her or his own practice. Fifth, the accountability movement galvanized and politicized practitioners. In response to the accountability movement, practitioners have adopted the self-monitoring role as a proper means of justifying practice and generating sensitive critiques of the working conditions in which their practice is conducted. Sixth, there was increasing solidarity in the teaching profession in response to the public criticism which has accompanied the post-expansion educational politics of the 1970s and 1980s; this, too, has prompted the organization of support networks of concerned professionals interested in the continuing developments of education even though the expansionist tide has turned. And, finally, there is the increased awareness of action research itself, which is perceived as providing an understandable and workable approach to the improvement of practice through critical self-reflection. (pp. 166-167)

The focus of action research has, however, tended to be very practice-oriented. In introducing a survey of action research, for instance, Carr and Kemmis note:

A range of practices have been studied by educational action researchers and some examples may suffice to show how they have used action research to improve their practices, their understandings of these practices, and the situations in which they work. (p. 167)

Not surprisingly, with the notion of an extended professional in mind, workers have used action research to improve their practice. Other developments in teacher education have similarly focussed on practice. The work of Clandinin and Connelly has argued in innovative and interesting ways that would seek to understand teachers' personal practical knowledge. The addition of the personal aspect in this formulation is a welcome move forward hinting as it does at the importance of biographical perspectives.

But, again, the personal is being linked irrevocably to practice. It is as if the teacher *is* his or her practice. For teacher educators, such specificity of focus is understandable, but I wish to argue that a broader perspective will achieve more: not solely in terms of our understandings, but ultimately in ways that feed back into changes in practical knowledge. In short, what I am saying is that it does not follow logically or psychologically that to *improve* practice we must initially and immediately *focus* on practice. Indeed, I shall argue the opposite point of view.

Taking the teacher as researcher and action research as expressing defensible value positions and viable starting points, I want to argue for a broadened sense of purpose. In particular, I am worried about a collaborative mode of research which seeks to give full equality and stature to the teacher but which employs as its initial and predominant focus the practice of the teacher. It is, I believe, a profoundly unpromising point of entry from which to promote a collaborative enterprise. For the university researcher aspiring to collaborative and equalitarian partnership, it may seem quite unproblematic, for the teacher it might seem far less so. In fact, it may seem to the teacher that the starting point for collaboration focusses on the maximum point of vulnerability. We must, I think, constantly remind ourselves how deeply uncertain and anxious most of us are about our work as teachers whether in classrooms or in (far less contested) lecture halls. These are often the arenas of greatest anxiety and insecurity as well as, occasionally, achievement.

Hence, I wish to argue that to place the teacher's classroom practice at the centre of the action for action researchers is to put the most exposed and problematic aspect of the teacher's world at the centre of scrutiny and negotiation. In terms of strategy, both personally and politically, I think it is a mistake to do this. I say it is a mistake to do this—and this may seem a paradox— particularly if the wish is to ultimately seek reflection about and change in the teacher's practice.

A more valuable and less vulnerable entry point would be to examine the teacher's work in the context of the teacher's life. Much of the emerging study in this area indicates that this focus allows a rich flow of dialogue and data. Moreover, the focus may (and I stress, may) allow teachers greater authority and control in collaborative research than has often appeared to be the case with practice-oriented study. In the world of teacher development, the central ingredient so far missing is the teacher's voice. Primarily the focus has been on the teacher's practice, almost the teacher *as* practice. What is needed is a focus that listens above all to the person at whom development is aimed. This means strategies should be developed which facilitate, maximize and in a real sense legislate the capturing of the teacher's voice.

The Teacher's Life and Work

Bringing substance and strategy together points us in a new direction for reconceptualizing educational research and development. In the first section, I provided two somewhat episodic arguments for seeking to understand teachers' lives as part of the educational research and development enterprise. In the second section, I argued that the teacher as researcher and action research modes were productive and generative ways forward, but that the initial and immediate focus on practice was overstated and undesirable. Strategically, a broader focus on life and work is hereby recommended. Hence, for substantive and strategic reasons, I would argue for a broadening of focus to allow detailed scrutiny of the teacher's life and work.

Broadening Our Data Base for Studying Teaching

So far I have argued in somewhat anecdotal fashion that data on teachers' lives is an important factor for our educational research studies. I have argued that strategically this is desirable; so as to involve teachers as researchers and to develop a collaborative mode. But there is also a substantive reason. The primary reason is that in my experience when talking to teachers about issues of curriculum development, subject teaching, school governance, and general school organization, they constantly import data on their own lives into the discussion. This I take to be *prima facie* evidence that teachers themselves judge such issues to be of major importance. One of the reasons that these data, have not been much used, however, is that researchers edit out such data viewing it as too personal, idiosyncratic or soft. It is, in short, yet another example of the selective use of the teacher's voice. The researcher only hears what he/she wants to hear and knows will sound well when replayed to the research community.

There may, of course, be perfectly valid reasons for not employing data on teachers' lives in our educational research studies. But this would require a sequence of reasoning to show why such data were irrelevant or of no importance. The normal research strategy is, however, simply to purge such data. I have not come across any accounts which give reasoned explanations as to why such data are not employed. The most commonsensical explanation seems to be that data on teachers' lives simply do not fit in with existing research paradigms. If this is the case, then it is the paradigms that are at fault, not the value and quality of this kind of data.

The arguments for employing data on teachers' lives are substantial, but given the predominance of existing paradigms, should be spelt out:

1. In the research on schools in which I have been involved—covering a wide range of different research foci and conceptual matrixes—the consistency of teachers talking about their own lives in the process of explaining their policy and practice has been striking. Were this only a personal observation, it would be worthless but again and again in talking to other researchers they have echoed this point. To give one example: David Hargreaves (1975) in researching for *Deviance in Classrooms* noted in talking about the book that again and again teachers had imported autobiographical comments into their explanations. He was much concerned in retrospect by the speed with which such data had been excised when writing up the research. The assumption, very much the conventional wisdom, was that such data were too personal, too idiosyncratic, too soft for a fully fledged piece of social science research.

    Of course, in the first instance (and some cases the last instance), it is true that personal data can be irrelevant, eccentric, and essentially redundant. But the point that needs to be grasped is that these features are not the inevitable corollary of that which is personal. Moreover, that which is personal at the point of collection may not remain personal. After all, a good deal of social science is concerned with the collection of a range of often personal insights and events and the elucidation of more collective and generalizable profferings and processes.

    The respect for the autobiographical, for the life, is but one side of a concern to elicit the teacher's voice. In some senses, like the anthropologist, this school of qualitative educational research is concerned to listen to what the teacher says, and to respect and deal seriously with those data which the teacher import into accounts. This is to invert the balance of proof. Conventionally, data which do not service the researcher's interests and foci are junked. In this model, the data the teacher provides have a more sacred property and are only dispensed with after painstaking proof of irrelevance and redundancy.

Listening to the teacher's voice should teach us that the autobiograph-ical, the life, is of substantial concern when teachers talk of their work. And at a commonsensical level, I find this essentially unsurprising. What I do find surprising, if not frankly unconscionable, is that for so long, researchers have ruled this part of the teacher's account out as irrelevant data.

2. Life experiences and background are obviously key ingredients of the person that we are, of our sense of self. To the degree that we invest ourselves in our teaching, experience and background, therefore, shape our practice. A common feature in many teachers' accounts of their background is the appearance of a favourite teacher who substan-tially influenced the person as a young school pupil. They often report that "it was this person who first sold me on teaching"; "it was sitting in her classroom when I first decided I wanted to be a teacher." In short, such people provide a role model, and, in addition, they most probably influence the subsequent vision of desirable pedagogy as well as choice of subject specialty.

Many other ingredients of background are important in the teacher's life and practice. An upbringing in a working class environment may, for instance, provide valuable insights and experience when teaching pupils from a similar background. I once observed a teacher with a working class background teach a class of comprehensive pupils in a school in the East End of London. He taught using the local cockney vernacular and his affinity was a quite startling aspect of his success as a teacher. In my interview, I spoke about his affinity and he noted that it was "coz I come from round 'ere, don't I?" Background and life experience were then a major aspect of his practice. But so they would be in the case of middle-class teachers teaching children from the working class or teachers of working class origins teaching middle-class children. Background is an important ingredient in the dynamic of practice (see Lortie, 1977; Hargreaves, 1986).

Of course, class is just one aspect as are gender or ethnicity. Teachers' backgrounds and life experiences are idiosyncratic and unique and must be explored, therefore, in their full complexity. [Treatment of gender issues has often been inadequate—see Sikes, Measor & Woods, 1985. Recent work is more encouraging—see Nelson (1992) and Casey (1992).]

3. The teacher's lifestyle both in and outside school, his/her latent identities and cultures, impact on views of teaching and on practice. Becker and Geer's (1971) work on latent identities and cultures provide a valuable theoretical basis (pp. 56-60). Lifestyle is, of course, often a characteristic element in certain cohorts; for instance, work on the generation of Sixties teachers would be of great value. In a recent study of one teacher focussing on his lifestyle, Walker and myself (Goodson & Walker, 1991) stated:

    > the connections between youth culture and the curriculum reform movement of the Sixties is more complex than we first thought. For Ron Fisher there definitely is a connection; he identifies strongly with youth culture and feels that to be important in his teaching. But despite his attraction to rock music and teenage life styles, it is the school he has become committed to, almost against his own sense of direction. Involvement in innovation, for Ron, at least, is not simply a question of technical involvement, but touches significant facets of his personal identity. This raises the question for the curriculum developer, what would a project look like if it explicitly set out to change the teachers rather than the curriculum? How would you design a project to appeal to the teacher-as-person rather than to the teacher-as-educator? What would be the effects and consequences of implementing such a design? (p. 145)

    This I think shows how work in this area begins to force a reconceptualization of models of teacher development. We move, in short, from the teacher-as-practice to the teacher-as-person as our starting point for development.

4. Focus on the life cycle will generate insights, therefore, into the unique elements of teaching. Indeed, so unique a characteristic would seem an obvious starting point for reflection about the teacher's world. Yet our research paradigms face so frankly in other directions that there has been little work to date in this area.

    Fortunately, work in other areas provides a very valuable framework. Some of Gail Sheehy's somewhat populist work in *Passages* (1976) and

Pathfinders (1981) is, I think, important. So also is the research work, on which some of her publications are based, carried out by Levinson. His work, whilst regrettably focussed only on men, does provide some very generative insights into how our perspectives at particular stages in our life crucially affect our professional work.

Take for instance the case study of John Barnes, a university biologist. Levinson (1979) is writing about his dream of himself as a front-rank, prize-winning biological researcher:

> Barnes's Dream assumed greater urgency as he approached 40. He believed that most creative work in science was done before then. A conversation with his father's lifelong friend around this time made a lasting impression on him. The older man confided that he had by now accepted his failure to become a "legal star" and was content to be a competent and respected tax lawyer. He had decided that stardom is not synonymous with the good life; it was "perfectly all right to be second best." At the time, however, Barnes was not ready to scale down his own ambition. Instead, he decided to give up the chairmanship and devote himself fully to his research.
>
> He stepped down from the chairmanship as he approached 41, and his project moved into its final phase. This was a crucial time for him, the culmination of years of striving. For several months, one distraction after another claimed his attention and heightened the suspense. He became the father of a little boy, and that same week was offered a prestigious chair at Yale. Flattered and excited, he felt that this was his "last chance for a big offer." But in the end Barnes said no. He found that he could not make a change at this stage of his work. Also, their ties to family and friends, and their love of place, were now of much greater importance to him and Ann. She said: "The kudos almost got him, but now we are both glad we stayed." (p. 267)

This quotation I think shows how definitions of our professional location and of our career direction can only be arrived at by detailed understanding of people's lives.

5. Likewise, career stages and career decisions can be analysed in their own right. Work on teachers' lives and careers is increasingly commanding attention in professional development workshops and courses. For instance, The Open University in England now uses *Teachers Lives and Careers* (Ball & Goodson, 1989) as one of its course set books. This is symptomatic of important changes in the way that professional courses are being reorganized to allow concentration on the perspective of teachers' careers.

Besides the career studies in *Teachers Lives and Careers*, a range of new research is beginning to examine this neglected aspect of teachers' professional lives. The work of Sikes, Measor and Woods (1985) has provided valuable new insights into how teachers construct and view their careers in teaching.

6. Moreover, the new work on teachers' careers points to the fact that there are critical incidents in teachers lives' and specifically in their work which may crucially affect perception and practice. Certainly work on beginning teachers has pointed to the importance of certain incidents in molding teachers' styles and practices. Lacey's work has pointed to the effects on teachers' strategies and the work of Knowles (1992) has further elucidated the relationship to evolving teacher strategies.

Other work on critical incidents in teachers' lives can confront important themes contextualized within a full life perspective. For instance, Kathleen Casey has employed life history narratives to understand the phenomenon of the teacher drop-out, specifically the female and activist teacher drop-out (Casey, 1988; Casey & Apple, 1989). Her work is exceptionally illuminating of this phenomenon which is currently receiving a great deal of essentially uncritical attention given the problem of teacher shortages. Yet, few of the countries at the hard edge of teacher shortages have bothered to fund serious study of teachers' lives to examine and extend our understanding of the phenomenon of teacher drop-outs. I would argue that only such an approach affords the possibility of extending our understanding.

Likewise with many other major themes in teachers' work, the question of teacher stress and burn-out would, I believe, be best studied through life history perspectives. Similarly the issue of effective teaching and the question of the take-up innovations and new managerial initiatives could profit from this approach. Above all, in the study of teachers' working conditions, this approach has a great deal to offer.

7. Studies of teachers' lives might allow us to see the individual in relation to the history of his or her time, allowing us to view the intersection of the life history with the history of society thus illuminating the choices, contingencies, and options open to the individual. Life histories of schools, subjects, and the teaching profession would provide vital contextual background. The initial focus on the teachers' lives, therefore, would reconceptualize our studies of schooling and curriculum in quite basic ways.

Essentially collaborative study of teachers' lives at the levels mentioned constitutes a new way of viewing teacher development—a way which should redirect the power relations underpinning teachers' lives in significant and generative ways.

Collaboration and Teacher Development

Strategically, I have argued that to promote the notion of teachers as researchers and to develop an action research modality where collaboration with externally situated researchers was fostered, we need to avoid an immediate and predominant focus on practice. I have further argued that this focus on practice should, at least partially, be replaced by a focus on the teacher's life.

What is at issue here seems to me almost anthropological: we are looking for a point for teachers (as researchers) and externally located researchers to trade. Practice promises maximum vulnerability as the trading point. This is a deeply unequal situation in which to begin to trade—for it could be argued that the teacher may already feel vulnerable and inferior in the face of a university researcher.

Talking about his/her own life, the teacher is, in this specific sense, in a less immediately exposed situation; and the exposure can be more carefully, consciously, and personally controlled. (This is not, it should be noted, to argue that once again exploitation might not take place, nor that there are no longer major ethical questions to do with exposure.) But I think this starting point has substantive as well as strategic advantages. Some have already been listed, however, in terms of the trade between teacher/researcher and external researcher, this focus seems to me to provide advantages.

Much of the work that is emerging on teachers' lives throw up structural insights which locate the teacher's life within the deeply structured and embedded environment of schooling (see Goodson, 1992; Goodson, in press). This provides a prime trading point for the external researcher. For one of the valuable characteristics of a collaboration between teachers as researchers and external researchers is that it is a collaboration between two parties who are differentially located in structural terms. Each sees the world through a different prism of practice and thought. This valuable difference may provide the external researcher with a possibility to offer back goods in the trade. The teacher/researcher offers data and insights; the external researcher, in pursuing glimpses of structure in different ways, may now also bring data and insights. The terms of trade, in short, look favourable. Under such conditions, collaboration may at last begin.

I noted earlier that this possible route to collaboration does not suspend issues of ethics and exploitation. This is, above all, because the collaboration between teacher/researcher and external researcher takes place in an occupational terrain which is itself inequitably structured. In terms of power, the external researcher still holds many advantages. Moreover, the conditions of university careers positively exhort researchers to exploit research data; the requirements of publications and peer review have their own dynamics. So whatever the favourable aspects of a focus on teachers' lives, we must remain deeply watchful. For if the teacher's practice was a vulnerable focus, the teacher's life is a deeply intimate, indeed intensive, focus. More than ever, procedural guidelines are necessary over questions relating to the ownership and publication of the data. These issues, themselves, must be conceived of in terms of a collaboration in which each party has clear rights, and in this case, the teacher's power of veto should be agreed on early and implemented, where necessary, late.

Note

*   Permission granted to reprint article by *Education Policy Analysis Archives.*

Chapter Eight

Teacher Development Partnership Research: A Focus on Methods and Issues[*]

Ardra Cole and J. Gary Knowles

~~~~~~

Over the last few decades, research on teaching and schooling has gone through a period of conceptual and methodological change. Increasingly, research involving teachers and teaching practice is situated not within the tradition of positivistic thinking but, rather, within an interpretive framework reflecting more phenomenological, hermeneutic, and interactionist perspectives.[1] This conceptual shift has moved us successively forward in our approaches to understanding life in and around classrooms. The use of methods which better capture and reflect the complexity of classroom life and the individuality of those who constitute it are becoming commonplace.

To study classroom phenomena and the work of teachers, researchers have moved inside classrooms and schools to observe, participate, and discuss teaching and learning with those who know it best—the teachers and students. These recent conceptual and methodological changes related to the research process have given rise to a whole new set of issues—technical, procedural, ethical, political, personnel, and educational. We are teacher development researchers operating within this new research paradigm. Our purpose in writing this article are to reflect on our own research practices and to raise for discussion some of the issues associated with alternative approaches to studying teaching and teacher development.

Situating our work within a personal and contextual research framework built on the foundations of a hermeneutic perspective (Gadamer, 1975; Hodges, 1952; Ryle, 1949), we briefly review the progress towards alternative approaches to research on teaching and teacher development. Drawing examples from our own research with teachers, which we characterize as partnership research, we focus on the researcher-teacher relationship with specific reference to the phenomenon of collaboration. The relationship between researcher and teacher and the roles each plays throughout the research process both characterize partnership research that is grounded in a hermeneutic perspective and give rise to the methodological issues we identify and discuss.

Our approach to educational research, and particularly research on teaching and teacher practice, is based on certain assumptions about teaching, teacher knowledge, and teacher practice. We articulate those assumptions before moving into a discussion of methods and issues associated with inquiry into these phenomena.

Assumptions About Teaching and Teacher Development

Our views find company in what might be described broadly as the constructivist camp, in which teaching is understood to be a complex and personal phenomenon continually influenced and made meaningful by factors and conditions both inside and outside classrooms and schools. Also implicit is our belief that each teacher's practice is idiosyncratic, an expression of a personal and professional way of knowing that is shaped and informed by events and experiences, both past and present, that take place at home, school, and in the broader societal and political spheres. Personal and professional backgrounds, experiences, perceptions, attitudes, beliefs, and goals underlie and inform the manner in which teachers carry out their lives and work in classroom communities and within the larger communities of schools and society.

Likewise, our perspective of teacher development rests in both personal and professional ways of knowing, set amid a complex array of historical, political, societal, local community, school, and personal circumstances. We view teacher development along a continuum beginning before entry into formal programmes of teacher education and continuing through formal preparation, into the early induction years, through experienced practice, to the time of eventual retirement from the teaching profession. In this view, teacher development represents emerging and ongoing, individual and collective, professional and personal development.

We view teaching *as* inquiry and inquiry *as* development; hence, our commitment to teacher development partnership research. From this perspective, teacher development represents a commitment to lifelong learning and ongoing inquiry into one's practice, a commitment to ongoing sense-making through reflection and interpretation of one's "minded actions" (Ryle, 1949).

The Rise of Alternative Approaches to Research on Teaching

Phillip Jackson's *Life in Classrooms* (1968) in some ways marked the beginning of a new era in educational research in North America; an era of interpretive contextual inquiry into classroom life for purposes of understanding and describing events as lived, and for directly informing practice and its embedded and related theories. In the United Kingdom, at about the same time, Lawrence Stenhouse initiated the action research movement, which gave prominence to the idea of teacher as researcher and challenged academic authority over research. Over the last two decades, the term "research" has begun to take on new meaning. In many circles, research is no longer the sole province of the academy undertaken mainly for the articulation of formal or "theoretical" knowledge usually of little consequence to practitioners. There is an increasing demand for research to inform theory and practice both in the academy and the classroom.

Traditional and Contemporary Approaches to Research

Traditional approaches to research on teacher development, based on assumptions reflecting an objective, logical-deductive view of knowledge and a conception of teaching as a rational set of predictable behaviours essentially devoid of person and context, increasingly are being passed over in favour of alternative approaches. Hypothesis testing and theory generation by rating, classifying, and correlating observational and verbal report data gathered under contrived (or, at least, controlled) conditions are no longer readily accepted ways of apprehending and representing teaching and classroom life.

Examples of studies of teacher thinking conducted in the 1970s illustrate the traditional researcher-controlled, empirical-analytic approach to understanding teacher development. Studies of teachers' interactive thought and decision making produced conceptualizations of teachers as interactive decision makers (e.g., Shavelson, 1976; Shavelson, Atwood, & Borko, 1977; Shavelson & Stern, 1981; Peterson & Clark, 1978; Marx & Peterson, 1981); as information processors (e.g., Marland, 1977; MacKay & Marland, 1978; Fogarty, Wang, & Creek, 1983); and as clinical information processors (e.g., Shulman & Elstein, 1975; National Institute of Education, 1975). It was generally held in these studies that, "Any teaching act is the result of a decision, whether conscious or unconscious, that the teacher makes after the complex processing of available information" (Shavelson, 1973, p. 149). This overly-simplified and purely rational conceptualization of teaching was challenged by those who held to the belief that teacher action is an embodiment of a complex and personal, hence subjective, mode of teacher knowing. It prompted Saphier (1982), for one, to assert:

> We're not going to get anywhere anymore with correlation studies of isolated teacher behaviours and student outcomes. They served their purpose but their purpose is past. Researchers need the collaboration of teachers to steer clear of the trivial and increase the savvy and sophistication of their questions. (p. 92)

Research on teacher thinking recast as research on teacher practice, an expression of teacher knowing, both changed the content of accumulating information on the epistemology of teacher practice and initiated a whole new focus of inquiry. The reorientation of teacher development research has led to a variety of epistemological characterizations and portrayals of teachers' personal and practical perspectives. For example, teachers' perspectives are represented in autobiographical accounts, oral and life histories, and narratives (e.g., Ball & Goodson, 1985; Beattie, 1991; Conle, Eastman, & Nitsis, 1991; Conle, Connelly, & Nicholson, 1991; Goodson, 1992; Goodson & Cole, 1993; Knowles, 1988, 1989, 1991, 1992; Knowles & Hoefler, 1989). Teachers' personal and practical theories have been described, for example, by Cole (1990), Handal and Lauvas (1987), Holt and Johnston (1988), Hunt (1980, 1987), and Hunt and Gow (1984). The concept of personal practical knowledge developed by Clandinin and Connelly in a series of studies beginning in 1985 (e.g., Connelly & Clandinin, 1985, 1990; Clandinin, 1986; Clandinin & Connelly, 1986) has attained a level of prominence in the literature on teacher knowledge. Image and metaphor as representational modes of teacher thought and action also have become prevalent in recent research on teaching (e.g., Bullough, Knowles, & Crow, 1991; Clandinin, 1986; Cole, 1988, 1990; Fox, 1983; Hunt, 1987, 1991; Knowles, 1991; Marshall, 1990; Munby, 1986, 1987; Russell, Munby, Spafford, & Johnston, 1988).

Insights into the complexity of teaching practice have developed with the emergence of case studies and ethnographic accounts of teaching practice (e.g., Britzman, 1991; Brucherhoff, 1991; Bullough, 1989; Bullough, Knowles, & Crow, 1991; Grossman, 1990; Louden, 1991; McLaren, 1986; Nias, Southworth, & Yeomans, 1989; Palonsky, 1986; Perl & Wilson, 1986). And, these various foci are evidenced in the attention to specific aspects of teacher development such as socialization and induction (e.g., Bullough, 1989; Bullough, Knowles, & Crow, 1991; Cole, 1990,

1991a, 1992; Crow, 1987; Thiessen, 1991; Zeichner, 1983).

Teachers recently have begun to assume their rightful position at the head and heart of inquiry into classroom practice. They are joining researchers in the recording, playing back, and analysis of their experiences. The recent rise in popularity of action research (e.g., Cassidy, 1986; Elliott, 1981, 1991; Kemmis & McTaggart, 1988; Oja & Smulyan, 1989; Noffke, 1990) is perhaps the best illustration of how teachers are participating in and initiating alternative modes of inquiry that involve them in the interpretation and representation of their own experiences. Action research typifies inquiry, which accords centrality to relevance and context to bring about change in practice and in the contexts in which practice is expressed. The phrase "teacher as researcher" is not uncommon now in current literature on teacher knowledge and practice (see, for example, Daiker & Morenberg, 1990; Duckworth, 1986; Mohr & MacLean, 1987; Oberg & McCutcheon, 1990).

Teachers' voices increasingly are being heard in literature on teacher education and development and at academic conferences. Examples of media that devote extensive, if not exclusive, space to the works of inquiring teachers include: *The Teacher's Journal* published by Brown University in cooperation with Rhode Island Public Schools; *Among Teachers*, a journal; *Voices* (teacher collections), a writing series; and *Explorations* (teacher monographs)[2]; *Teacher Lore: Learning From Our Own Experience* (Schubert & Ayers 1992), a more comprehensive publication that is an "attempt to systematically collect the stories, insights, knowledge—the lore—of experienced teachers" (p. 152); and, four edited collections of teacher research accounts (Bissex & Bullock, 1987; Daiker & Moreberg, 1990; Goswami & Stillman, 1987; Mohr & MacLean, 1987.

In sum, research on teacher development that does not appear to have any direct relevance or benefit to classroom practice and that takes into account few if any of the exigencies and complexities of teaching and classroom life is not only detached from the complex meaning of teaching and teachers' lives but is also removed from informing the professional development of teachers. Traditional approaches to educational research, broadly characterized as ahistorical, acontextual, and apersonal, have been pushed aside to make room for alternative approaches in which the intensity of human actions and their meanings are centrally located. Perhaps the most fundamental distinction to be made between traditional and contemporary teacher development research models, however, is found in the relationship between the "researcher" and the "researched." It is to this relationship that we not turn.

Partnership Research: Redefining the Relationship

Through the transition in the way educational research activities are viewed, research into teaching has become more subjective, more intensive, more demanding of the participants, and less controlled by researchers affiliated with academic and research institutions. In some cases, research has become more personally and professionally intrusive. (This is particularly so with research using methods of biography, autobiography, narrative, and life history). In most cases, research has become more collaborative—a shift that has challenged the hierarchical relationship between the researcher and the researched embedded in the traditional research model.

In operational modes within traditional research, as Figure 1 suggests, teachers or other "subjects" usually assume a largely passive role, their involvement often limited to their consent to participate and provide essential data. Primary or sole responsibility for decision making about activities at every phase of the research process is assumed by the researcher.[3]

Figure 1: Relationship and Responsibilities in Traditional Research

Phases of Research Activity

	Planning and Preparation	Information Gathering	Interpretation and Representation	Reporting and Use
Teacher (person affiliated with an institution primarily oriented towards practice)	Consent	Some Involvement	Usually No Involvement	Usually No Involvement
Researcher (person affiliated with a research institution)	Primary Responsibility	Primary Responsibility	Sole Responsibility	Sole Responsibility

In contrast, new forms of partnership research are based on fundamental assumptions about the importance of mutuality in purpose, interpretation, and reporting, and about the potency of multiple perspectives. Also implicit in this model is the understanding that each partner in the inquiry process contributes particular and important expertise, and that the relationship between the classroom teacher and the university researcher, for example, is multifaceted and *not* powerfully hierarchical.

> The energy which fuels the act of collaborative interpretation comes from the sparking of the two perspectives: that of the *insider*, who has the intimate knowledge of the setting but whose eyes are dulled by routine reconstruction of events in their own image...and that of the *outsider*, whose wares include ways of "seeing" and thinking about the events of the classroom which he or she has developed through broad experience of classrooms and through critical reflection on different conceptual frameworks for analyzing classrooms.... Thus, in a sense, the academic is moving into the pragmatic world of classroom knowledge-building, but bringing into it a perspective that strengthens the practitioner's framework for analysis. Each partner can learn from what the other has to offer. (Rudduck, 1987, p. 139)

In cases where the co-researchers—that is, the university-researcher and the teacher-researcher—are engaged in a mutual exploration of their own and each other's practice (e.g., Fortin, 1991), there may be few discernible distinctions between actions of the researcher and those of the researched.

The characterization of teacher and researcher as partners in theory building (Cole, 1989) has given rise to a new set of issues associated with the relationship between researcher and teacher and the collaborative nature of the research partnership. University researchers essentially have to reconceptualize traditional research roles and reconstruct the way in which the research agenda is derived.

Respecting, listening to, and giving attention to how the research act and process fit with the everyday lived experiences of teachers, for example, are among the items on the new agenda. There are new technical and procedural matters of concern, such as workloads and responsibilities connected with locating and interpreting information and with developing the formal representations of the research. There are new ethical and political concerns at issue with the move from ahistorical, acontextual, apersonal foci (the procedural aspects of classroom practice) to the realm of inquiry which centres on the personal, historical, and contextual. Issues of control associated with interpreting, representing, and reporting outcomes also emanate from new terms of teacher involvement in alternative paradigm research.

Our belief in the importance of attending to this complex relationship of persons in research has prompted us to place the matter at the centre of our thinking. For the remainder of our article, we focus our thoughts on the researcher-teacher partnership and relationship. We identify and discuss some methodological dilemmas and issues which have arisen in our own research with teachers and that we continue to address as we carry out our work. Besides the central issue of the negotiation of the research relationship and responsibilities, the main issues we address are: research as intrusion into teachers' lives; collaborative versus cooperative research; deriving mutual benefit from research; and representation and voice.

We use three organizing frameworks: (a) examples of our own research with teachers; (b) a matrix displaying the phases of research activities and the roles of researcher and teacher (see Figure 2); and, (c) a matrix displaying the phases and scope of the issues in teacher development partnership research (see Figure 3), that suggests a series of guiding questions that we think need to be asked at the outset and throughout any inquiry.

Examples and Issues from our Work

Examples from some of our recent research activities serve to highlight some of the central issues associated with researching the contexts and lives of teachers for purposes of comprehending teacher development. Because the examples derive from separately conducted research projects, we take turns writing in our own voice. In the research accounts themselves (reported elsewhere) the teachers' voices are also clearly represented. These reflections on research, however, are primarily *our* thoughts, *our* attempts to critically analyze our own research practice; therefore, in some cases there may be a noticeable absence of the teacher's voice.

The examples are *not* intended to represent exemplary research practice, nor do they represent or convey the scope of questions, issues, or dilemmas connected to this line of research. They simply serve to jog *our* memories, reminding us of the potentially tentative nature of research activities involving the lives of teachers, and provide concrete examples on which to base discussion of some of the issues. Primarily, we focus on the issue of collaboration in partnership research.

A Beginning Teacher Withdraws from a Study: Issues of Intrusion, Roles and Relationships, and Representation (Example 1)

Elizabeth was a first-year secondary school teacher whose entry to the profession I (Knowles) was studying (see Knowles, 1988, 1989). I had known her for over a year, both in my capacity as university course instructor and as supervisor of her student teaching. We had, I believed, a congenial, mutually respectful relationship.

When I approached Elizabeth, seeking her participation in allowing me to trace her evolving professional development in the context of life history influences and her use of classroom coping strategies, she readily agreed to my research plan. After a series of initial interviews, classroom observations of the first days and the first two weeks of school, I sought permission to talk to her parents and husband about their perceptions of her decision to become a teacher, about her familial and other life experiences associated with becoming a teacher and thinking about teaching, and about her ongoing development as a classroom professional. She, and they, readily agreed, and family members subsequently provided rich data triangulation of her experiences, intents, and preparation for practice.

Thus, by the end of the second week of Elizabeth's first year, I had already amassed a large amount of information focussing on her thinking about her classroom practices, the actual classroom practices themselves, classroom coping strategies, life history data pertaining to her ways of coping and dealing with problems in general, and her educational experiences and emerging professional beliefs. Together, these various complementary sources and topics provided considerable insights into Elizabeth as an emerging professional.

The information-gathering intrusions into her life were taken in stride by Elizabeth, that is, at least nominally and superficially, until the beginning of the third week. Then, pandemonium broke out; in turn, her classroom structure, organization, and relationships with students were threatened and then rapidly dismantled. A particularly difficult student in a particularly difficult class—her worst—broke the pattern of her teaching. The classroom management problem escalated, forcing many disturbing issues to the foreground of her practice and of her thinking about teaching. The effect also rippled through her other classes. Rumour spread like wildfire.

In response to the extremely difficult circumstances that resulted and in an effort to survive and get on top of the confounding situation, Elizabeth chose to make drastic changes in the manner of her teaching and in the structure of her classroom. These changes, in effect, represented a complete reversal in her teaching strategies and their representation.

In addition, Elizabeth chose to remove herself from the study. She knew the changes in her practice were antithetical to some of my views about working in schools and classrooms, and she felt embarrassed by the changes. She also began to view my inquiry into her professional and personal life as an invasion; not only did the inquiry simply take too much time, but it became uncomfortable. She also named other causes as being at the root of her decision to withdraw, all seemingly related to my role and involvement in her classroom.

At the onset, and even after about four weeks of working together, we had not successfuly resolved the nature and form of my involvement in the work of researching her emerging development. Over the first week of the research, my involvement in her professional activities presented an ongoing concern. Was I merely a researcher? Or, was I still university practicum supervisor? Was my role still that of teaching methods instructor? (At the time, I believe that I relinquished the latter two roles; Elizabeth was not convinced that I had. She was probably correct.) Or, was one of my roles (to be defined more productively after the fact) that of providing constructive feedback, a mirror, as it were, on her teaching?

In talking about the research process, we never clearly articulated each other's expectations and roles. And this role confusion seemed to be at the root of our disequilibrium and the ultimate demise of the study as it was originally conceived. For example, providing extensive feedback on her teaching was one expectation that Elizabeth had for my role in her classroom; however, it was not on my agenda to act substantially in that capacity. If I had been savvy, perhaps more informed, I may have articulated a vision of a more interactive, reflexive, research agenda. As Elizabeth explained, though, she "suffered from overload" and "coping with difficult students was enough, let alone [dealing with] anything or anyone else." There was simply too much going on in her classroom, and in her personal and professional life. The research activity, rather than being beneficial to her, was perceived as yet another burden, and an intrusive one at that—and it was. (As an aside, although she curtailed my classroom visitations, journal writing, and regular interviews, she eventually continued some months later and at irregular intervals to talk to me about her teaching and her professional development.)

Relationships and Responsibilities in the Research Phases

The central issues, then, in considering research on Elizabeth's development as a new teacher are multiple and complex. In my thinking I have frequently raised a number of issues and questions, wondering to what extent I could have orchestrated a much different representation of the score. Upon reflection, it seems that my research approach, although responsive and personal, contextual and historical, was carried out in a mainly traditional mode (compare Figure 1).

The planning and preparing for the effort did not greatly involve Elizabeth, apart from my early interactions with her in uncovering what I perceived to be important issues associated with her professional development, and outlining and negotiating with her alternative courses of action. Further, Elizabeth was only involved in the data collection in as much as she was the major source of information. She specified appropriate times for me to enter into her classroom for observations and interviews, and granted permission for me to collect information from family members. In the process, she was a keeper of the gate of information but not a primary player in any other part of the research. Through ongoing interviews and discussions, she verified or corrected my analyses and made known some of her interpretations of events and circumstances. The final analysis and representation of her experiences, however, were mine. She had little influence on the manner in which I reported the study and, although pertinent sections of the final report of her experience were presented to her as a *fait accompli*, the extent to which they proved beneficial is not known with certainty.

Collaboration or Cooperation?

Collaborative partnership research requires substantial investments of time and energy by both parties. For research to be truly collaborative, it needs to be a process of ongoing negotiation (Cole, 1991b). The research associated with Elizabeth included no serious attempts to collaborate; it was more cooperative in nature reflecting a more traditional researcher-teacher relationship (see Figure 1). She cooperated, for a time, with my agenda. Issues such as roles and responsibilities, status, commitment, and available energies, left unnegotiated, became roadblocks to true collaboration. In addition, the issue of mutual benefit and growth was not adequately addressed, and Elizabeth opted out of an agreement that she viewed as more burdensome than advantageous. The isolation of Elizabeth in role and process during the research activities, and my hazy definition of role and contribution to her development, were at the heart of the matter.

The following example presents a contrasting picture of partnership research. We use it as an example of a response to the central question in collaborative research, "Who is the research for?" and to illustrate the use of the "Matrix for Considering Relationships and Responsibilities in Teacher Development Partnership Research" (Figure 2).

Figure 2: Matrix for Considering Relationships and Responsibilities in Teacher Development Partnership Research (Illustration from Example 2)

Phases of Research Activity

	Planning and Preparation (purpose, procedure, access, roles, logistics of time and place)	Information Gathering (participation, observation, interviews, taping, written accounts)	Interpretation and Representation (verification, validation, voice)	Reporting and Use (voice, control, benefits, public/ private use)
Teacher (person affiliated with an institution primarily oriented towards practice)	Negotiated participation in terms of perceived benefit, commitment, and procedure	Identification of information sources and negotiation of appropriate strategies	Responsive to preliminary analyses; mutual interpretation leading to final analysis	Negotiated representation in report and editing of personal accounts; perceived mutual benefit
Researcher (person affiliated with a research institution)	Primary responsibility for articulation of purpose, coordination of research, and negotiation of activities	Identification of possible strategies and primary responsibility for gathering mutually agreed upon information	Preparation and presentation of preliminary analysis; mutual interpretation of preliminary analysis leading to final analysis	Primary responsibility for writing account; responsive to teachers' editorial and representational comments; perceived mutual benefit

A Study of Teacher Practice through an Exploration of Teacher Beliefs: The Issues of Mutual Benefit and Voice (Example 2)

Beth and Martin are two experienced classroom teachers who joined me (Cole) in an exploration of the knowledge embedded and expressed in their daily classroom practice. We were interested in gaining insight into the spontaneous aspect of their teaching through an examination of their implicit attitudes, beliefs, and theories about teaching and learning (Cole, 1987, 1989). The questions governing our work related to the phenomenon of "just knowing" inherent in experienced practice: "In the immediacy of classroom action, how do experienced teachers 'just know'?" and further, "What does it mean for a teacher to 'just know'?"

To explore these questions, we used the following information-gathering methods: my weekly participation and observation in each teacher's classroom, for a period of four months, recorded by field notes and audiotapes; audiotaped interview-discussions following each visit; the teachers' written statements and reflections about their work and my visits; and my ongoing written descriptive summaries of our work, presented to the teachers each week for their reflection and our discussion.

From the outset of the initial contact through to the interpretation and representation, our work was intended to be a collaborative endeavour. Indeed, the final report was subtitled, "A Mutual Interpretation." Periodically throughout the study and at the end of our work, I asked each teacher to reflect on their involvement in the research. The following comments from one of the teacher-researchers, Martin, illustrate the mutual benefit that can be derived from collaborative partnership research.

I think it's been a very valuable experience....It's given me renewed confidence in my teaching, and I appreciate that. I think a lot of it has been because you've been very encouraging, very positive. It has to do with your style I suppose....You looked specifically for items relating to the study and chose to ignore or not comment on negative things, and that has made the experience much more palatable for me. It made me less defensive and less afraid.

It's much closer scrutiny than a teacher normally gets. Staying on track looking for specific things has made it a positive thing....I came away feeling better about my teaching, and I also think I had a better understanding of some of the processes that go on in my teaching.

I think it helped you too.

I think this kind of research has to go on because it takes place in the actual context. You paid attention to context, and I think that's very important in research. It's the kind that should yield useful information.

In looking over some of the summaries of your visits I'd say, "Oh, yeah, I am accomplishing many of the things I want to accomplish." An outsider can sometimes see that better than the person in the middle of it. I've found it to be an encouraging experience, and I've been feeling better about my teaching than I did before you came, so that's good.

I'm finding it helpful to have someone take such a close look and mention things [about my teaching]. I find it encouraging that you see some of my ideas in practice because I'm not always so sure that they're coming through.

I think I have a deeper awareness of what's going on when I'm teaching now. By having isolated certain aspects of what's going on in the classroom, laid them on the table, and looked at them more closely, I think it's deepened my awareness of what's going on when I put it back into that integral whole.

Relationships and Responsibilities in the Research Phases

Martin characterized the research project as a "joint" effort and Beth described it as an endeavour in which she "came out benefitting as much from the experience as [I]." Clearly, both teachers felt very much partners in the research. I attribute their (and my) satisfaction with the research activities and our successful collaboration to ongoing attention to mutuality throughout the project. At each phase of the research (see Figure 2) from planning and preparation through to reporting and use, our roles and responsibilities were continually re-negotiated (though not always explicitly). Logistical matters of time and place, my participation in their classrooms, the use of an audiotape recorder, interpretation and representation of their practice, and the issue of benefit were among the many items we considered together.

A look at Martin's comments also highlights the importance of ongoing attention to other issues. Maintaining my commitment to a nonevaluative stance and adopting the motto, "accentuate the positive" gave Martin the confidence and security he needed to examine critically his own teaching. In addition, the dialectic of interpretation made possible by the melding of our perspectives gave new clarity to his insights (and mine). Once again, we point out the centrality of the researcher-teacher relationship at all phases of an inquiry.

The matrix in Figure 2 is helpful for depicting the research relationship. It provides a way of determining the nature and extent of classroom-teacher/academic-researcher involvement throughout an inquiry that is intended to be collaborative. Questions related to participation in decision making about various activities associated with each phase of the research and about how the various participants are so involved can provide insights into the authenticity of the collaboration. If answers to such questions lead to a matrix similar to Figure 1, then clearly the collaborative nature of the research is called into question and merits further consideration.

Applying the Figure 2 framework to the research with Beth and Martin results in a depiction of a project that could be described as authentically collaborative, at least, for the most part. Some might say, however, that it, too, fell short at the reporting phase. In the actual writing up of the research report, the teachers assumed two primary roles: one editorial, the other representational. Although verbatim quotes from our interviews and the teachers' written statements contributed a generous portion of the report, the teachers were not involved directly in the actual creation of the final text.

The dilemma of equality in participation is a persistent one. Given the differences in our day-to-day professional lives and our varying institution-ally assigned roles and responsibilities, is it reasonable to expect equal involvement in all aspects of the research? As long as responsibilities are negotiated and mutually agreed upon, does it not make sense that time, opportunity, workload, and personal preference be key factors in decision making about activities such as writing?

Collaboration for collaboration's sake seems counter-productive. True collaboration is more likely to result when the aim is *not* for *equal* involvement in all aspects of the research; but, rather, for *negotiated* and *mutually agreed upon* involvement. In our final example, we recount another story of collaboration, this one with a bit of a twist.

An Exploration of "Failure" in Student Teaching: Issues of Persistence and Voice (Example 3)

In a study of student teachers' emerging conceptions and development, I (Knowles) was also interested in examining my own practice as a practicum supervisor. Several weeks into Angela's final period of student teaching, both the cooperating teachers and I agreed that Angela, one of the participants in a yearlong, graduate preservice teacher education programme, was experiencing considerable difficulty and headed for possible "failure" in the classroom. And, despite some final desperate remedial efforts, she eventually did "fail."

In the meantime, I had collected considerable data about aspects of Angela's development as a prospective teacher; I had recorded her progress as an emerging teacher from the time she entered the programme. She kept an extensive journal, talked freely with me about aspects of her ongoing development, and placed considerable trust in me as I vainly attempted to guide and facilitate her professional development. I, too, kept a journal and maintained field notes of my visits to her classroom. Even throughout her obvious difficulties Angela continued to place confidence in my supervisory actions, talking freely about her experiences and our efforts to nullify her inappropriate classroom practices. Eventually a consensus was reached by all parties involved with her practicum, including the principal and cooperating teachers, and she was removed from the classroom.

Although I wrote about the experience (Knowles, 1988, 1992), I had not intended to explore the matter further with Angela as well. But, at Angela's insistence, further explorations of the circumstances surrounding the "failure" did occur. Indeed, she refused to let the mind-crushing and potentially disabling experience get the better of her and would not let me lay the matter to rest. For this reason, we called the subsequent coauthored article "The Student Teacher Who Wouldn't Go Away: Learning From Failure" (Knowles & Hoefler, 1989).

Relationships and Responsibilities in the Research Phases

Only after the authentic exploration of the events associated with her "failure" in the student teaching component of her teacher preparation— her participation in the programme, the failure itself, and the subsequent painful exploration of its cause and antecedents—did we mutually decide to proceed with the public presentation of the experience. Only then did we turn to the actual data—our individual journals and my field notes—to write the account. In so doing, we essentially excluded the intent of my original study and focussed on the circumstances surrounding her failure. And, it was written together. I took the lead in framing the circumstances, the overall process, and developing the final written product; she took the lead in the interpretation and presentation of the data, while verifying and correcting my separate analyses. In some respects, she gave me an unforgettable lesson in collaborative, partnership research.

The original intent of my work with Angela (to explore her development and my own supervisory practice) faded into the background because the agenda as originally conceived became quite inappropriate and *her* agenda became compelling. The point at which the change occurred was *not* her removal from the classrooms in which she attempted to shape her practice; rather, it was somewhere within the initial period after her failure during which, daily, she pounded my door seeking answers to her own actions and my, and others', responses to them, and general and specific understandings of the complex circumstances. Flexibility in both framing the information we had accumulated and thinking about its potential usefulness was the key to our subsequent actions.

Representation of Angela's voice came about quite naturally in a sense, once we decided that a written account would serve us both well. Although I was the initiator of this process, she was keen to extend the meanings associated with her experience. Correctly, she sensed that my analysis of the circumstances would be enhanced by my writing about the events; she, being a prolific journal writer, also clarifying much of her thinking about the matter through careful attention to writing. Thus, writing became a tool for us to work through the analyses. Often she would turn up at my door with new analyses that she had derived in the previous night's writing. And, this kind of reflexivity, with written statements regularly exchanged between us, ensured that the representation of her voice was entirely at her discretion.

It seems ironic that a study which we characterize as a highly successful collaborative venture came about as a result of the unintended failure of one of the participants. If it had not been for Angela's insistence on negotiating closure, we wonder how truly collaborative the original study might have been—since it was never completed. Referring again to Figure 2, we can apply the framework to the study with Angela and ask the following questions: Who was involved? How was each partner involved? and, How were roles and responsibilities negotiated at each inquiry phase? And we could conclude that the research was indeed a collaborative endeavour.

Issues and Questions in Teacher Development Partnership Research

Because teachers are no longer passive agents (or subjects in externally imposed research and driven research), their involvement is central at all stages of the research process from planning and preparing to do the research, through data gathering, interpretation, and representation, to reporting and use of the outcomes. But, once again, we point to the distinction between cooperation and collaboration, and emphasize the essentiality of negotiation. In making this point, we are also mindful of the depth of this new research agenda.

Figure 3: Issues in Teacher Development Partnership Research

	Planning and Preparation (purpose, procedure, access, roles, logistics of time and place)	Information Gathering (participation, observation, interviews, taping, written accounts)	Interpretation and Representation (verification, validation, voice)	Reporting and Use (voice, control, benefits, public/private use)
Technical Issues (e.g., logistics, finances, implementation of research design)				
Personnel Issues (e.g., relationships and responsibilities)				
Procedural Issues (e.g., time frame, monitoring of research, information flow)				
Ethical Issues (e.g., care, equity, confidentiality, control of information)				
Political Issues (e.g., policy, legislative, curriculum implications)				
Educational Issues (e.g., informing and improving practice)				

At each phase of the inquiry, from planning to reporting and use, and throughout the various activities in which collaborative researchers (and others) engage, are layers of issues that require attention so that the research can be truly collaborative and mutually developmental. In Figure 3, we identify multiple issues that reflect some of the complexity inherent in alternative approaches to research on teaching and teacher development. We also offer a series of questions related to each issue. Although our list is far from exhaustive, we hope to encourage university and teacher researchers to begin to consider some of the difficult issues in teacher development partnership research. The matrix in Figure 3 is intentionally open-ended. We intend it as a vehicle to assist those engaged in teacher development partnership research to raise questions about the research process; therefore, as with Figure 2, we invite you to use the framework and pose these, and other, questions at each phase of an inquiry.

Technical Issues

Technical issues present themselves at every phase of the research process from determining logistics of time and place in the planning phase to working out techniques of information gathering to management and organization of data for interpretation and reporting. Central to these issues are questions such as:

- How will the planning of the project proceed?
- Is external resource support required? How much? When?
- Where will financial support be found? What kind of request for funding is required and who participates in preparing the formal request? How is the budget managed? Who controls the budget?
- What arrangements need to be made for data collection, storage, analysis, reporting, and so on?
- What existing facilities and resources need to be made available for the activities of the research?
- How are research and practice activities coordinated and negotiated?
- How flexible and responsive is the planning?

Personnel Issues

The personnel issues associated with intense collaborative research on teacher development are very complex. At each phase mutually acceptable relationships and roles are essential for the ongoing development of collaborative work; yet, because of the differing nature of institutional commitments, negotiating who does what, and when and how it is done is a challenging task. We do not mean to imply that these and other issues, once negotiated, are set in stone. When participants are open to negotiation, roles and responsibilities can be modified at any time. The following questions, however, may be useful for addressing personnel issues:

- How is responsibility to be shared throughout the research?
- How are strengths of research partners identified and taken into account?
- How are time and responsibility demands of partners taken into consideration in determining roles and responsibilities?
- Have roles and responsibilities been negotiated and agreed upon? Is there flexibility to make changes to the negotiated roles and responsibilities.

Procedural Issues

Addressing and negotiating procedural issues is essential to actually carrying out the research. Among the things to be considered are: establishing a time frame for the research work; deciding how the information gathering will actually proceed; and making arrangements for ongoing responsivity to the data and the research design and for the mutual interpretation and reporting of the information. The following questions are potentially useful to consider:

- When, where, and how does the research project proceed? How do participants coordinate their activities?
- How might the research activities interfere with normal routines? What allowances need to be made? Do special provisions and care need to be taken to ensure ongoing benefits for all parties?
- What arrangements need to be made to ensure opportunities for ongoing reflexivity, responsivity, and mutual involvement?

Ethical Issues

Ethical issues permeate collaborative research projects at every point of their implementation. Too often, we sense, questions concerning ethical issues are inadvertently overlooked because of their complex and interwoven nature. With the advent of more intrusive research methods, and the requirements of personal investment in research, consideration of ethical issues takes on a new prominence. Some questions to consider include:

- How will confidentiality of informants be assured? Or, conversely, are

there potential negative consequences if participants wish to reveal their identities?
- How will consent be given?
- Who will have access to the data during and after the study?
- What happens in the case of conflicting impressions and interpretations? How are differing positions negotiated?
- How will control be negotiated throughout the study?
- How will equity of influence be maintained?

Political Issues

Political issues associated with researching teachers' lives and practices are too often not considered as being an integral part of the research process; yet, in collaborative research, addressing political issues is essential for maintaining authenticity. Although political issues are subtle, their effect may be monumental. Collaborative research implies equality in issues of control, authority, and autonomy. The politics of collaborative research demand that these issues be considered. Such consideration might be facilitated by the following questions:

- Who will use this research? Why? When? For what purpose? Are there hidden agendas associated with participation? How can openness be assured?
- What are the long-term goals of the study? Are there short-term goals?
- Who has authority over the data and their use? What are the purposes of the research report(s)?
- How will participation in the study be viewed by others in the school community or educational context in which the work is embedded?
- What is the extent of institutional commitment? Why? What are the institutional expectations? Have these been clearly expressed?
- Is the institutional commitment sufficient to allow for the individual commitment necessary? What is the form of the institutional commitment, and how does it directly have an impact on each participant in the research process?
- Are there institutional privileges or benefits associated with participation in the research? Are there potential disadvantages to participation?

Educational Issues

The root purpose of research into teachers' professional development is, we maintain, to inform and enhance teachers' practice and children's learning. The educational issues, then, associated with research of the nature we have described may inform the methods and the implementation of those methods. Questions that may usefully inform and direct collaborative partnership researchers include:

- How is participation in this project likely to influence development and inform practice in the classroom, university, and beyond?
- How will participation in the project inform the professional development of *all* persons involved?
- To what extent is participation in the research empowering?
- Does the research work propel others to engage in similar proccesses?
- How will the outcomes be disseminated? By whom? To whom? For what purpose will the research be disseminated?

The Ongoing Dialectic and Development of Partnership Research

Teacher development partnership research, as we have described and discussed it, is supported and carried out within a small but growing community of educators concerned with understanding the initial and continuing development of teachers and the contexts in which practical and professional action reside. The epistemological perspective in which this kind of work is situated makes methodological demands that set partnership research apart from other similar kinds of inquiry; thus, attention to these demands is essential for paradigmatic and methodological coherence.

A hermeneutic approach to understanding teaching and teacher development assumes a dialectical relationship between knowledge and action, theory and practice. Understanding of such a dialectical relationship, therefore, requires a dialectical perspective on inquiry. With teachers as holders and users of the tools for theory building and researchers as companions in conversation, such understanding is attainable. Thus, researcher and teacher become engaged as joint theorists/researchers in a mutual apprehension and interpretation of meaning in action. True collaboration—not just cooperation—therefore, is integral to partnership research grounded in a hermeneutic perspective. If we are to take seriously the notion of mutuality in research in the interests of advancing our understanding of teachers and their work then we need to pay careful and thoughtful attention to the kinds of dilemmas and issues we raised and engage in ongoing responsivity throughout any inquiry. Such attention is essential for equitable, mutually educative, and authentically collaborative research.

Notes

* Reprinted with permission from the *American Educational Research Journal*, Fall 1993, Vol. 30, No. 3, pp. 473-495.

Earlier versions of this article were presented at the Continuity and Change in Teacher Education Conference, Faculty of Education, The University of Western Ontario, London, Ontario, Canada, Oct. 30-Nov. 1, 1991, and The Human Sciences Research Conference, Oakland, Michigan, June 9-13, 1992.

1. We deliberately have avoided presenting the shift in perspective as a move from quantitative to qualitative research because, for us, such a characterization does not adequately represent the essence of the shift. Due to loose and overuse, these terms more often are used to represent differences in method rather than in perspective; we do not wish to confuse the two. "Paradigm" and "method" are not synonymous. For a comparative discussion of competing research perspectives, see, for example, Eisner (1991), Eisner and Peshkin (1990), Jacob (1987), Morgan and Smircich (1980), Reason and Rowan (1981), and Smith (1983).

2. These three publications are written by and for teachers as part of another recent attempt to bring together "a community of teachers across Canada and the world who want to explore our teaching and tell our stories" (Among Teachers Community, 1991).

3. To be fair, however, as one of our examples shows, these kinds of circumstances are *not* exclusively relegated to traditional empirical-analytical approaches. What we have labelled traditional research modes may be found across all teacher development research despite the impropriety of such.

Chapter Nine

Teacher Education: Problem Solving Within a "Holding Environment"

Anne L. Cummings and Ernest T. Hallberg

One of the many challenges facing teacher education programmes today is preparing preservice teachers to cope with the complexity of classroom interactions. Too often in the past, teacher education has focussed on the behavioural aspects of teaching which has led to more simplistic formulations for teacher performance. This emphasis is exemplified in the "how to" prescriptions: how to motivate students, how to reinforce positive behaviours, etc. What is lacking in this approach is the impact of teachers' thought processes, judgments, and decisions on the way that students learn and teachers teach (Peterson, 1988).

Given the complexity and ambiguity that is inherent in the interactive teaching experience, Clark (1988) believes that research about teacher thinking will provide helpful, new avenues of understanding about these processes. He asserts that much of a teacher's energy is directed to predicting problems and reacting to the interruptions that surface daily in the classroom. In fact, he states that teachers encounter interactive decision-making situations at approximately two-minute intervals while teaching. If we can better understand this interactive decision-making process utilized by teachers, teacher educators may then be better able to aid preservice teachers in learning to think in ways that will help them cope with the complexities of the classroom. By viewing teachers as active, thoughtful problem solvers, an external perspective focussing on what teachers do is then replaced by an internal perspective of what teachers perceive and understand (Kagan, 1988).

With this more internal perspective, the role of teacher educators as supervisors and facilitators of reflective decision making also becomes more complex. Yet, as Berliner (1986) attests, the supervising teacher can have a great impact on the development of the preservice teacher and thus, it behooves us to consider carefully the optimal supervisory situation. One helpful metaphor for conceptualizing the supervisory role is Winnicott's (1965) "holding environment." This concept has been applied successfully to the supervisory experience in psychotherapy (Jarmon, 1990; Watkins, 1990). Within an educational context, the holding environment would involve the teacher educator providing the safety, stability, and anchor from which the preservice teacher can experiment with new thought processes.

With this brief introduction, the remainder of this article will review the social problem-solving literature as it applies to novice and experienced teachers, describe a supervisory model for teacher education based on Winnicott's holding environment, and finally, present a research study on the social problem solving of preservice teachers with applications to the holding environment model of teacher supervision.

Social Problem Solving

While much research has studied well-structured problem solving in the classroom using impersonal science or math problems (e.g., Frederiksen, 1984; Leinhardt & Smith, 1985; Peterson, 1988), little research has examined the problem solving of teachers with the more ill-defined, social problems that arise daily in the classroom. Social or personal problem solving is here defined as the process used by people to cope effectively with the problematic situations of everyday life (D'Zurilla & Goldfried, 1971). This type of problem solving is further conceptualized as being highly interactive, complex, and intermittent rather than being in a stage or linear sequence (Heppner & Krauskopf, 1987).

In summarizing research findings about teachers' interactive decision making, Clark (1988) reports several characteristics of effective teachers. The interactive decision-making style of more effective teachers was composed of quick judgment, chunking of information into a few categories, differentiation of the importance of various cues in the problem situation, and a flexibility about changing the direction of the classroom interaction when necessary.

Other authors (Berliner, 1986; Peterson & Comeaux, 1987) claim that novice teachers, compared to more experienced teachers, tend to be at a disadvantage in problem situations because of their lack of both declarative and procedural knowledge of common teaching practices. They have not yet acquired a broad repertoire of schemata or hypotheses for responding to the continually changing classroom environment. Peterson and Comeaux

(1987), in particular, found in their study of teachers' schemata during classroom instruction that experienced teachers were more able to view problem events through a lens of higher-level principles of effective classroom teaching. In other words, these teachers were able to activate schemata to help them organize a variety of incoming information.

These findings are consistent with research comparing experts and novices who are solving well-defined problems in a variety of fields. Chi, Glaser, and Farr (1989) state that novices work more on the surface features of a problem, while experts are better able to use the underlying structures inherent in the problem. In addition, experts have more domain-specific schemata that they use to obtain problem solutions, while novices tend to become entangled in the details of the problem (Voss, Green, Post, & Penner, 1983).

One principle emerging from the preceding research on both teaching and other fields is the importance of possessing effective schemata for solving problems efficiently. One advantage of such schemata is that they can be used to predict problem situations in contrast to merely responding to events as they arise. For example, Housner and Griffey (1985) found that their experienced teachers were better at anticipating problem situations in the classroom and developing appropriate contingency plans than were their novice teachers.

The problem-solving process, itself, is complex in that it involves encoding incoming information, retrieving knowledge from memory, and applying this knowledge to new situations. Of these elements, probably the most critical aspect of the process is the accurate encoding of the problem (Heppner & Krauskopf, 1987). Before a problem can be solved, problem solvers must be able to identify the central elements of the problem, assess their own role in the problem, and analyze the interactive environmental components of the problem.

Heppner and Krauskopf (1987) identify three other aspects of encoding that can facilitate the problem-solving process: speed, accuracy, and completeness. Speed of encoding is important because many interpersonal problems in the classroom require quick responses. Accuracy of perception about the problem is necessary so that the problem solver is not misled by irrelevant or distorted aspects of the situation. Finally, grasping the complete problem is needed to ensure that the problem solver focusses on the entire problem rather than a tangential element.

The supervisory process within teacher education programmes has the potential of impacting directly the encoding process of preservice teachers in problem situations. Much work could be done to help preservice teachers develop a more analytical approach to problem situations by encouraging them to activate their reflective selves before moving into action patterns. The need for this type of work is evidenced in a study of expert and novice teachers solving discipline problems (Swanson, O'Connor, & Cooney, 1990). The expert teachers were better at defining and representing the problem, plus evaluating possible strategies, while the novice teachers tended to view problems more in relation to the possible solutions they would use.

Besides the information processing elements involved in solving problems, social problem solving is influenced by individual difference variables of the problem solver. While it is beyond the scope of this article to examine all of the possible individual difference variables that can affect social problem solving (e.g., personality characteristics, values, self-concept), we do want to highlight one area that is particularly applicable to the holding environment model: the individual's developmental level of the self.

Adult learners are not static entities. Rather, the developmental process of the self continues throughout the lifespan. One research team (Cavanaugh, Kramer, Sinnott, Camp, & Markley, 1985) has highlighted the aspects of adult development that are especially related to social problem solving. They believe that as adults are required to adapt to an increasingly complex social environment, they must become more relativistic and differentiated in their problem solving to be able to deal effectively with the everyday problems of life.

Adopting this view as teacher educators would mean challenging preservice teachers who are more undimensional and undifferentiated in their problem-solving approach to become more relativistic and differentiated in their thinking about problem situations. In other words, we need to resist the temptation to provide quick solutions to preservice teachers' "how to" questions. Instead, the focus should be on helping them to develop broad schemata for use in developing more relativistic approaches to a particular problem situation. As Lampert and Clark (1990) assert, expertise in managing people in teaching requires learning to think in highly responsive ways to the social details of the problem situation.

Thus, facilitating effective social problem solving in preservice teachers becomes closely linked to facilitating effective teacher thinking. Additionally, developing a thoughtful teacher involves preservice teachers having a self-awareness of their cognitions and being encouraged to reflect on their thoughts as they approach social problems (Peterson, 1988).

In summary, social problem solving within the classroom is a highly complex, interactive process that requires careful preparation for preservice teachers. As teacher educators, we need to help preservice teachers accurately encode problem situations, develop a reflective orientation to problem solving, and build effective schemata for approaching a wide variety of interpersonal problems within the classroom. One of the ways to accomplish these goals is to create a holding environment within which preservice teachers can develop these new skills.

Developmental Phases of Self-Identity Within a Holding Environment

When one discusses the capabilities of preservice teachers to solve ill-defined social problems, it is useful to place such abilities within the context of the development of the teacher's professional identity. The self-identity (Erikson, 1959) of a beginning teacher involves the development of the self beginning with excitement and anticipation mixed with self-doubts and anxiety, then progressing toward self-confidence and professional self-constancy (Watkins, 1990). This development and maturation optimally occur within a social environment that is supportive, safe, and challenging.

In providing such a social climate, the holding environment metaphor (Winnicott, 1965) serves as a guide to supervisory strategies for the nurturance of the self of the preservice teacher within the developmental process. The holding environment metaphor in supervisory practice mirrors the essential elements of good parenting in providing empathy-based interventions for the purpose of supporting and facilitating the personal growth for the preservice teacher.

In this section of the chapter, we will describe the phases of the developmental model suggested for viewing the preservice teacher's growth toward professional self-identity. Second, we will discuss the essence of the holding environment metaphor in terms of implications for the supervisory relationship. Subsequently, we will focus upon the preservice teacher's characteristics at different stages of development and possible supervisory strategies at each phase.

Developing a professional self-identity is a process arising from the complex interactions of the preservice teacher with the tasks of teaching and the instructional and supervisory environment. This model suggests four overlapping stages or phases, each having different demands upon the self-identity of the preservice teacher. The stages are (a) involvement and connection, (b) differentiation, (c) practice and experimentation, and (d) professional self-constancy (Watkins, 1990) (see Table 1).

Table 1: Developmental Phases of Self Identity in Teaching

Preservice Teacher Characteristics and Supervisor Functions

Phase	Pre-service Teacher Characteristics	Supervisor Functions
1. Involvement & Connections	1. Eager to connect and to be involved, with high hopes and expectations. 2. May be confused and anxious, feeling of unsureness, experiencing early vulnerability. 3. Initial dependence on supervisor. 4. Need to do something concrete as quickly as possible. 5. Tendency to be egocentric, concerned about own role and function.	1. Provides holding environment emphasizing early structure, empathic sensitivity, and nurturance. 2. Sets ground rules and initial schedule, to facilitate confidence and trust.
2. Differentiation	1. Feels belonging. 2. Expands attention outward, away from self, toward students, the curriculum and the supervisor. 3. Beginning ability to receive discriminating feedback. 4. Experiences excitement about early successes in teaching and relating with students. 5. Beginnings of analytical thinking.	1. Model teaching behaviours, with willingness to discuss self skills without defensiveness. 2. Uses empathy, concrete examples, and affirming interventions in supervisory meetings. 3. Begins to focus on preservice teacher and student relationships. 4. Helps the reflection process concerning class management policies and strategies, as well as educational goals and teaching strategies, only in a beginning sense.

Developmental Phases of Self-Identity in Teaching

Preservice Teacher Characteristics and Supervisor Functions (cont'd)

Phase	Pre-service Teacher Characteristics	Supervisor Functions
3. Practice and experimentation	1. Open to experimentation—trial, success, error, and feedback. 2. Manifests increased confidence and independent thought. 3. Beginnings of thinking within a framework about connections between strategies and consequences. 4. Manifests first rudiments of self identity as a teacher. 5. Difficulties seem to focus on self hesitancy and/or self doubt or the proneness to inflated self estimates.	1. Encouragement of independency. 2. Self disclosure of trial and error experiences. 3. Recognizes and reinforces growth and gains. 4. Focus on the pre-service teacher's understanding and reflection about the teaching and learning process. 5. Serves as a reality check, emphasizing objective and reflective attitudes.
4. Professional self constancy	1. Consolidation of self as a teacher. 2. Increased need for supervisor in dealing with specific students and educational issues. 3. May feel overwhelmed and/or cynical of educational enterprises. 4. Increased objectivity about self and influence of self on perceiving ill-defined problems. 5. Regards supervisor in a more wholistic and integrated fashion. 6. "Letting go" of supervisor. 7. Readiness for job search.	1. Uses collaborative and egalitarian forms of relating. 2. Recognizes and deals with ambivalence and related behaviours. 3. Assists preservice teacher in reflective understanding of self as an educator.

When the preservice teacher enters practice teaching, the first needs are to become involved and to make meaningful connections with the supervising teacher, the class, and the school. The preservice teacher is likely to be full of enthusiasm and feel varying degrees of anxiety, fear of failure, and general misgivings about self as a teacher. To cope with these anxieties, a high degree of dependency upon the supervisor may occur (Jarmon, 1990). The preservice teacher seeks global reactions and support from significant others.

As adequate involvement and connections occur, the preservice teacher is enabled to extend attention outward, away from self-preoccupation. The preservice teacher's perceptual field broadens to consider problems and tasks in the areas of more complex lesson planning, classroom management, and relationships with students in the class. The broadened perceptual field allows the preservice teacher to become more differentiating about the elements of facilitating learning.

The third stage is that of practice and experimentation (Watkins, 1990). With a broadened perspective, increased successes in teaching and a corresponding increase in confidence and independence, the preservice teacher begins to practise favoured teaching styles and experiment with more creative strategies both in relationships and curriculum delivery. There are beginning attempts to predict and prevent management and instructional problems. The manifestations of self-identity as a teacher begin to occur, perhaps bringing conflicts about deeper needs and self-doubts.

The last stage of this developmental model focusses on the beginning teacher acquiring a more constant self-identity as a professional (Watkins, 1990). The individual is now more able to participate fully as a colleague, to share mutual strategies and consequences, and to acquire increasing objectivity about the self in interaction with peers and pupils. This stage involves a lifetime of identity definition and self-clarification. We believe that most preservice teachers only begin to establish some sense of professional self-constancy, and that its establishment is highly important to beginning teachers in the first two to three years of employment.

The holding environment metaphor, coined by Winnicott (1965), describes the "good enough parent" in providing a loving, trusting, and safe yet stimulating social climate, in which natural growth and maturation are fostered. Care-giving is the primary facilitative strategy available to the supervising teacher. It implies psychological holding, when needed, as well as disclosure of teaching strategies, challenging the preservice teacher at the appropriate stage.

This relationship environment is not restricted to practicum placement supervisors, but includes supervisors, instructors, and peers at all instructional levels, including faculties of education. Care-giving, within this metaphor, emphasizes the empathic functions that facilitate expression of personal needs and attitudes by the preservice teacher. The supervising teacher provides a safe, trusting environment through empathic listening and initial structuring of the environment and the scheduling of time. Thus, the preservice teacher is more likely to identify with the supervisor. Identification is seen as a process basic to the needs of the self to establish and maintain meaningful relationships.

The four-stage developmental model and the care-giving metaphor give us a basic guide for supervisory conceptualizations and behaviours. In the involvement and connection phase, the supervisor helps the pre-service teacher become as fully involved and trusting as possible, being aware that the supervisee may regress to dependency, be needy, and be unsure. The supervisor sets time and function ground rules and together both parties arrange for opportunities for early success in delivering lessons.

Phase two, differentiation, is ambiguous, complex, and thus often a more difficult stage. Still providing the empathic relationship base, the supervisor delivers more personalized feedback and helps the preservice teacher expand the field of awareness and keep several factors in focus.

In the third stage, the first rudiments of self-identity as a teacher are manifested as the supervisee begins to show self-confidence, creativity, and wishes to experiment with self-developed ideas. The supervisor recognizes the need to encourage independence within a structure while urging the individual to reflect on the reasons and rationale for differing strategies and consequences. Sometimes there is a tendency for the preservice teacher to exaggerate self-estimates; in this event the supervisor provides a reality base by gently and firmly challenging the supervisee to reflect upon the many complexities of teaching and learning.

Finding a professional self-identity, the last stage of this model, is a life-long endeavour which is entered near the end of the preservice year and follows the supervisee's decision about commitment to the teaching profession. At this stage, the supervisor enters a more collaborative and egalitarian relationship with the preservice teacher. The mutuality of "self-in-relationship" takes on a new depth and is likely to help meet the professional needs for challenge and support for both mentor and beginning teacher.

A Study of Preservice Teacher Social Problem Solving

To understand better the social problem solving of preservice teachers with in a holding environment, we examined the thought processes of pre-service teachers during problem solving. One difficulty in researching the thinking processes involved in social problem solving is that thinking cannot be accessed directly. One of the more effective ways of assessing problem-solving and thinking processes is the think-aloud methodology (Clark, 1988; Ericsson & Simon, 1984). This methodology involves teachers talk-ing out loud while they solve problems, thus giving researchers a close approximation of the cognitive and metacognitive processes utilized by teachers as they reflect on their own knowledge and actions in a problem situation.

Using the think-aloud methodology, we asked 29 (22 women and 7 men) education students to solve four problems that preservice teachers typically face. The four problem situations included the following: (a) "You have just taught a new concept to the class. The brighter students under-stand the concept, while the slower students do not understand it" (instruc-tion); (b) "Two students together have been gradually escalating their disruption of your class presentations over time and have not responded to your requests to be quiet" (discipline); (c) "You are having conflict with your associate teacher because of differences in style and approach" (asso-ciate teacher); and, (d) "You are finding it difficult to balance the demands of school work and the needs of your personal life" (time demands). The last problem with a more self emphasis was included to examine whether there were differences in problem-solving approaches between more school-related problems and a more personal problem.

Preservice teachers solved these problems out loud with a research assistant at the beginning, middle, and toward the end of their preservice year. Problem solutions were taped, transcribed, and then analyzed for eight different cognitive problem-solving elements. The strategies generated for each problem were also content analyzed to determine the relationship be-tween the type of problem and the types of strategies used by the preservice teacher. Previous research (Cummings, Murray, & Martin, 1989; Kagan, 1988) has found that the type of social problem can influence the kind of problem-solving approach employed. Understanding how different types of problems might elicit different strategies from preservice teachers could aid teacher educators in better preparing students for typical classroom situa-tions. For example, do preservice teachers use different types of strategies for instruction problems than they do for discipline problems? The problem solutions were also examined over time to determine what effect experience, knowledge, and the holding environment might have on the problem-solving processes and content of the problem solutions.

Protocols were scored for eight mutually exclusive categories intended to describe the total process of social problem solving using a scoring manual developed by Cummings et al. (1989). The scoring categories were based on problem-solving elements from prominent social problem-solving models (D'Zurilla & Goldfried, 1971; Platt & Spivack, 1975). The eight categories were the following: (a) analysis (directly or indirectly assessing the problem); (b) strategy (idea, action, or approach for solving the problem); (c) elaboration (detail about a strategy or the situation); (d) reason (explanation for a strategy, feeling, or evaluation); (e) evaluation of a strategy or situation (judging the feasibility or desirability of a strategy or situation); (f) evaluation of self (problem solver judges self within the problem situation); (g) feeling (how the problem solver feels about the problem, strategy, or outcome); and, (h) if-then thinking (assumption about the problem, followed by a possible solution).

For the initial analyses, the four problems were grouped into two Conflict problems (discipline, associate teacher) and two Balancing problems (instruction and time demands). The Conflict problems involved solving an interpersonal conflict between the preservice teacher and other people (associate teacher in one problem and students in the other). Balancing problems involved two opposing needs or pressures (balancing the needs of work versus personal life in the self problem and balancing the needs of slow versus fast learners in the instruction problem. A second grouping was also used by combining the two Classroom problems (discipline, instruction) and the two Non-Classroom problems (associate teacher, time demands).

Another level of analysis was also employed: a qualitative, content analysis of the strategies generated for the four problems. Using protocol analysis techniques (Ericsson & Simon, 1984), seven strategy categories were developed for three of the problems and six categories were developed for the fourth problem (see Table 2). The instruction and discipline problems shared four common categories, while the supervising teacher and time demands problem shared four common categories. For all of the coding in this study, two trained raters were used who achieved an inter-rater reliability of .88 on category agreement using Cohen's (1960) coefficient of interjudge agreement.

The first goal of the study was to assess whether preservice teachers varied their cognitive processes for different types of problems. Using MANOVA analyses, we found that when Conflict problems were compared with Balance problems, preservice teachers used more evaluation of strategies, $F(1,28) = 5.08$, $p = .03$, and provided more reasons, $F(1,28) = 22.76$, $p .001$, on Conflict problems. Thus, preservice teachers were more analytical and evaluative of their actions when the problem involved conflict with other people.

When Classroom problems were compared with Non-Classroom problems, for Non-Classroom problems the preservice teachers used more elaboration, $F(1,28) = 6.51$, $p .02$; more evaluation of strategies, $F(1,28) = 10.04$, $p .004$; and more evaluation of self, $F(1,28) = 42.04$, $p .001$. However, on Classroom problems, participants generated more strategies, $F(1,28) = 35.50$, $p .001$. Figure 1 presents the mean values for the problem-solving elements highlighted in these analyses.

Figure 1: *Significant differences in mean number of problem-solving elements on classroom versus non-classroom problems.*

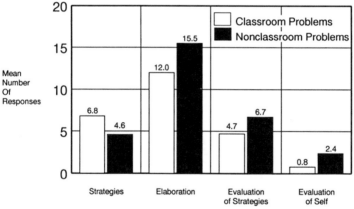

These preservice teachers were more evaluative on problems outside of the classroom while being more prone to action strategies for classroom problems. Having a greater number of strategies for classroom problems is not surprising given that much of teacher education focusses on specific ways of handling various classroom dilemmas. However, it is interesting that participants used more evaluation on non-classroom problems. When this result is combined with the greater number of strategies for classroom problems, it may indicate that these preservice teachers were inclined to be less reflective about their actions when dealing with classroom situations. This finding is congruent with research on problem solving that consistently finds that compared to experts, novices do not reflect on their problem solving and work more on the surface features of problems (Chi, Glaser, &

Farr, 1989; Eylon & Linn, 1988; Glaser, 1990).

Table 2: Problem-solving strategy categories

Instruction Problem	Discipline Problem
1. try a different approach 2. assess the situation 3. deal with the problem out of class 4. seek help from others 5. repeat or review 6. deal with the problem in class on an individual basis 7. deal with the problem in class with an emphasis on small groups	1. try a different approach 2. assess the situation 3. deal with the problem out of class 4. seek help from others 5. talk about the problem 6. take direct action 7. use an indirect solution
Supervising Teacher Problem	**Time Demands Problem**
1. talk about the problem 2. use self-talk 3. assess the situation 4. compromise/find a balance 5. seek help from others 6. use an indirect solution 7. look for the positive	1. talk about the problem 2. use self-talk 3. assess the situation 4. compromise/find a balance 5. organize/establish priorities 6. take direct action

The second goal of the study was to determine the relationship between different types of problems and the types of problem-solving strategies used by preservice teachers. This second stage of analysis was a more fine-grained approach focussing only on the specific strategies used rather than including all of the cognitive elements. Again, MANOVAs were used to compare the strategy categories common to two problems (see Table 2). The first comparison was between the common categories for the two Classroom problems, discipline and instruction (try a different approach, assess the situation, deal with problem outside of class, and seek help from others). Participants used "try a different approach," $F(1,27) = 11.85$, p= .002, and "assess the situation," $F(1,27) = 6.72$, p $= .015$, more often on the instruction problem than they did on the discipline problem. It appears that the preservice teachers were more flexible in trying different approaches and taking the time to assess with the instruction problem. This difference may be due to preservice teachers feeling more pressured to take action immediately with a discipline problem.

The second comparison examined the two Non-Classroom problems (associate teacher and time demands) on their four common strategy categories (talk about problem, use self-talk, assess the situation, and compromise/find a balance). The preservice teachers used "talk about problem" more often for the associate teacher, $F(1,27) = 25.75$, p$= .001$ and "assess the situation" more often for dealing with time demands, $F(1,27) = 5.02$, p$= .03$.

The final comparison assessed the two Conflict problems (discipline and associate teacher) on their four common strategies (assess the situation, seek help from others, talk about the problem, and use an indirect approach). Participants used an indirect solution more often with the associate teacher, $F(1,27) = 5.86$, p$= .02$, and "assess the situation" more often on the discipline problem, $F(1,27) = 6.67$, p $.015$.

Interesting patterns are present in these three analyses of types of strategies. From the different comparisons, the strategy, "assessing the situation," was used significantly more often on three of the four problems. The problem which had the least frequency of this strategy involved conflict with the associate teacher. When this result is combined with the finding that preservice teachers also used an indirect solution more often with the associate teacher problem than with the discipline problem, a possible interpretation emerges. Perhaps when preservice teachers are in a position of less power and control, they are less likely to reflect or assess and more likely to take an indirect approach. In other words, indirect solutions may be elicited by the unequal power in the relationship between the preservice teacher and associate teacher. This hypothesis is further strengthened by considering that when the participants were in a position of greater power relative to pupils on the discipline problem, the most frequently occurring strategy was "take direct action."

In congruence with previous research (Cummings et al., 1989), these results seem to suggest that the type of problem influences the type of cognitive processing and strategies used by preservice teachers. As Kagan (1988) concludes, the kinds of interactive decisions made by teachers are shaped by the specific task environments encountered.

The preceding analyses provide information about the problem-solving processes of preservice teachers in general through aggregating the data over the three testing times. However, the third goal of the study was to determine any effect of experience, knowledge, and a holding environment on the problem solving of preservice teachers. This goal was addressed in two ways. First, the cognitive elements from all four problems were combined and compared at the first, middle, and last testings periods using a MANOVA. Over the course of the teacher preparation year, these preservice teachers used less analysis, $F(2,26) = 4.08$, p= .03; fewer strategies, $F(2,26) = 3.55$, p= .04; and more evaluation of strategies, $F(2,26) = 3.62$, p= .04 (see Figure 2).

The increase in evaluation of strategies over the course of the year is a promising finding in that one goal of teacher education programmes is to help students learn to think reflectively in dealing with classroom problems. The movement toward greater evaluation can also be viewed as an example of increased differentiation of self as a problem solver within the holding environment model.

On the surface, the decrease in strategies and analysis over time is puzzling. One would expect that the experience and knowledge gained during teacher education would lead to more analysis and a wider range of strategies rather than fewer of each. To gain clarity about these results, it became necessary to analyze the problem responses for each participant for each problem over the three testings. While there were many individual differences in the responses, several patterns emerged from this analysis. We need to emphasize that the following patterns can only be seen as trends in the data, as they were not able to be assessed through statistical tests.

Figure 2: Means for six of the eight problem-solving elements at three times of testing.

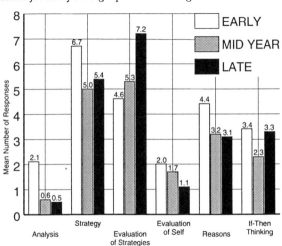

In reading the problem solutions, it became clear why there was a decrease in strategies and analysis over time. On the first testing for the discipline problem, many participants would list a number of strategies that they might try. At this point in their programme, the preservice teachers had not experienced a practice teaching assignment and, thus, much of their problem solutions were speculative about what might work. For example, in response to the discipline problem, one participant said, "I would go to that part of the room where the students are being disruptive. If that doesn't work, I would go back again and ask them to please be quiet. If that didn't work again, I would go and sit behind them and lecture right behind them. If they were still being disruptive, I would start directing questions at them so they would have to be on their toes and get them involved. If there is still a problem after that, then I would ask them to leave the room...."

At the second testing after a practice teaching period of four weeks in the schools, the same participant had a better idea of what would work. "I had some general level classes and I had a lot of kids who were disruptive. I tried to break up the class into three different teaching styles. We had 75-minute periods so I had a lesson, a lecture, and I moved into individual work where a student had to hand in an assignment afterwards, and then I moved to group work. I was hopefully trying to keep them busy to avoid the situation. It didn't always work but I tried to keep them quiet as best as I could." In this case, the preservice teacher did not have to consider a lot of different strategies, as in the first answer, because she had found a strategy that worked for her from her experience. The student now appears to be at Stage 3 of experimentation and practice. This change is consistent with research on expert-novice differences in problem solving (e.g., Chi, Glaser, & Farr, 1989) which shows that experts more than novices activate a parsimonious set of schemata to solve problems efficiently. The student had also learned to take a preventative approach to the situation rather than a reactive one.

When the developmental phases of self-identity within a holding environment were considered, some evidence emerged in the problem solutions on the second and third testings. For example, the first nonpunitive ways of dealing with the discipline problem appeared on the second testing. One student stated, "challenge their energy" which is a very different response from "send them to the principal." A preservice teacher who can think about challenging the energy of disruptive students has greater self-confidence and is thinking more reflectively than the preservice teacher who is relying on an outside authority to solve the problem.

In addition, evidence of analyzing why the students were disruptive or analyzing one's own influence did not appear until the second testing. This inclusion of looking beneath the students' behaviour or the preservice teacher's own behaviour for underlying reasons provides support for the preservice teacher becoming more differentiated and expanding attention away from self to include the students. Asking for input from the students themselves, either about the class sessions or about possible solutions to their disruptive behaviour also did not appear until the second testing. Again, involving the students in the problem solving indicates movement away from an authority position to a more confident partnership model that includes the students in the problem solving.

Unfortunately, these positive examples were not present in all protocols. At least three of the participants described more punitive strategies over time on the discipline problem. These participants may not have progressed as far as Stage 3 where different frameworks for classroom management can be considered. What individual difference variables might be contributing to such an outcome needs to be the subject of future research.

The most disturbing problem solutions occurred on the associate teacher problem. While some participants stated direct approaches such as talking about the problem, the primary strategy employed for this problem was an indirect approach. Participants at all three testings made the following types of statements: "Adjust to their style," "Tell yourself it is only for three weeks." These statements suggest the idea that viewing oneself as an equal colleague is less likely to occur during the preservice period.

When we consider that one of the goals of developing self-identity in preservice teachers is the encouragement of independence and experimentation, it is distressing to see the resignation in these responses to a non-collaborative and nonegalitarian relationship with the associate teacher. Teacher education was not successful in these instances at providing a safe, holding environment to empower the preservice teachers to become independent, professional selves with their associate teachers.

One would hope, instead, that preservice teachers would experience growth in coping with this type of conflict as evidenced by one participant. On the first testing she said that she "would probably just let it ride." By the second testing, she was analyzing herself, assessing exactly what the differences were between the two of them, and considering talking to the associate: "I would ask, is it me or is it him? I probably would look at their style and try to figure out what the actual differences are and then maybe talk to the person about it." On the third testing, she had progressed to considering how to reach a compromise: "You have to sit down and go through the problem step by step and somehow come to a compromise. You need to give your reasons because maybe they didn't think about why you are doing it your way and visa versa." Thus, this participant appears to have developed an increased sense of professionalism.

While the generalizability of this study is limited by the analogue nature of the problem situations, it is still possible to consider how these results could potentially contribute to thinking about alternate models of teacher education. An examination of the strategies in Table 2 shows that similar problems (e.g., classroom problems of discipline and instruction) elicited both some similar strategies and some different strategies. On the other hand, problems that were quite different (e.g., time demands and instruction) elicited very few similar strategies. Thus, while there are some commonalities in approaches to similar problems, the more disparate problems become, the less commonality there appears to be in efforts to resolve them.

Given this finding, teacher education programmes might best meet the needs of preservice teachers by facilitating the development of very specific problem-solving schemata for specific problems as well as providing general strategies that would apply across similar situations. In reviewing studies on transfer of learning, Perkins and Salomon (1989) found that effective thinking was quite dependent on context-bound knowledge and skills that do not easily transfer to other domains, thus supporting the need for specific schemata for specific problems. However, they also discovered in more recent research that transfer can occur when general principles of reasoning are taught in conjunction with self-monitoring activities and potential applications to other possible contexts, thus accenting the need for more general schemata in addition to specific schemata.

As Swanson, O'Connor, and Cooney (1990) note, if pattern recognition is important in fields such as physics and medicine, chances are high that it will be helpful for classroom problems also. Therefore, instead of teacher education being focussed on delivering facts and rules, the emphasis needs to shift to joining context-specific knowledge for solving ill-defined human problems with more general strategic knowledge.

In addition, teacher education programmes should be encouraging flexibility of student thinking that is matched to different classroom problem situations. Adoption of present models of problem solving across situations is likely to be of relatively less value. One way to encourage flexible thinking could be to ask pre-service teachers to think aloud about their classroom problems during teacher education experiences as a means of enhancing their cognitive monitoring and evaluative functioning. In addition, using the identification concept, it would be equally important for teacher educators in a supervisory relationship to think aloud as they reflect on problematic situations.

However, an even greater change that needs to occur is for teacher education programmes to adopt a holding environment model of teacher development that recognizes the developmental nature of acquiring a professional self-identity. Preservice teachers will be better able to become flexible, efficient, social problem solvers of complex human problems within a safe supervisory relationship that encourages both differentiation in thinking and collaboration in relating to others.

*Innovative Approaches to
Teacher Education*

Chapter Ten

Learning to Live New Stories of Teacher Education*

D. Jean Clandinin

Collaboration is a way of thinking about teaching, living, and working relationships. Recently, with increasing frequency, we read about collaborative relationships between schools and universities. However, "collaboration" in the late 1980s seems more often to be used as a mere word, perhaps even a buzzword, rather than as a term. It is used almost interchangeably with collegiality and cooperation. While these words share some aspects of the meaning of collaboration, it is important to look closely at what we mean by the term "collaboration" and how our relationships can be seen as collaborative ones.

In this article, I will explore the notion of collaboration through an exploration of my experiences working in teacher education settings. In particular, I will explore my work with teachers and student teachers in an alternative programme in preservice teacher education.

In my experience, university-school relationships in teacher education have been characterized by relationships of inequality, relationships where schools and teachers play out the scripts written and directed by university teacher educators. The relationships come into clearest focus in practicum situations when university programmes require students to fulfil practicum experiences. At most Canadian universities, the form, timing, cycles of evaluation, and evaluation criteria are determined by the universities. School board senior administrators and teachers' federations often play a consultative, monitoring kind of role but, for the most part, the university maintains control of the story outlines, the characters involved, the timing of the various story events throughout the school year and the evaluation of student teachers' performances. Teachers and schools provide the settings for the performances but have little say in the broad story outlines. In some ways, our institutions acknowledge the lack of meaningful involvement of teachers and schools in shaping the story of teacher education when they define teacher and school participation in teacher education practica as fulfilling a service role.

In this way, there is a tacit acknowledgement that the learning is only for the benefit of student teachers, that is, for our future teachers and for the profession. There is no acknowledgement in most places in Canada that work with teacher education practica is professional development, that is, part of ongoing teacher education for university teachers *and* cooperating teachers as well as for student teachers.

Recently there has been much talk of collaboration in teacher education. For example, in *Tomorrow's Teachers* (1986), the report of the Holmes Group, we read,

> The very definition of a Professional Development School as a site where educators learn and inquire presumes a high degree of collaboration. Master teachers spend time observing novices teach and confer regularly with them. Novices closely observe veterans. Staff development becomes a regular, ongoing feature in the life of the school, rather than an infrequent add-on, so school faculties work together to provide mutual learning opportunities. Research is conducted in joint projects among university and school faculty. Common standards get forged out of sustained dialogue. A Professional Development School pursues its distinctive mission by organizing to ensure teamwork. (p. 79)

In this short quotation, we see the rhetoric of collaboration. Words and phrases such as "mutual learning opportunities," "joint projects," "common standards" and "teamwork" flow from the notion of collaboration. Just what meaning the term "collaboration" has in these pages and other similar documents is left somewhat vague. Some of us are left with the uncomfortable feeling that while the language has changed, the familiar story of university-school relationships in teacher education has not.

What we see happening, as new stories such as those suggested in the Holmes Group report begin to be lived out, are stories of mandated collaboration. These stories of mandated collaboration are, however, still versions of the old story although frequently now they are ones in which senior university teacher educators have joined hands with senior school board administrators and governments to mandate collaboration among schools and teacher educators. For many teachers and some university teachers, the story of mandated collaboration remains a story in which teachers', student teachers', and children's voices are not heard.

This chapter is not about a generic view of university-school relationships. At best, in my view, these overarching relationships provide a space that allow the possibility of collaborative working relationships between teachers, university teachers, and student teachers. At worst, they are another form of the story of mandated collaboration.

The Alternative Programme in Teacher Education

In a recent project, a group of university teachers, cooperating teachers, and student teachers agreed to participate in an alternative programme in teacher education in order to explore what we might learn when we set ourselves the task of telling and living a more collaborative story of teacher education (Clandinin, Davies, Hogan, & Kennard, 1993).

In our work we used the term collaboration to refer to a way of constructing a relationship that involves "receptivity of the other" (Kennard, 1989), one that pays careful attention to the other's voice. Kennard points out that collaboration is "a way of exploring with the other," something that requires "trust and caring that comes with knowing, with relationship." This notion of collaboration underscored our inquiry into a collaborative teacher education programme.

Dewey's (1938) theory of experience provided a theoretical context for developing a collaborative notion of relationships in our programme. For Dewey teaching and learning are reciprocal processes which mutually influence one another. Furthermore, in Dewey's view, social transmission and social reconstruction of purpose occur simultaneously in a joint inquiry undertaken by teachers and students. The process is collaborative because the enquiry is shared by teachers and learners and because meaning, in the form of social purpose, is jointly constructed in the inquiry.

Dewey's theory of experience offered some guide to our work of imagining, telling, and living a new story of teacher education in which all participants could live and tell a story of learning and teaching. As we imagined more collaborative ways of working in teacher education settings, we drew heavily on work in collaborative research, an area where we had some experience in collaboration. We saw collaborative research as an outgrowth of participant observation methodologies. Participant observation, along with terms such as "co-participants," are commonly found in the indexes of methodology books. Many of those claiming to use collaborative methods in the late 1980s were actually using participant observation methods, something quite different. Basically, participant observation is a process in which the researcher participates in the participant's activities. This is fundamentally different from a researcher observing what a participant does. But it is also fundamentally different from collaborative research where the participant enters into, and shapes, the research agenda. From the point of view of research, both observation and participant observation are one-way streets defined by the researcher. Collaboration is a two-way street in which the researcher participates in the participant's practical agenda and the participant participates in the researcher's research agenda. It was this latter kind of notion that we wanted to pay attention to in our attempts to figure out a more collaborative story of teacher education.

Noddings (1986) became an important resource for our thinking in her emphasis on the collaborative nature of the research process as one in which all research participants see themselves as part of a community which is valued by both researchers and teachers. We found what she had to say about the relationship between researchers and teachers fit with what we imagined as the relationships among university teachers, cooperating teachers, and student teachers.

Other work (Clandinin & Connelly, 1988; Feiman-Nemser & Floden, 1986; Day, 1987) called into question the role that researchers normally play in classrooms. This work draws attention to the ways in which researchers situate themselves in relation to the persons with whom they work, to the ways in which they practise, and to the ways all participants model in their practices a valuing and confirmation of the other. Other work on space for researcher and teacher voice (Britzman, 1989; Clandinin, 1988; Eisner, 1988) addresses the ways in which collaboration is worked out in relationships. Eisner (1988) sees collaborative relationships as providing a context in which we can gain understanding by "participating sympathetically in the stories and in the lives of those who tell them" (p. x). In other work we have written about collaborative research relationships as ones that imply a sharing, an interpenetration of two or more person's spheres of experience (Connelly & Clandinin, 1988).

These notions of collaborative research were helpful to us as we imagined a new story of teacher education. As university teachers and cooperating teachers worked together, we were trying to imagine teacher education as a collaborative inquiry in which collaboration was essential between student teachers, university teachers, and cooperating teachers. We saw this collaborative process as akin to what we had experienced in collaborative research, that is, a process in which there was a joint living out of all participants' narratives so that participants were continuing to tell and live their own stories but the stories were being lived out in a collaborative setting.

Describing the Programme

The alternative programme in teacher education involved 28 students who were enrolled in the elementary route B.Ed. or B.Ed After Degree programme at the University of Calgary in 1989-90. Six university teachers and 28 teachers in 20 Calgary schools worked together to create the programme. We first met as a group of university teachers to discuss possibilities for an alternative programme in teacher education. When we had begun to feel comfortable in discussing our ideas in teacher education, we invited teachers and principals to work with us. Eventually student teachers joined us and we all became participants in the inquiry.

The programme was designed so each student teacher worked with a cooperating teacher from late August, 1989 until the end of April, 1990. The students worked in the schools Mondays, Wednesday mornings, and Fridays. Tuesdays and Thursdays they participated in integrated methods of instruction courses on campus. Wednesday afternoons they participated in small response groups with other student teachers and a university teacher. A more detailed account of the programme can be found in *Learning to Teach, Teaching to Learn: Stories of Collaboration in Teacher Education* (1993), a book which tells stories of the experiences of many of the participants in the programme.

Narrative Themes in the Inquiry

In the planning sessions for the programme and as we lived out the programme, we saw our inquiry as guided by what we came to call five narrative themes. These themes guided our telling and living of the story of the alternative teacher education programme.

One important narrative theme in the inquiry was a view of teacher education as part of the ongoing writing of student teachers' lives, not a separate preparation for something that is disconnected from what came before and a readying for what is to come after. Teacher education was seen as part of the ongoing storying and restorying of student teachers' lives. Teacher education experiences were part of ongoing narratives of experience, narratives that were being continually revised and rewritten as individuals found new ways of making sense of their work as teachers and as people, and as they found themselves in new situations.

A second narrative theme was a questioning of the separation of theory and practice, a questioning of the view that we learn theory in order to apply it to practice. In our inquiry, we tried to make new sense of how theory and practice might be connected, that is, we tried to engage in a dialogue between our practices and theory, a dialogue mutually informing to both theory and practice. In this view, theory was not seen as superior to practice but as in a kind of dialectical relationship to practice. The dialogue or conversation between theory and practice resulted in new understandings for both.

A third narrative theme, and the one that is most central to this chapter, was collaboration. In our inquiry, we wanted to learn to listen to each other so that together we might all learn to make new sense of practice and learn to live more moral lives in our teaching. We engaged in making sense of teacher education with each other, that is, with our student teachers, with cooperating teachers and with university teachers. When we worked with others, we were able to see more clearly new possible stories. We did not see our work as teachers as changing or transforming children or each other. That was not our project with student teachers. We did not see ourselves as the ones who held the power to transform others. As we worked with each other, our attention was drawn to other plot lines and other ways of living and telling our own stories. This happened because we engaged with intensity with each other, paying careful attention to how others were telling and living their stories. When we became participants in their stories, their stories changed. When they became participants in our stories, our stories changed. The experience was educative for each of us.

A fourth narrative theme was a search for language to talk about the ways each of us made sense of ourselves as people and as teachers. We were attempting to develop a language of teacher education that allowed description of ways of finding a place in order to feel part of a personal and professional community. We wanted a language of teacher education to talk about who we were and about what lives we were writing for ourselves.

A fifth narrative theme was improvisation or what Bateson (1989) calls "desperate improvisation." We engaged in an inquiry in which there were many ways of knowing, many ways of making sense and many institutional stories. Improvisation became a theme for the ways we learned to live new stories of practice. There were many improvisations as student teachers, cooperating teachers, and university teachers tried to figure out what it meant to learn to live a new story. As we worked together in the programme, we frequently made reference to our work together as work guided by an ethic of caring (Noddings, 1986). We tried to think of our improvisatory actions from within an ethic of caring, examining actions taken and actions imagined as being ones that were caring.

Telling Stories from the Inquiry

While there is much to be said about each of the narrative themes in our programme, the purpose of this article is to explore the ways in which we struggled to tell and live a new story of teacher education in which the university and the schools, the university teachers, student teachers, and cooperating teachers, worked more collaboratively. In this section, I relate "telling stories" of the inquiry which helped us see the difficulty of restorying the relationships.

The first story is one which illustrates the ways in which the "old" story of university-school relationships bounds the knowing of both university teachers and cooperating teachers. These stories are adapted from the book *Learning to Teach, Teaching to Learn.*

Barbara: Naming "The University" as Knowing

We were excited to have Barbara participate in the programme because we knew her well. We had worked with her in the classroom, in a research project, and in graduate studies. She had come to understand what it meant to construct her own knowledge during her master's programme. She too was excited about taking that new way of knowing into the classroom and into her work with a student teacher.

She participated with us on the steering committee, attending meetings with us, and worked closely with us on all aspects of the Alternative Programme. We were surprised when, during a discussion of evaluation at a steering committee meeting, Barbara turned to us and said, "What does the university want us to do?" At the time we laughed and joked about how she was turning us, her friends and colleagues, into an institution. We teased Barbara about it for the remainder of the year. However, when we considered the narrative meaning behind her question, we understood how easy it is to go back into the old story of received knowing. The story of received knowing is a comfortable one in the face of the uncertainty that was the context of our inquiry. Barbara's experience reminded us of how difficult it must have been on many occasions for other cooperating teachers to have confidence in the construction of their own knowledge within the context of this work. Many times in their conversations with us we heard echoes of Barbara's question as they too sought their answers in knowledge that came from outside themselves. For all of us the inquiry was being lived out in a series of new situations. We had to remember that new situations could put us back into the silence of being received knowers. Barbara's question became a reminder of the difficulty of learning to live a new story, or unlearning the old lesson.

Sonia: Getting Down the Teacher's Words

Sonia tended to be quiet during our Wednesday afternoon seminars. She said she liked to listen and take in what everyone was saying. However, as it became time for the first assignment to be written, Sonia initiated a discussion about what it was that the university wanted. Other members of the group offered their perceptions on how the assignment might look. Pat also spoke for a few minutes about how papers might look. It was a surprise to her at this point to see Sonia pull out a pencil and attempt to write down everything she said. When Pat finished, Sonia looked a little frustrated and asked Pat to repeat her words. Sonia had not managed to record everything. Pat explained that she had been just imagining a possibility rather than giving a model for the paper. She couldn't repeat her words exactly, much to Sonia's disappointment. Others in the group laughed and made a joke about how Pat had actually said something worth writing down. Pat laughed too but later thought about the narrative meaning of Sonia's actions. As is the case with many university students, Sonia was accustomed to recording the professor's words at the moment of utterance in order to take them away and use them as a prescription for completing assignments and papers. The professor's words are used to frame the task and to give shape to the paper. It is a story of received knowing in our universities. Sonia's actions were particularly surprising to us because she had impressed us with her stunning practices in the classroom and her insights in her journal. As we reflected on how difficult it was for Sonia to move to a new story of writing papers to a constructed knower, we wondered about the difficulties being experienced by other students as they struggled with the new ways of knowing we were asking of them. As she came to trust her own voice, Sonia wrote unique papers that told us a great deal about how she had learned to construct her knowledge from theory, from her own story, from the children's stories, and from her work with Jude McCullough, her cooperating teacher.

Collaboration: A Metaphor of Middle Ground

As we worked together in the programme, we attempted to make spaces which would allow a more collaborative story of teacher education to be lived and told. When we tried to think about the features that marked the programme and what we learned in the inquiry, a metaphor of creating a middle ground, a new space for teacher education emerged. When we began the inquiry, we saw teacher education as situated in the gap between the universities and the schools. For student teachers, their practicum experience was supposed to bridge that gap. For many of them, however, they felt lost within it. The gap silenced those of us who worked at the university as well as those of us who worked in the schools. As we tell the story now, we see that we wanted to figure out how to create and live in a middle ground of connection.

When we began the inquiry, we had no metaphor of middle ground as a guide. We began our work with our stories. We wanted to acknowledge our own stories, stories of who we were and how we were making sense of our lives and our practices. As the year progressed, we shared stories of how we were making sense. Theory in the shape of research papers, philosophical books, other teachers', students', and children's stories were all used to help us reflect upon our own stories. Initially, we had seen our purpose as making connections between who we were and how we were writing our lives and between our lives and how others had envisioned writing their lives in teaching. We approached each of the pieces, that is, the written stories of teachers, children, researchers and philosophers, with a sense of conversation. In these conversations, we responded within an ethic of caring in which we were able to question our actions as moral actions. It is only now that we can see how the sharing and responding to each other's stories was a beginning step in creating that middle ground, a new space for teacher education.

As we lived out the year, we came to see the complexity of creating and living in this middle ground. The year was a year of restorying for each of us. For university teachers, we saw how important it was to be more connected to teachers and student teachers in the schools. For cooperating teachers, we saw the importance of telling our stories and feeling heard even as we listened to university teachers' stories in more attentive ways.

We see the middle ground as peopled with teacher educators who are university teachers, cooperating teachers, and student teachers. We have to acknowledge, we are all learning from each other, from our experiences, and from our conversations with theory and practice. This acknowledgement of each of us, as a teacher educator, blurs the distinctions we have traditionally made between teaching and learning in teacher education.

The small group seminars held each week were places to make connections between a university teacher, a small group of student teachers, and
their cooperating teachers. It was in these small groups held in schools that
we came together and asked our wonders, shared our journals, and laughed
and cried about the complexities of teaching and living our stories. The
journals were a three-way written dialogue in which all participants shared
stories and responded to each other. They were a place for figuring out
experience through writing. We became aware of the importance of having
all participants see journals as places to make sense. As university teachers
and cooperating teachers wrote responses, they came to see their practices
in changed ways. Because the journals brought stories of practice to university classrooms and because the journals reflected university discussions to
the cooperating teachers, they became an important feature of the middle
ground. The journals became a way for the teachers to be represented at
the university and for the university teachers to be represented in the
classrooms. This allowed the teacher's voice to be heard in the university
and the university teacher's voice to be heard in the classrooms. All
participants came to feel comfortable with the sounds of the other's voice
in what had been their own place. This sharing of journals and stories, this
feeling of being comfortable, of being at home, was an important part of the
middle ground of connection.

In the large classes on campus and in the small group seminars, one of
our tasks was to figure out ways of giving students each other. We had, for
too long, seen the dialogue as existing only between teacher and student.
In this programme, we wanted the students to come to value each other
and their ways of knowing. We wanted them to figure out how to be invited
into each other's stories so they could make a connection and live a story
different from the one usually lived and told within the university. We
encouraged them to see each other as colleagues learning with, and from
one another, rather than as competitors for grades.

As we worked in the programme, we came to new insights into evaluation. While we all started with the notion of self-evaluation and wanted
to encourage our students to engage in that process, we came to see that
evaluation was both in the person and in the situation. We needed to figure
out ways to help students and ourselves understand evaluation as contextualized. It was, for us, important to acknowledge that our knowing is an
expression of ourselves but it is drawn out in the particular situations in
which we work. Because we are always changing, storying, and restorying
ourselves, and because the situations in which we work are always changing,

we came to see that evaluation must give a sense of the changing, growing, developing sense of knowing each of us has in our practice. This view of evaluation in the middle ground requires that we give up our privileged stance of expert to be attentive to all voices. In collaborative evaluation, one voice does not carry more authority than another.

We now see this view of multiple voices in evaluation as reflected in our renegotiation of the assignments. Initially, we had attempted to write assignments prior to making connections with student teachers and cooperating teachers in their classrooms. In the initial construction of the assignments, we could not allow spaces for their voices. When we became aware of the ways in which the assignments were being lost in the gaps between the university requirements and the requirements of practice, we came together to talk about ways to make connections in that gap. We wanted the assignments to bring together the work of the student teachers at the university and at the schools; to bring together cooperating teacher, student teacher, and university teacher; and, to allow student teachers an opportunity to do and write assignments that would help them figure out the lives that children in their classrooms were writing and the ways they were writing their lives as teachers. The renegotiated assignments formed another connection between the student teacher, cooperating teacher, and university teacher. In the middle ground, we came to see the assignments that each student teacher completed as an expression of each person's conversation between theory and practice.

What Have We Learned?

Collaboration between teacher and learner, and teacher and researcher has begun to be the focus of inquiry (Noddings, 1986; Lieberman, 1986; Kennard, 1989). Researchers such as Noddings (1986) and Kennard (1989) see important implications for the ways in which we conduct research. They suggest that collaboration, as a way of thinking through our relationships with teachers, researchers, and others, will "require restructuring of our institutions on new ideals, that would require all of us to work in ways not requiring hierarchical ordering and power" (Kennard, 1989).

As we worked together in the alternative programme, we began to see that we know little about collaboration in teacher education. In our telling and living of the alternative programme, we see we have only begun to construct new narrative texts to restory the old story of teacher education, the story in which we ask, "What does the university want us to do?"

Note

* Parts of this chapter appear in D.J. Clandinin, A. Davies, P. Hogan, & B. Kennard, (Eds.). (1993). *Learning to teach, teaching to learn: Stories of collaboration in teacher education*. New York: Teachers College Press.

Chapter Eleven

Negotiating Fair Trade: Towards Collaborative Relationships Between Researchers and Teachers

Chris Fliesser and Ivor Goodson

Introduction

During the 1950s and 1960s, research on education was largely a positivist enterprise, dominated by quantitative research methods, focussing on the process-product model (Dunkin & Biddle, 1974).

> As education professors attempted to establish academic creden-
> tials and forge academic careers their research became more and
> more methodologically sophisticated and thereby less and less
> accessible to practitioners (Johnson, 1989, p. 87).

Classroom teachers (insiders) involved in research projects usually played the role of a "subject" being studied, manipulated, and probed by university professors (outsiders).

In the past 20 years, particularly in England, Australia, and the United States, symbolic interactionists, ethnomethodologists, and sociologists of knowledge began studying schooling using the subjective perceptions and constructions of reality of teachers (see Goodson & Walker, 1991). This increasing interest in qualitative methodologies has developed the view of schools as complex organizations, and teaching as a complex activity (Lieberman, 1986). Some of the university researchers of teaching began viewing teachers as participants in the research as opposed to subjects being studied or as Ward and Tikunoff (1977) stated a "working with posture rather than working on." Involving teachers as partners in research on schooling is the essence of collaborative research (Tikunoff & Ward, 1983; Lieberman, 1986).

Feldman (1991) contends that the relationships between teachers and researchers are collaborative only in the generic sense of the term (people labour together) and do not meet the specifications of what he calls "equitable collaborations." If the relationship between university professors and teachers is to be equitable, the goals of both parties in the research must be met.

> Therefore, an equitable collaboration is one in which the following is ideal for all the actors: work with parity; assume equal responsibility for problem identification, data collection, analysis, and report-writing; share the same set of goals; and, needs are met (respect, payment for services, kind and caring treatment). (p. 5)

Collaboration on this view is a process that empowers teachers. Ideally, it also represents a nonhierarchical form of power where academics and teachers negotiate and live in equitable working relationships. Negotiating equitable relationships is problematic in most collaborative research projects because the participants themselves enter the relationship as unequal partners. Thiessen (1991) describes three types of inequality—social status and influence, expertise, and position.

There are other impediments to equitable collaboration: the differences between university interests and teacher interests, associated with different structural locations; differences in job descriptions; hierarchical and bureaucratic relationships; the way teacher voices are represented in reports where the academic's voice drowns out the teachers voice; and, where the relationship between school teacher and outsider researcher has grown into dependency, with a form of mutual confirmation being pursued (often indicated by questions like "Am I giving you what you want?"). Outsider researchers may be unwilling to give up their power base, which is based on the notion of their having "specialized knowledge" (Feldman, 1991).

Yet, these impediments and inequalities might be viewed as differences which can enrich research projects and the collaborative nature of the interaction; they should not be viewed as insurmountable problems which cannot be overcome. The trick is to turn differences in voice, vision, and validity into advantages.

Fair Trade: En Route to Equitable Collaboration

In this chapter, we will argue that cultivating collaborative relationships is incremental in nature. Feldman's concept of equitable collaboration is useful as a long term goal of some research projects. However, it is unlikely that a group of strangers who may have little understanding of each other's world can share Feldman's definition of collaboration from the start of the project.

In order for a working relationship to develop into a collaborative one, it requires that all parties have mutual respect and trust, which is built upon understanding the complexities and intricacies of each other's world and role (outsiders, insiders). This deep understanding may be acquired over time during which research roles can be negotiated and renegotiated so that they become equitable and collaborative. The reality may well be that only some outsider/insider relationships will evolve during the course of the research project into equitable collaborations, but it is worth exploring how this process can be sponsored.

An appropriate starting point for negotiations between outsiders and insiders may be the notion of a "fair trade."[1] Outsider and insider can negotiate their roles and relationships by answering these questions: At this point in time, what I am willing to offer to the research project (e.g., time, skills, resources)? What do I expect to get out of my involvement in this research project (e.g., professional development, published articles, tenure)? Both should have the opportunity to disclose honestly what they are bringing to the bargaining table and what they expect to take away. Further negotiations can take place during the course of the project as participants' interests change and, more importantly, if and when mutual trust and respect develops.

In this article, drawing on our project experience, we try to answer the following questions. How did we negotiate roles and relationships between participants in our research projects so that all partners perceive themselves as getting a fair trade? Did we move towards more collaborative working relationships? What are some of the issues and complexities involved in the dynamic process of conducting a research project?

Background to the Research Project

In 1988, as part of the requirement for a Master's of Education, Chris Fliesser, a teacher at Fanshawe Community College, completed a thesis entitled *The Induction of Technical Vocational Teachers in a Community College Setting* (Fliesser, 1988). This qualitative study illuminated issues related to the first one to three years of teaching in a community college from the subjective perceptions and constructions of four new technical-vocational teachers. After presenting interpretations of personal accounts, he put forth a number of recommendations describing ways in which the colleges and similar institutions could assist new teachers when making the transition from the shop floor to the classroom. In the summer after he graduated, Chris was encouraged by his thesis advisor, Ivor Goodson, to develop and submit a proposal for a research project where we would set up a pilot induction programme for new community college teachers. The proposal resulted in a grant from the Ontario Ministry of Colleges and Universities for a two-year project.

During the summer of 1989, seven, newly-hired, full-time community college teachers agreed to participate in a two-year pilot induction programme. Ivor Goodson and Ardra Cole, another university professor (outsider), would be involved in mapping out the contextual elements in the college setting, as well as in documenting and evaluating the induction programme, itself, over a two-year period. They would complete life histories of each new teacher (Goodson, 1984), direct bi-annual reflective sessions for the new teachers, and analyze tapes from bi-weekly sharing sessions as well as the journal Chris kept. Chris was to develop and deliver the induction programme. As part of this role, he was to undertake classroom observations, facilitate bi-weekly sharing sessions, be available for individual consultation, attend project meetings, provide some workshops, and keep a detailed journal. At the end of the two-year induction programme, in the summer of 1991, the three members of the research team began analyzing the data and writing up a final report.

Negotiating a Fair Trade

The expertise each of us brought to the project was different. Ardra was a researcher having a wide range of experience working with new teachers both in the elementary and secondary setting. Ivor had experience in using and developing qualitative research methods and had done work studying and writing about teachers's careers and lives. Chris was familiar with the college setting and had some experience with the research methods used as well as experience working with new teachers. The new teachers brought with them their rich and varied backgrounds from their occupational fields and were very enthusiastic about being involved in the research project.

Ardra, Ivor, and Chris had similar, as well as different, reasons for studying new teachers. All were interested in helping this particular group of teachers make the transition from their working worlds in diverse disciplines to becoming teachers. We all hoped that the college would set up a permanent programme which would help future teachers. However,

Ardra and Ivor were mainly interested in adding to the growing literature on new teachers—Ardra adding to the induction literature and Ivor, the literature on teachers careers and lives. Chris was mainly interested in the induction programme, itself, and to a lesser degree, the research. The new teachers were interested in getting assistance during the first few years as well as setting up a permanent induction programme.

The differences in status, position, expertise, and interests were all possible impediments to developing equitable relationships. How did we negotiate our roles in the beginning of the project? Ivor and Chris had known each other for two years. The relationship was evolving from one of teacher-student to a more collegial one, and therefore we trusted and respected one another and knew each other's strengths and limitations. When the research proposal was developed, we both worked on it. We also decided who should be hired as the other researcher. After a few meetings among the three team members, we felt that all of us knew what expertise we were willing to lend to the project and in turn what we would get out of the project for our efforts. Decisions were made by consensus, although formally, for the record, Ivor held the position of principal investigator; Ardra, the position of co-investigator, and Chris, the position of coordinator of the induction programme. The new teachers in the study had the status of probationary teachers.

The new teachers in the study were what Houser (1990) calls "minimally informed participants." They were new teachers, who on the urging of the president at the college, participated in the study. Most of them participated because they believed it would help them keep their jobs and that they would learn from the activities planned during the project. At the beginning of the research project, Ivor, Ardra, and Chris met with the group of new teachers. It was at that meeting that we informally negotiated a "trade." The participants were willing to give some of their time to the project. In return, they would get an induction programme which might help them become better teachers. They were willing to be the "guinea pigs" as one participant put it, so that new teachers in the future would benefit from a permanent induction programme. As we shall see, at the beginning stages of the project, the participants did not have equal status with the research team, but as the project progressed had a louder and louder voice in how the project proceeded.

Chris' Role within the Project

Some factors which created tension, or at least were potential sources of conflict, were related to the roles and relationships we negotiated. For example, Chris' location within the project and his unique role in it, the question of what the research would give to the participants as part of the fair trade, and Chris' changing perceptions and interests as a result of his involvement in this research project were areas of tension. In the following pages, he describes these issues as well as how we attempted to resolve them through mutual negotiation.

Chris' Reflections

I was the one who had to be there to observe new faculty, facilitate their professional development, reinforce them, and support them. It was a role I had freely negotiated. Ardra and Ivor on the other hand would watch us, observe us, and evaluate us. I recall feeling like I was on the front line that, technically, I was part of the research team, but I had the difficult job of "doing it now and analyzing it later." I did not realize at the time when we were negotiating our roles how two-sided my position was. I was alone facing the day-to-day pressure of trying to juggle all the pieces to make the induction programme work. This journal entry shows some of my anxiety which I felt at the beginning of the two-year programme:

> I feel somewhat squeezed because I have so much work to do to get this programme going...yet once again I feel I have very little support (from the research team). All of the day-to-day arrangements are falling on my shoulders....Can I pull it off and still do the other things I have to do? (Journal entry, Sept. 1, 1989)

I recall meeting with Ivor and Ardra and telling them how I felt. They were sympathetic to my feelings, but there was little they could do to help me. The following events precipitated me changing some of my attitudes and perceptions: having an office at the university where I spent at least one day a week; the continuing discourse I had with Ivor and our growing friendship; the meetings and conversations I had with Ardra as well as professors at the Faculty of Education; and, my turning 40 years old. In this section I will describe: how critical reflection began to inform more of my day-to-day actions; how I became more interested in more direct participation in academic (university) life; and finally, how my perceptions of my work within my institution changed. Most of these changes in attitudes and perceptions translated into direct action in the induction programme and this points out the importance of re-negotiating roles throughout the course of a research project.

When the research project started, I believed that the success of the induction programme would be measured by the increase in skills of new teachers, and I would be the one to help the teachers acquire them, and not the researchers at the university. The research component of the project was simply the vehicle to get funds, while playing a part in the criticism and construction of professional knowledge was of minor importance in my view. I believed the project was all about action, about helping new teachers, about measurable results, and that these actions were only marginally related to reflection or to developing educational theories.

All of us spend some time reflecting about our lives but few of us have or take the time to reflect in a regular systematic way. At the beginning of the project I did not see the value of keeping a journal to aid reflection.

It's Saturday evening. Again one day after our Friday session. I'm really finding it difficult to sit down and journal. Maybe I should be more succinct....(Oct. 14, 1989)

....This is a pain...I can see why people quit writing in diaries.(Oct. 10, 1990)

In the course of being involved in this research project I moved from what van Manen (1977) calls the technical level of reflection to more critical reflection. I also began reflecting in a more systematic and formal way; I now keep a personal-professional journal (Holly, 1987). I began to realize that critical reflection (of which keeping a journal was one method I could use) was an excellent way of informing my day-to-day actions.

It has taken me two years to get to the point where I believe writing a journal is important enough to deserve at least a commitment of 30 minutes a day and at least an hour on Sundays. Why do I believe this is important now? First, I believe my life is getting busier and busier. Unless I reflect on this busyness "it" will give my life direction instead of me. Second, maybe my life is important enough to write about. Maybe my journey of becoming a more reflective person is significant to others that follow. (April 25, 1991)

Adding to the critical literature on teacher development was important to both Ardra and Ivor, but it was of little significance to me at the start of the project. I had a limited understanding of the specialized knowledge and theories related to teacher development. They had the expertise in constructing the professional knowledge about teachers careers and lives.

However, during the course of the research project I too started becoming interested in being a part of the discourse in which Ivor and Ardra were involved. I realized that there was value in reflecting and writing about important issues and sharing these thoughts with others. I wanted to write a few articles and present a few papers. I began to gain confidence that I had something to offer from my practitioner's perspective.

As both Ivor and Ardra became aware of my growing interest in participating more extensively in the academic (university) life, they helped me to realize my goal. In essence, we renegotiated our roles, and I became an equal partner. They let me "in" rather than shut me "out." The three of us are now analyzing the data and working on a number of papers and articles related to this project.

The following are three fairly lengthy quotes from my journal that outline some changes in my attitudes and perceptions about my working life, my life within academic institutions. We will see why they changed and how they impacted on the project.

> At various times between Thursday and today (after Ivor and I had lunch), I have from time to time reflected about my life, life in academia, working life in general. In the past few years I have defined my own job. "You define your own space and then you spend some time protecting it." (Ivor) I have in fact defined my own space at Fanshawe College. I remember when I first started my job as curriculum consultant (5 years ago). I felt like I had to be at the college from 8 to 5. I had to appear to be working hard and look like an administrator. After all, in the academic world in order to advance and change the place you had to take on a position of power. Over the course of the past few years, I began to realize that I did not need real power (administrative position) to impact and change an institution. I am also coming to the realization that institutions can't be changed but their inner workings can be exposed or manipulated. People with real power are too busy to be able to be involved with the many interesting things I was doing. (April 25, 1991)

> In reflecting on my career, I believe that for a while, about ten years ago until two years ago, I did give up "the fight" and I allowed the status quo to engulf me. I felt I needed to be one of the people that had real power and status in order to get on to the gravy train. Now

that I better understand how the gravy train works, I can be myself, I can begin to critically look at the train, the people on it, and the regions it passes through. In fact I can unpack and expose, I can assume a "subversive" posture, one that I feel much more comfortable with. (April 17, 1991)

In one way I feel blessed that I met Ivor, who over the course of a few years exposed this weakness in institutions as well as rekindled the fire in me which is to critically study the status quo. On the other hand, I feel sad that my naive and ideal view of institutions is shattered. No longer can I go about my merry way helping people. I now must uncover, expose in some cases and play the hard-ball politics which is at the essence of institutional life. 'Life was simpler then...' However, I never want to go back to the good old days. I now have much greater control of my life. I work harder than I ever have, not working on others' agendas, but my own. (April 17, 1991)

These changes in my attitudes and perceptions in turn influenced the direction of the induction programme at the college. For example, after our first group reflective session, the new teachers decided that they wanted a series of workshops during the second year of the programme. The one workshop everyone wanted was entitled: "The micro-politics of Fanshawe College: How things really get done around here." During the course of the second year of the project the new teachers and I spent countless hours discussing the micro-politics of academic life within our institution. Some of these discussions spun out of the new teachers' frustrations with institutional life, and many of the discussions were sparked by my increasing awareness of how to get things accomplished in an institution, to "uncover, expose, and in some cases play hard-ball politics." It was obvious to me that teachers had to step out of their classrooms from time to time and make their voices heard. Teachers not only required classroom teaching skills, but they had to be able to manoeuvre in the political backwaters of the institution in skilful and informed ways. By the end of the induction programme, all of the new teachers knew what "micro-politics" was, and that they had to get good at playing politics in order to get the things that they and their students required.

Conclusion

Chris' discussion captures some of the aspects of our collaborative discussions, our negotiated "trade." In these sections, we see how the role of change agent within a research project and within an institution plays out. The role that Chris played resembles that of a "broker" who is at the "sharp end" of programme delivery, but also prompted and pushed by the findings and falterings of the outsider researchers. Above all, Chris' role shows how the negotiations over "trade" took place—how the project teachers began to express their own emerging needs and how, albeit in limited ways, the project team responded. Caught between insider and outsider worlds, Chris mediates between these worlds, and in doing so elucidates some of the tensions and resolutions at work when developing collaborative trades.

Drawing from some of our experience, the following guidelines might form the basis from which to negotiate "fair trade" and enhance more collaborative relationships during the research process.

1. Negotiate a fair trade by addressing these two questions: At this point in time, what am I willing to offer to the research project (time, skills etc.)? At this point in time, what do I expect to get out of my involvement in this research project (professional development, publish articles, tenure)?

2. Make a commitment to forming an equitable working relationship with all members of the project once there is sufficient trust and understanding amongst researchers and teachers.

3. Consider the impediments to equity in research projects such as: the differences between university researcher interests and teacher interests (expectations); differences in job descriptions; hierarchical teacher-student relationships; the way teacher voices are represented in reports where the academics voice drowns out the teacher's voice; and, where the relationship between school teacher and researcher has grown into dependency, usually the school teacher needing confirmation from the researcher; differences in interests, social status, job description, expertise; everyone having access to the same data during the course of the project; and, researchers not willing to give up their power base, which is based on them having specialized knowledge, to teachers.

4. Negotiate and renegotiate roles at various times throughout the dynamic process of a research project, keeping in mind that participants'

interests and needs change. Project members should be able to renegotiate their roles when they feel it necessary.

5.   Time and energy should be committed to developing strong, trusting, and equitable relationships.

6.   As part of the research design, develop an evaluation strategy to determine how the relationship between researchers and teachers influences the research process.

This case study is only one project as seen through the eyes of a teacher. Only certain elements may be applicable to other projects. However, one major theme holds true for most research projects studying the complexities of teaching: researchers and teachers must work as equals so that they may both uncover the complexities of learning and teaching.

Note

1.   The notion of a "fair trade" was initially and tentatively conceptualized by Ivor Goodson (1991).

Chapter Twelve

Forging Partnerships:
Faculty and Field Perspectives on French Immersion Teacher Education

Suzanne Majhanovich

Historical Perspective

Ever since the expansion of French as a Second Language into the elementary schools in the 1960s and 70s, as well as the phenomenal growth of French immersion programmes, the Department of Education and later the Ontario Faculties of Education have been scrambling to provide programmes to train French teachers and to meet the demand for FSL teachers. In Ontario, French as a teachable subject was traditionally an option open to prospective secondary teachers. Elementary French teachers of the 1960s and early 70s in the worst case scenario were often qualified elementary teachers with no training in French methodology, and probably little knowledge of French beyond the high school courses they had followed years before. However, secondary French teachers who either could not find a position at the secondary level or who wished to change to the elementary panel also became oral French teachers, although the methodology they had received had little to do with the elementary oral French programmes of the time. In the 1960s, French in the elementary schools was considered to be mainly a conversation class, and qualified teachers who also held professional qualifications in French at the elementary level were practically non-existent.

In 1965, Ontario Regulation 352 amended Regulation 88 (on teacher qualifications) to include a new certificate: "The Temporary Certificate as Teacher of French to English-Speaking Pupils in Elementary Schools." This certificate could be gained in one summer session through a Department of Education course. One did not have to be otherwise a qualified teacher, but only had to have Grade 13 standing in French or the equivalent and pass an oral entrance examination. This certificate could be renewed annually on the approval of an inspector. Even in the 1970s, when the renamed Ministry of Education (rather than Department) moved to regularize teaching qualifications for elementary French, those who held the "Temporary Certificate as Teacher of French..." were allowed to continue teaching French as long as they remained in the same board (O. Reg. 352, 1965, s.35).

By the 1970s, the teacher training colleges became faculties of education connected with universities, and courses previously offered through the Department of Education were turned over to the faculties which would, henceforth, offer them through their continuing education programmes. The oral French certificate was phased out and replaced by a three-part French as a Second Language programme including Parts I, II, and Specialist by 1978. Entrance qualifications varied widely from faculty to faculty. Some required only demonstrated ability in oral and written French as determined by a faculty prepared test. Others required as much as the equivalent to a major in French or university courses in the French language plus the aforementioned demonstrated ability in oral and written French.

In order to ensure that elementary French teachers had some kind of qualification, the Ministry required in 1978 that any French as a Second Language teacher possess at least the FSL I qualification (Reg. 262, 20(8)(c), 1978), or its equivalent. The FSL I qualification (or equivalent) was also the minimal qualification for immersion teachers as they are also FSL teachers (Reg. 262, 1(d), Reg. 269, 4(3), Reg. 262, 20(9), 1980).

French immersion teachers usually were hired from among those teachers who had qualified to teach in the French language schools, from francophones from Ontario or other provinces, or from other French-speaking countries. As the demand increased, anglophones with native-like ability increasingly joined the ranks of immersion teachers. Claire Mian (1984) reported that at that time (1984) in her Toronto High School immersion programme, there were teachers from Quebec, New Brunswick, Ontario, Egypt, France, Greece, and Italy, 50% of whom were native French speakers. Still, the faculties of education in Ontario generally had no specific courses to train immersion teachers.

Elementary teachers often added the FSL I course to their regular preservice programme in the 1970s, and often prospective secondary French teachers chose the same option, knowing that the French methodology they were receiving in their teachable subject course was not particularly applicable to elementary French teaching. Yet, they were most likely to be hired at the elementary level as there were very few jobs in any subject at the secondary level during the 1970s.

Teacher training was reorganized in Ontario in 1978 such that candidates were to choose to train for either the Primary-Junior (K-6) division, the Junior-Intermediate (4-10) division, or the Intermediate-Senior (7-13) division instead of the old arrangement of elementary (K-10), or secondary (7-13). On successful completion of the new programme, the candidates would receive the Ontario Teachers Certificate.

About that time, it was agreed by the faculties and the Ministry of Education that additional qualification courses such as FSL I (and many other specialty subjects) would no longer be available to students during their preservice year. The immediate result was that candidates who opted to train in the Primary-Junior division no longer could receive any preparation to teach French until after they had completed the OTC qualification, and that meant that probably no school practicum could be arranged for these teachers. Furthermore, boards who needed to hire P-J teachers for French, particularly French immersion, would have to hire conditionally without any evidence that even if the prospective teachers passed the FSL I course, they could cope in an FSL or an immersion class. Junior-Intermediate students could still take French as a teachable subject, and the course they received often closely paralleled the FSL I course. In addition, they could receive up to half their practicum time (a minimum of four weeks) in an elementary French class. These graduates were, and remain, the most sought-after French teachers, but for reasons of the make-up of most Ontario faculty programmes, fewer Junior-Intermediate FSL candidates can be accepted than those opting for teacher preparation at the secondary level (see Majhanovich, 1990, p. 457).

Intermediate-Senior French candidates, no longer able to add on the FSL I course during the preservice year, would receive a qualification deemed equivalent to FSL I but, in fact, the content of the course had little to do with elementary French methods. At most, some would receive two or three weeks teaching French in an elementary school giving them at least some familiarity with programmes and methods at that level. This problem has recently been alleviated to some extent by the change in the regulation for teacher education (Reg. 297), which now permits candidates for the Primary-Junior programme to qualify for French as a Second Language (Ontario Reg. 557/93, October 9, 1993). So far few candidates have availed themselves of the option.

Although the preparation offered for French teachers may have been adequate in other times when French was a secondary school subject only, and where there was no great variety of texts and programmes, somehow the programmes described above do not seem to meet the needs of French teachers today. Over the years, the general approach to French teacher preparation has been viewed with a critical eye (Massey, 1980). Much has been written regarding what a second-language teacher training programme should comprise (Strevens; 1981, Stern, 1983, especially Chapters 19-22). Calvé (1983) has outlined an elaborate programme to prepare core French teachers, and Obadia (1984, 1985), Frisson-Rickson and Rebuffot (1986), and Tardiff (1984) have proposed plans for the training of immersion teachers. Majhanovich and Fish (1988) have discussed a special course to train immersion teachers for particular levels and Brine and Shapson (1989) comment on retraining courses to upgrade French teachers to immersion standards. Finally, Moeller (1989) has argued for national standards for French teachers.

The Problem: Teacher Education for French Immersion

Meanwhile, the traditional tension over ownership of teacher education and preparation continues between the faculties of education and the field. With regard to the preparation of elementary French immersion teachers, the problem is particularly serious since, as the historical perspective above shows, there is no real place in Ontario faculty of education programmes preparing teachers for the Ontario Teacher Certificate to provide a programme in elementary French immersion teaching. The schools and boards have had to take responsibility for induction of new immersion teachers or have simply had to take on faith a candidate who had completed a summer programme in basic second language methodology without ever having taught a core French let alone a French immersion class. Is it any wonder that some question the value of teacher education in a faculty at all—especially in this area? Such an attitude is problematical since after decades of entrusting teacher education largely to universities' faculties or colleges of education, a reversion to an earlier apprenticeship model of teacher training housed mainly in the schools seems to be reasserting itself. Is this simply a manifestation of a narrow view of "social efficiency" (Labaree, 1991; Zeichner & Tabachnick, 1991)? Or have two of the main players in teacher education, namely, the schools and faculties, simply been working at cross purposes? It is evident that all is not working as well as it might. If one were to characterize the traditional relationship between many faculties of education and the field in Ontario, Canada, at least, such terms as wary cooperation, collaboration at a distance, or even benign neglect (on the part of some faculties) spring to mind.

The only contact many faculty members have had with schools since they left teaching to enter the next level of education (if, indeed, they ever did teach in a school setting) may well have involved hasty visits to various schools to observe and evaluate student teachers with only a few minutes, if any, spent with the associate teacher, as well as the odd workshop presented to groups of teachers on professional development days. Many teachers, once armed with their certificate, do not return to a faculty of education for further upgrading through inservice or graduate courses, and remain firmly convinced that "teachers' college" is exactly the same as it was when they attended perhaps 15 or 20 years earlier. It is little wonder then that myths abound on both sides as to what really transpires in the "ivory tower" of the faculty or "down in the trenches" of the schools.

Surely, there must be a way of utilizing the knowledge and expertise of the faculty professors and school practitioners such that their expectations can be harmonized effectively, and teacher education can be enhanced. However, as long as the faculty and field do not communicate any better than is often the case now, misconceptions will prevail, and teacher education—and the profession—stand to lose. Closer collaboration with the field would seem to provide a solution. A common ground where both have a vested interest is the practicum.

A Possible Solution: Field and Faculty Collaboration

This chapter describes a case where the faculty and field had to cooperate in order to meet a goal that both had but could not fulfil without the assistance of the other partner. It is derived from a two-year collaborative project involved in the preparation of elementary French immersion teachers. The teacher certification programme in Ontario did not really allow for the preparation of French immersion teachers during the preservice year. (In Ontario, most teacher education takes place at a faculty of education consecutive to the completion of a B.A. or B.Sc. degree at a university.) Elementary French immersion teachers were in demand, and immersion schools preferred to hire teachers who had received some training in the theory of second language acquisition at a faculty, but who also had some experience in teaching in an immersion setting during their preservice year. By adapting the existing programme in the faculty, methods courses could be provided to the teachers, but they had little meaning for the trainee teachers without school-based experience in an immersion setting.

When the school that was chosen to collaborate in the experiment agreed to participate, a programme was set up that would make best use of the expertise of both institutions. As such, the faculty advisers and school staff planned together how the programme would evolve; the faculty instructors devised a course, but it was a teacher in the school who came to the faculty to teach it to the students in the programme. As a staff member in the school, he was able to work closely with colleagues who were to accept the students during the practice teaching sessions, and as a result adapted and tailored the course to the needs of the actual classes. Naturally, the administrators in the school also were involved in the experiment, especially in the selection of the associate teachers. In part, the school had been chosen because of the philosophy of the administrators toward teacher education, mentoring, and induction. It was felt that the ambience of that particular school would be most beneficial to student teachers, who by participating in a programme that added another dimension to their preparation, that of teaching in a French immersion school where all subjects would be taught in a second language, needed considerable support and encouragement.

This chapter draws on the testimony of some of the key players in the experiment—the faculty advisers, the principal of the school, the teacher who also served as instructor for the course, and a graduate of the programme, now a full-time teacher. Their comments reveal the potential for working in the field to develop a greater understanding between two of the key com- ponents of teacher education as well as to provide greater support for stu- dent teachers during their preparation to enter the profession. Most of all, the experiment shows that such a collaboration between faculty and field can forge the best links between theory and practice without underemphasizing one or the other, and in a way that is meaningful to student teachers.

At the conclusion of the two-year programme, some of the key players were gathered together for a round-table discussion. The goal was to revisit the project from the various perspectives of those who had been central to it. The programme had been a success; everyone was satisfied with the process and outcomes within the parameters of the project. Now it was time to explore what exactly it was about the programme that each of the key participants had found particularly striking or conducive to improved teacher education. Naturally, as faculty advisers, we wondered how closely our perceptions of the programme coincided with those of the principal, instructor, and student teachers. From the perspective of the faculty, the programme had afforded a chance to prepare teachers for the first time for immersion classrooms during the preservice year and to provide them with practicum time in an immersion school. The project also enabled the faculty to get to know one school very well—to develop a close working relationship with the principal and vice principal, to meet and speak with teachers with whom we would not have had contact under normal circumstances since they were not associates, and to appreciate better the routines of this particular school. Because as faculty advisers, we concentrated our time in one school instead of the previous "flying visit" to numerous schools, each with one or two students only, we felt more comfortable and welcome when we visited "our" project school. I believe that this approach certainly informed our teaching back in the faculty, and, as an added benefit, the school staff saw us more as colleagues than as "teachers college masters."

The principal was completely supportive of the project. He could see the advantage of forging closer ties with the faculty, and it was an added bonus that as a final assignment in the project, each student teacher developed a unit of work geared to provide enrichment materials or remedial work for designated groups of students within the school—thus, the school got some concrete curriculum development from the project.

The principal also agreed with the faculty advisers that if collegiality was to be a central feature in the experiment, the contact had to go beyond assigned practice teaching sessions. Collegiality was promoted by early visits to the school by the student teachers accompanied by the faculty advisers. At an early meeting, the faculty advisers met with the staff as a whole to outline the way they anticipated the programme would work. That set up the necessary two-way communication between the faculty and staff, but also prepared all concerned for the slightly different role the student teachers would be playing. As the principal explained:

Our candidates came to us. They visited the school before they taught in a very social setting where they had an opportunity to appreciate the lay of the land in terms of the school and the staff.

They had a chance to discover the style of the school. They had a chance to interact informally. They had the opportunity of making contacts not just with the associate teacher, but with other members of the staff. Too often, I believe there's a tendency within the teacher-training process for the contact to be only two-way— associate and student. And this project has a lot of strengths in as much as it brings the student into a setting where they become, in essence, a member of the school staff almost immediately. I think that's extremely important because no one associate teacher can provide the kind of insights that are key in being an effective teacher within an 8 to 10 month period. The communication links were very powerful in the project: three-way communication, faculty, student teacher, and associate teacher. There was a lot of communication in the process. Very quickly in this project, team-play came into place, and I think that was a key in the effectiveness of the training.

The principal was not referring to the assigned practicum time; in fact, the students in this project received only three out of ten assigned practice teaching weeks in the project school itself. He meant that the student teachers needed to interact with staff members in the school outside of the practicum in order to appreciate the ambience of an immersion school.

It is interesting, though, that he did not think the schools could take over the teacher preparation completely but accepted the faculty role in providing the theory and background methodology necessary for FSL teaching. He just stressed that in order to relate theory and practice, and to turn theory into practice, it helped to include early visitation to the school.

The student from the project confirmed this attitude and also spoke in favour of an early teaching experience in the immersion school:

> ...it is critical to understand and believe in the philosophy behind immersion, and the turning point for me was my experience [at the immersion school]...All the methods and wonderful philosophy didn't come together for me until I had been out there. I just can't say enough about that early introduction. Just get out there and see; yes, it does work.

The melding of theory and practice by combining faculty lectures, readings, and presentations with concurrent visits to the classroom is of particular importance in immersion situations because it is a different approach. Those involved in immersion schools as well as aspiring teachers of immersion always confirm that one never really believes that immersion works until one sees it in action. However, it would seem to be sensible to use the same approach in regular teacher education to bridge the gap between what goes on in the faculty and what transpires in the field.

A feature of the collaborative approach that this project encouraged was increased communication among all the participants. Both the instructor of the course and the student teacher stressed the importance of the classroom discussions at the faculty among the student teachers regarding their observations in the school. Through these discussions and through the journal entries that the students provided and the instructor responded to, the students began to relate the theory and methodology they were learning at the faculty to what they had observed in the school.

The instructor, himself, entered into a new sort of collaboration with his colleagues at the school in that he observed the classes of those who would serve as associate teachers in order to tailor his course at the faculty to the classes the students would be teaching during the practicum. This task involved some delicate negotiations with colleagues, but led to growth in the instructor, himself. As he reported:

> When I was approached to instruct the course, it was with a sense of awe and somewhat overwhelming because of the implications of what teaching this course would involve. I began by approaching my colleagues at the school to ask for their participation...My viewpoint was that I needed to be in their classroom at least once to see what kind of teaching styles they had,...to reassure myself that I was going to be on track with where they were headed.

> What I found most interesting from teaching the course over the two-year period was how individual teachers are, and how difficult it is to address everyone's needs.

The peer collaboration and observation that the instructor undertook in his school in order to develop the faculty course is probably not typical of most schools. Nevertheless, it could be adapted in schools that wish to develop a peer coaching model, where individual teachers could consult with any other teacher who wanted to share a new approach, work out a new curriculum, or collaborate on solving a classroom problem.

Conclusions

This article has dealt with the benefits of close cooperation between the faculty of education and the field, but the specific project discussed involved teacher education of French immersion teachers. As such, there are elements particularly pertinent for immersion teaching. In teacher education, close cooperation between the faculty and the field is important, but in the preparation of immersion teachers, it is essential. As the principal pointed out, immersion education is a relatively new phenomenon, and normally, student teachers cannot draw on personal experience to understand immersion. Indeed, none of the practising teachers at the immersion school had experience with it before they became immersion teachers. None of the students teachers in our programme had received their elementary or secondary education in an immersion school. Hence, they had no more than a superficial familiarity with the programme. Certain features of immersion schools cannot be adequately covered in a faculty course or during a short practicum assignment in a school. The issue of scepticism about the feasibility of immersion in general is a case in point. The student teacher mentioned that she did not really believe immersion could work—all positive research reports notwithstanding—until she spent time in an immersion school.

The principal underlined that position and commented that administrators and teachers in French immersion schools routinely face parents who are sceptical about the phenomenon—who are worried that they may have made an unwise choice in placing their child in immersion. Staff members in a French immersion school know that the approach works and generally very successfully, but have to be well-informed about immersion teaching and confident about it in order to allay the fears of parents. The principal stressed the need for a nurturing environment in an immersion school that supports children when they take the necessary risks of trying to express themselves in a language that is not their first language or try to learn subject content taught in a second language. He also stressed that immersion schools are both different from and similar to first language schools but that one cannot appreciate the similarities and differences without exposure to the phenomenon. Finally, he mentioned that because of the uniqueness of immersion education, teachers in such programmes must be prepared to be observed in action far more often than regular teachers—parents, trustees, board officials, and others are curious about French immersion, and are welcomed into the schools where it is the approach used to see what it is all about. One of the main benefits the principal saw in the special project was the chance for future French immersion teachers to begin to accustom themselves to the realities of this type of teaching before they actually accepted an immersion post.

Undoubtedly, it can be argued that there are realities of any school that can only be appreciated through familiarity with the school. The kind of cooperative experience we undertook for French immersion teaching could benefit teacher education, in general. The kind of mentoring encouraged at the school in our project was necessary to make the programme work. If the model were adopted in other schools, mentoring and peer coaching for student and novice teachers would become a part of the induction into the profession. Such an approach would surely help to alleviate the isolation that new teachers feel when beginning their career—an isolation that all too often contributes to young teachers leaving the profession after only a brief tenure.

In the United States, 30% of beginning teachers abandon teaching during the first five years (Rosenholtz, 1987). In Canada, the figures are lower, but there is still considerable drop-out. This unfortunate loss to the profession of promising candidates points not to poor preparation necessarily, but rather to the need for an induction programme or peer coaching for beginning teachers (see Cole & McNay, 1988).

With regard to our programme to prepare French immersion teachers, it benefited student teachers who, through the programme, not only became more familiar with life in an immersion school than they would have under normal teacher training, but also they were better able to link what they learned at the faculty with the practice of teaching in the field. It benefited our faculty because our own teaching was informed by our experiences in working closely with one school in the field. We also benefited from a diminution of suspicion with which the members of the field often regard us. Finally, the field benefited because they had access to some fine student teachers who worked with them and developed specialized materials for them. In fact, after the project ended, the board hired one or two of the students who wished to stay in the region. The immersion teachers in the school also worked more collaboratively among themselves as a result of the project.

Because of this French immersion teacher development project and some others that ran simultaneously with it, our faculty has now altered our practicum arrangements to reflect more closely the objectives we followed in the projects. So far, it seems to be working well.

References

Allen, D. W., & Ryan, K. (1969). *Microteaching*. Reading, MA: Addison-Wesley.

Allender, J. A. (1982). Fourth grade fantasy. *Journal of Humanistic Education, 6*, 36-41.

Amarel, M. (1988). Developmental teacher education. In *Dialogues in teacher education* (Issue paper 88-4). East Lansing, MI: Michigan State University, National Center for Research on Teacher Education.

Among Teachers Community. (1991). *An invitation to join*. Toronto, ON: The Ontario Institute for Studies in Education and the Faculty of Education, University of Toronto, Joint Centre for Teacher Development.

Association of Teacher Educators. (1991). *Restructuring the education of teachers* (Report of the Commission on the Education of Teachers into the 21st Century). Reston, VA: Author.

Atkin, J. M., & Raths, J. D. (1974). *Changing patterns of teacher education in the U.S.* Paris: Organization for Economic Cooperation and Development.

Ball, S. J., & Goodson, I. F. (Eds.). (1985). *Teachers lives and careers*. Philadelphia: Falmer Press.

Bateson, M. (1989). *Composing a life*. New York: The Atlantic Monthly Press.

Beattie, M. (1991). *The making of a music: The construction and reconstruction of a teacher's personal practical knowledge during inquiry*. Paper presented at the meeting of the International Society for Educational Biography, Toronto, ON.

Becker, H. S., & Geer, B. (1971). Latent culture: A note on the theory of latent social roles. In B. R. Cosin, I. R. Dale, G. M. Esland, D. Mackinnon, & D. F. Swift (Eds.), *School and society: A sociological reader* (pp. 52-56). London: Routledge and Kegan Paul.

Berliner, D. C. (1984). The half-full glass: A review of research on teaching. In P. Hosford (Ed.), *Using what we know about teaching* (pp. 51-77). Alexandria, VA: Association of Supervision & Curriculum Development.

Berliner, D. C. (1986). In pursuit of the expert pedagogue. *Educational Researcher, 15*(7), 5-13.

Bestor, A. (1953). *Educational wastelands*. Urbana, IL: University of Illinois Press.

Bissex, G. L., & Bullock, R. H. (Eds.). (1987). *Seeing for ourselves: Case-study research by teachers of writing*. Portsmouth, NH: Heinemann.

Blumberg, A. (1989). *School administration as a craft: Foundations of practice*. Boston: Allyn & Bacon.

Booth, W. C. (1988). *The vocation of a teacher: Rhetorical occasions 1967-1988*. Chicago: University of Chicago Press.

Borg, W. (1970). *The minicourse.* Beverly Hills, CA: Macmillan Educational Services.

Borrowman, M. (1956). *The liberal and the technical in teacher education: A historical survey of American thought.* New York: Teachers College, Bureau of Publications.

Borrowman, M. (1965). Liberal education and the professional preparation of teachers. In M. L. Borrowman (Ed.), *Teacher education in the U.S.: A documentary history* (pp. 1-53). New York: Teachers College Press.

Bowman, J. (Ed.). (1991). *A report to the College of Teachers on teacher education in British Columbia.* Vancouver: B.C. College of Teachers.

Brine, J. M., & Shapson, S. M. (1989). Case study of a teacher retraining program for French immmersion. *The Canadian Modern Language Review, 45,* 464-477.

British Columbia Commission on Education. (1974). *Teacher education in British Columbia - Final report.* Victoria, BC: Author.

British Columbia, Royal Commission on Education. (1988). *A legacy for learners: The report of the royal commission on education.* Victoria, BC: Author.

British Columbia Teachers Federation. (1974). *Proposed teaching profession act.* Vancouver, BC: Author.

Britzman, D. (1989). Who has the floor: Curriculum, teaching, and the English student teacher's struggle for voice. *Curriculum Inquiry, 19,* 143-162.

Britzman, D. (1991). *Practice makes practice: A critical study of learning to teach.* Albany, NY: State University of New York Press.

Broudy, H. S. (1956). Teaching—craft or profession? *Educational Forum, 20,* 175-184.

Brown, H. (1938). A challenge to teachers colleges, *Social Frontier, 4,* 327-329.

Brucherhoff, C. E. (1991). *Between classes: Faculty life at Trueman High.* New York: Teachers College Press.

Bullough, R. V., Jr. (1989). *First year teacher: A case study.* New York: Teachers College Press.

Bullough, R. V., Jr., Knowles, J. G., & Crow, N. A. (1991). *Emerging as a teacher.* New York: Routledge.

Calvé, P. (1983). La formation des enseignants en FSL: Le parent pauvre d'un riche patrimoine. *The Canadian Modern Language Review, 40*(1), 14-18.

Canter, L., & Canter, M. (1976). *Assertive discipline.* Santa Monica, CA: Canter and Associates.

Carnegie Forum on Education and the Economy. (1986). *A nation prepared: Teachers for the 21st century.* New York: Author.

Carr, W., & Kemmis, S. (1986). *Becoming critical: Education, knowledge and action research.* London: Falmer Press.

Casey, K. (1988). *Teacher as author: Life history narratives of contemporary women teachers working for social change.* Unpublished doctoral dissertation, University of Wisconsin, Madison.

Casey, K. (1992). Why do progressive women activists leave teaching? Theory, methodology and politics in life history research. In I. F. Goodson (Ed.), *Studying Teachers' Lives* (pp. 187-208). London: Routledge.

Casey, K., & Apple, M. W. (1989). Gender and the conditions of teachers' work: The development of understanding in America. In S. Acker (Ed.), *Teachers, gender and careers* (pp. 171-186). London: Falmer Press.

Cassidy, T. (1986). Initiating and encouraging action research in comprehensive schools. In D. Hustler, A. Cassidy, & E. C. Cuff (Eds.), *Action research in classrooms and schools* (pp. 133-142). London: Allen & Unwin.

Cavanaugh, J. C., Kramer, D. A., Sinnott, J. D., Camp, C. J., & Markley, R. P. (1985). On missing links and such: Interfaces between cognitive research and everyday problem-solving. *Human Development, 28,* 146-168.

Charters W. W., & Waples, D. (1929). *Commonwealth teacher training study.* Chicago: University of Chicago Press.

Chi, M., Glaser, R., & Farr, M. J. (Eds.). (1989). *The nature of expertise.* Hillsdale, NJ: Erlbaum.

Chubb, J., & Moe, T. (1990). *Politics, markets, and America's schools.* Washington, DC: Brookings Institution.

Clandinin, D. J. (1986). *Classroom practice: Teachers images in action.* London: Falmer Press.

Clandinin D. J. (1988, June). *Understanding research on teaching as feminist research.* Paper presented at the meeting of the Canadian Society for the Study of Education, Windsor, ON.

Clandinin, D. J., & Connelly, F. M. (1986). Rhythms in teaching: The narrative study of teachers' personal knowledge of classrooms. *Teaching and teacher education, 2,* 377-387.

Clandinin, D. J., & Connelly, F. M. (1988). Studying teachers' knowledge of classrooms: Collaborative research, ethics, and the negotiation of narrative. *The Journal of Educational Thought, 22,* 269-282.

Clandinin, D. J., Davies, A., Hogan, P., &, Kennard, B. (Eds.). (1993). *Learning to teach, teaching to learn: Stories of collaboration in teacher education.* New York: Teachers College Press.

Clark, C. M. (1988). Asking the right questions about teacher preparation: Contributions of research on teacher thinking. *Educational Researcher, 17*(2), 5-12.

Clark, C. M. (1991). Teachers as designers in self-directed professional development. In A. Hargreaves, & M. Fullan (Eds.), *Understanding teacher development* (pp. 105-120). London: Cassell.

Clifford, G. J., & Guthrie, J. W. (1988). *Ed school: A brief for professional education.* Chicago: University of Chicago Press.

Clift, R. T., Houston, W. R., & Pugach, M. C. (Eds.). (1990). *Encouraging reflective practice in education: An analysis of issues and programs.* New York: Teachers College Press.

Cochran-Smith, M. (1991). Learning to teach against the grain. *Harvard*

Educational Review, 61, 279-310.

Cochran-Smith, M., & Lytle, S. L. (1990). Research on teaching and teacher research: The issues that divide. *Educational Researcher, 19*(2), 2-11.

Cohen, D. (1977). *Ideas and action: Social science and craft in educational practice.* Chicago: Center for New Schools.

Cohen, S. (1976). The history of the history of American education. *Harvard Educational Review, 46*, 298-330.

Cohn, J. (1960). A coefficient of agreement for nominal scales. *Educational and Psychological Measurements, 20*, 37-46.

Cole, A.L. (1987). *Teachers' spontaneous adaptations: A mutual interpretation.* Unpublished doctoral dissertation, The University of Toronto, Toronto, ON.

Cole, A. L. (1988). Personal signals in spontaneous teaching practice. *International Journal of Qualitative Studies in Education, 2*(1), 25-39.

Cole, A. L. (1989). Researcher and teacher: Partners in theory building. *Journal of Education for Teaching, 15*, 225-237.

Cole, A. L. (1990). Personal theories of teaching: Development in the formative years. *Alberta Journal of Educational Research, 36*, 203-222.

Cole, A. L. (1991a). Relationships in the workplace: Doing what comes naturally? *International Journal of Teaching and Teacher Education, 7*, 415-426.

Cole, A. L. (1991b). Interviewing for life history: A process of ongoing negotiation. In I. F. Goodson, & J. M. Mangan (Eds.), *RUCCUS Occasional Papers, Vol. 1., Qualitative educational research studies: Methodologies in transition* (pp. 185-208). London, ON: University of Western Ontario.

Cole, A. L. (1992). Teacher development in the workplace: Rethinking the appropriation of professional relationships. *Teachers College Record, 94*, 365-381.

Cole, A. L., & Knowles, J. G. (1992). *Beginning teachers talk: Who listens? Who learns?* Paper presented at the meeting of the Canadian Society for the Study of Education, Charlottetown, PE, Canada.

Cole, A. L., & McNay, M. (1988). Induction programs in Ontario schools: Issues and possibilities. *Education Canada, 28*(4), 4-11, 44-45.

Collingwood, R. G. (1938). *The principles of art.* Indianapolis, IN: Hackett.

Combs, A. (1972). Some basic concepts for teacher education. *Journal of Teacher Education, 22*, 286-290.

Conle, C., Connelly, F. M., & Nicholson, K. (1991). *The telling of stories of experience as curricular events in a group context.* Paper presented at the meeting of the American Educational Research Association, Chicago.

Conle, C., Eastman, T., & Nitsis, V. (1991). *Narrative echoing: Resonance and reconstruction in stories of experience.* Paper presented at the meeting of the American Educational Research Association, Chicago.

Connelly, F. M., & Clandinin, D. J. (1985). Personal practical knowledge and the modes of knowing: Relevance for teaching and learning. In E. Eisner (Ed.), *Learning and teaching the ways of knowing: Eighty-fourth Yearbook for the National Society for the Study of Education* (pp. 174-198). Chicago: National Society for the

Study of Education.

Connelly, F. M., & Clandinin, D. J. (1988). *Teachers as curriculum planners: Narratives of experience*. New York: Teachers College Press.

Connelly, F. M., & Clandinin, D. J. (1990). Stories of experience and narrative inquiry. *Educational Researcher, 19*(5), 2-14.

Counts, G. (1932). *Dare the schools build a new social order?* New York: John Day.

Cremin, L. (1953). The heritage of American teacher education. *Journal of Teacher Education, 4*, 163-170.

Crook, P. (1974). *A study of selected teacher training programs in the U.S. committed to a philosophy of "open education."* Unpublished doctoral dissertation, Syracuse University, Syracuse, NY.

Crow, N. (1987). *Preservice teachers' biographies: A case study*. Unpublished doctoral dissertation, University of Utah, Salt Lake City, UT.

Cruickshank, D. (1986). *Models for the preparation of America's teachers*. Bloomington, IN: Phi Delta Kappa.

Cruickshank, D. (1987). *Reflective teaching: The preparation of students of teaching*. Reston, VA: Association of Teacher Educators.

Cummings, A. L., Murray, H. G., & Martin, J. (1989). Protocol analysis of the social problem solving of teachers. *American Educational Research Journal, 26*, 25-43.

Daiker, D. A., & Morenberg, M. (Eds.). (1990). *The writing teacher as researcher: Essays in the theory and practice of class-based research*. Portsmouth, NH: Boynton Cook.

Day, C. (1987). Professional learning through collaborative in-service activity. In J. Smyth (Ed.), *Educating teachers: Changing the nature of pedagogical knowledge* (pp. 207-222). London: Falmer Press.

Dewey, J. (1938). *Experience and education*. New York: Collier Books.

Diamond, C. T. (1991). *Teacher education as transformation*. Philadelphia: Open University Press.

Duckworth, E. (1986). Teaching as research. *Harvard Educational Review, 56*, 481-495.

Dunkin, M. J., & Biddle, B. J. (1974). *The study of teaching*. New York: Holt, Rinehart and Winston.

D'Zurilla, T. J., & Goldfried, M. R. (1971). Problem solving and behaviour modification. *Journal of Abnormal Psychology, 78*, 107-126.

Eisner, E. W. (1988). Foreword. In F. M. Connelly, & D. J. Clandinin (Eds.), *Teachers as curriculum planners: Narratives of experience* (pp. ix-xi). New York: Teachers College Press.

Eisner, E. W. (1991). *The enlightened eye: Qualitative inquiry and the enhancement of educational practice*. New York: Macmillan.

Eisner, E. W., & Peshkin, A. (Eds.). (1990). *Qualitative inquiry in education: The continuing debate*. New York: Teachers College Press.

Elliott, J. (1981). *Action research: Framework for self evaluation in schools* (TIQL

Working Paper No. 1.). Cambridge, England: Cambridge Institute of Education.

Elliott, J. (1991). *Action research for educational change*. Buckingham, England: Open University Press.

Erickson, F. (1991). *Teacher research and research on teaching: Perspectives and paradoxes*. Symposium conducted at the meeting of the American Educational Research Association, Chicago.

Ericsson, K. A., & Simon, H. A. (1984). *Protocol analysis: Verbal reports as data*. Cambridge, MA: MIT Press.

Erikson, E. H. (1959). *Identity and the life cycle: Selected papers*. New York: International Universities Press.

Eylon, B. S., & Linn, M. C. (1988). Learning and instruction: An examination of four research perspectives in science education. *Review of Educational Research, 58*, 251-301.

Feiman-Nemser, S. (1990). Teacher preparation: Structural and conceptual alternatives. In W. R. Houston (Ed.), *Handbook of research on teacher education* (pp. 212-233). New York: Macmillan.

Feiman-Nemser, S., & Featherstone, H. (Eds.). (1992). *Exploring teaching: Adventures of teachers and students in an introductory course*. New York: Teachers College Press.

Feiman-Nemser, S., & Floden, R. (1986). The cultures of teaching. In M. Wittrock (Ed.), *The handbook of research on teaching* (pp. 505-526). New York: Macmillan.

Feldman, A. (in press). Promoting equitable collaboration between university researchers and school teachers. *International Journal of Qualitative Studies in Education*.

Fennema, E., Carpenter, T., & Peterson, P. (1989). Learning mathematics with understanding: Cognitively guided instruction. In J. Brophy (Ed.), *Advances in research on teaching*. Vol 1, *Teaching for meaningful understanding and self-regulated learning* (pp. 195-221). Greenwich, CT: Jai.

Flexner, A. (1930). *Universities: American, English, German*. Oxford, England: Oxford University Press.

Fliesser, C. (1988). *The induction of technical/vocational teachers in a community college setting*. Unpublished master's thesis, University of Western Ontario, London, ON, Canada.

Fogarty, J. L., Wang, M. C., & Creek, R. (1983). A descriptive study of novice and experienced teachers' interactive thoughts and actions. *Journal of Educational Research, 77*(1), 22-32.

Fortin, N. G. (1991). *Collaborative stories: Teaching and the teacher-educator*. Unpublished doctoral dissertation, University of Alberta, Edmonton, AB, Canada.

Fosnot, C. T. (1989). *Enquiring teachers, enquiring learners: A constructionist approach for teaching*. New York: Teachers College Press.

Fox, D. (1983). Personal theories of teaching. *Studies in Higher Education, 8*(2), 151-163.

Frederiksen, N. (1984). Implications of cognitive theory for instruction in problem solving. *Review of Educational Research, 54,* 363-407.

Frisson-Rickson, F., & Rebuffot, J. (1986). *La formation et le perfectionnement des professeurs en immersion: Pour des critères nationaux.* Ottawa, ON: Association canadienne des professeurs d'immersion.

Fullan, M. G. (1991). *Overcoming barriers to educational change.* Unpublished manuscript.

Fullan, M. G. (1991, October). *Redefining the curriculum of teacher education.* Paper presented at the conference on "Continuity and Change in Teacher Education," Faculty of Education, University of Western Ontario, London, ON, Canada.

Fullan, M., Connelly, F. M., & Watson, N. (1990). *Teacher education in Ontario: Current practices and options for the future.* Toronto, ON: Ontario Ministry of Education and Ministry of Colleges and Universities.

Fuller, F. (1974). A conceptual framework for a personalized teacher education program. *Theory into Practice, 13*(2), 112-122.

Gadamer, H. (1975). *Truth and method.* New York: The Seabury Press.

Gage, N. L. (Ed.). (1963). *Handbook of research on teaching.* Chicago: Rand McNally.

Gage, N. L. (1985). *Hard gains in the soft sciences: The case of pedagogy.* Bloomington, IN: Phi Delta Kappa.

Gage, N. L., & Winne, P. (1975). Performance-based teacher education. In K. Ryan (Ed.), *Teacher education* (pp. 146-172). Chicago: University of Chicago Press.

Gardner, H. (1983). *Frames of mind.* New York: Basic Books.

Gentile, J. R. (1988). *Instructional improvement: Summary and analysis of Madeline Hunter's essential elements of instruction and supervision.* Oxford, OH: National Staff Development Council.

Glaser, R. (1990). The reemergence of learning theory within instructional research. *American Psychologist, 45,* 29-39.

Gomez, M. L. (1991). Teaching a language of opportunity in a language arts methods class. In B. R. Tabachnick, & K. Zeichner (Eds.), *Issues and practices in inquiry-oriented teacher education* (pp. 91-112). Philadelphia: Falmer Press.

Goodlad, J. (1990a). *Places where teachers are taught.* San Francisco: Jossey-Bass.

Goodlad, J. (1990b). *Teachers for our nation's schools.* San Francisco: Jossey-Bass.

Goodlad, J., Soder, R., & Sirotnik, K. (Eds.). (1990). *The moral dimensions of teaching.* San Francisco: Jossey-Bass.

Goodson, I. F. (1984). The use of life histories in the study of teaching. In E. Hammersley (Ed.), *The ethnography of schooling* (pp. 129-54). Chester, England: Bemrose.

Goodson, I. F. (1991). Sponsoring the teacher's voice. *Cambridge Journal of Education, 21,* 35-45.

Goodson, I. F. (1991, October). *The devil's bargain: Educational research and the teacher.* Paper presented at the conference on "Continuity and Change in Teacher

Education," Faculty of Education, University of Western Ontario, London, ON, Canada.

Goodson, I. F. (Ed.). (1992). *Studying teachers' lives*. London: Routledge.

Goodson, I. F. (in press). *Representing teachers*. London: Falmer Press.

Goodson, I. F., & Cole, A. L. (1993). Exploring the teacher's professional knowledge. In D. McLaughin, & W. G. Tierney (Eds.), *Naming silenced lives* (pp. 71-94). New York: Routledge.

Goodson, I. F., & Walker, R. (1991). *Biography, identity and schooling: Episodes in educational research*. London: Falmer Press.

Gore, J., & Zeichner, K. (1991). Action research and reflective teaching in preservice teacher education: A case study from the U.S. *Teaching & Teacher Education, 7*(2), 119-136.

Goswami, D., & Stillman, P. R. (Eds.). (1987). *Reclaiming the classroom: Teacher research as an agency for change*. Upper Montclair, NJ: Boynton Cook.

Grant, C., & Secada, W. (1990). Preparing teachers for diversity. In W. R. Houston (Ed.), *Handbook of research on teacher education* (pp. 403-422). New York: Macmillan.

Greene, M. (1984). How do we think about our craft? In A. Lieberman (Ed.), *Rethinking school improvement: Research, craft, and concept* (pp. 13-25). New York: Teachers College Press.

Grimmett, P. P. (1991, October). *Collaborative teacher development: The vital role of faculty*. Paper presented at the conference on "Understanding Teacher Development," University of Western Ontario, London, ON, Canada.

Grimmett, P. P., & Erickson, G. L. (Eds.). (1988). *Reflection in teacher education*. New York: Teachers College Press.

Grimmett, P. P., & MacKinnon, A. M. (1992). Craft knowledge and the education of teachers. In G. Grant (Ed.), *Review of research in education*, (Vol. 18, (pp. 385-456). Washington, DC: American Educational Research Association.

Grossman, P. L. (1990). *The making of a teacher: Teacher knowledge and teacher education*. New York: Teachers College Press.

Gutman, A. (1987). *Democratic education*. Princeton, NJ: Princeton University Press.

Handal, G., & Lauvas, P. (1987). *Promoting reflective teaching: Supervision in action*. Milton Keynes, England: The Society for Research into Higher Education & Open University Press.

Hargreaves, A. (1986). *Two cultures of schooling*. London: Falmer Press.

Hargreaves, D. H., Hester, S. K., & Mellor, F. J. (1975). *Deviance in classrooms*. London: Routledge.

Hartnett, A., & Naish, M. (1980). Technicians or social bandits? Some moral and political issues in the education of teachers. In P. Woods (Ed.), *Teacher strategies: Explorations in the sociology of the school* (pp. 254-274). London: Croom Helm.

Heppner, P. P., & Krauskopf, C. J. (1987). An information processing approach to personal problem solving. *The Counseling Psychologist, 15*, 371-447.

Herbst, J. (1989). And sadly teach: Teacher education and professionalization in American culture. Madison, WI: University of Wisconsin Press.

Hewson, P., Zeichner, K., & Tabachnick, B. R. (1990). *Developing appropriate conceptions of teaching science during preservice teacher education*. Madison, WI: Wisconsin Center for Educational Research.

Hirsch, E. D. (1988). *Cultural literacy*. New York: Vintage Books.

Hirst, P. (1965). Liberal education and the nature of knowledge. In R. D. Archambault (Ed.), *Philosophical analysis of education* (pp. 113-138). New York: Humanities Press.

Hirst, P. (1989). Implications of government funding policies for research on teaching and teacher education: England and Wales. *Teaching and Teacher Education, 5*, 272.

Hodges, H. A. (1952). *The philosophy of Wilhelm Dilthey*. London: Routledge & Kegan Paul.

Holly, M. J. (1987). *Keeping a personal-professional journal*. Victoria, Australia: Deakin University Press.

Holmes Group. (1986). *Tomorrow's teachers*. East Lansing, MI: Author.

Holmes Group. (1990). *Principles for the design of professional development schools*. East Lansing, MI: Author.

Holmes, H. (1932). The teacher in politics. *Progressive Education, 4*, 414-418.

Holt, L., & Johnston, M. (1988). *A collaborative case study of change: In-service education and teachers' understandings*. Paper presented at the meeting of the American Educational Research Association, New Orleans.

Houser, N. (1990). Teacher-researcher: The synthesis of roles for teacher empowerment. *Action in Teacher Education, 12*, 55-60.

Housner, L. D., & Griffey, D. C. (1985). Teacher cognition: Differences in planning and interactive decision-making between experienced and inexperienced teachers. *Research Quarterly for Exercise and Sport, 56*, 45-53.

Houston, W. R. (Ed.). (1990). *Handbook of research on teacher education*. New York: Macmillan.

Howard, V. A. (1982). *Artistry: The work of artists*. Indianapolis, IN: Hackett.

Howey, K., & Zimpher, N. (1989). *Profiles of preservice teacher education*. Albany, NY: State University of New York Press.

Hunt, D. E. (1980). How to be your own best theorist. *Theory into Practice, 19*, 287-293.

Hunt, D. E. (1987). *Beginning with ourselves: Practice, theory, and human affairs*. Toronto, ON: OISE Press.

Hunt, D. E. (1991). *The renewal of personal energy*. Toronto, ON: OISE Press.

Hunt, D. E., & Gow, J. (1984). How to be your own best theorist II. *Theory into Practice, 18*, 64-71.

Imig, D. G. (1988). Texas revisited. *American Association of Colleges for Teacher Education BRIEFS 9*(7), 2.

Industrial Relations Act, British Columbia Statutes. (1987)

Jackson, P. W. (1968). *Life in classrooms*. New York: Holt, Rinehart & Winston.

Jacob, E. (1987). Qualitative research traditions: A review. *Review of Educational Research, 57*(1), 1-50.

Jarmon, H. (1990). The supervisory experience: An object relations perspective. *Psychotherapy, 27*, 195-201.

Johnson, F. H. (1964). *A history of public education in British Columbia*. Vancouver, BC: Publications Centre, University of British Columbia.

Johnson, W. K. (1989). Teachers and teacher training in the twentieth century. In D. Warren (Ed.), *American teachers: Histories of a profession at work*. New York: Macmillan.

Joint Board of Teacher Education. (1981). *Preparation of teachers for the public schools of British Columbia: Major premises and recommendations*. Vancouver, BC: Ministry of Education, Science and Technology.

Joyce, B. (1975). Conceptions of man and their implications for teacher education. In K. Ryan (Ed.), *Teacher education* (pp. 111-145). Chicago: University of Chicago Press.

Joyce, B., Weil, M., & Wald, R. (1974). Models of teaching in teacher education. An evaluation of instructional systems. *Interchange, 4*, 47-73.

Kagan, D. M. (1988). Teaching as clinical problem solving: A critical examination of the analogy and its implications. *Review of Educational Research, 58*, 482-505.

Kemmis, S., & McTaggart, R. (Eds.). (1988). *The action research planner* (3rd ed.). Victoria, Australia: Deakin University Press.

Kennard, B. (1989). *Confessions of a reformed researcher*. Unpublished manuscript, University of Calgary, AB, Canada.

Kennedy, M. M. (1987). Inexact sciences: Professional education and the development of expertise. In E. Z. Rothkopf (Ed.), *Review of research in education*, (Vol. 14, 133-167). Washington, DC: American Educational Research Association.

Kennedy, M. M. (1990). Choosing a goal for professional education. In W.R. Houston (Ed.), *Handbook of research in teacher education* (pp. 813-825). New York: Macmillan.

Kilpatrick, W. (Ed.). (1933). *The educational frontier*. New York: Century.

Kirk, D. (1986). Beyond the limits of theoretical discourse in teacher education: Towards a critical pedagogy. *Teaching and Teacher Education, 2*, 155-167.

Kirk, G. (1988). Persistence and change in teachers education. In S. Brown, & R. Wake (Eds.), *Education in transition: What role for research?* Edinburgh: The Scottish Council for Research in Education.

Kliebard, H. (1986). *The struggle for the American curriculum, 1893-1958*. Boston: Routledge & Kegan Paul.

Knowles, J. G. (1988). A beginning teacher's experience: Reflections on becoming a teacher. *Language Arts, 65*, 702-712.

Knowles, J. G. (1989). *Beginning teachers' biographies and coping strategies*. Unpublished doctoral dissertation, University of Utah, Salt Lake City, UT.

Knowles, J. G. (1991). *Metaphors of windows on internal narratives: A beginning teacher's reflections on personal history.* Paper presented at "The Narrative and Education" conference the International Society for Educational Biography, University of Toronto, Ontario, Canada.

Knowles, J. G. (1992). Models for understanding preservice and beginning teachers' biographies: Illustrations from case studies. In I. F. Goodson (Ed.), *Studying teachers' lives* (pp. 99-152). London: Routledge.

Knowles, J. G., & Hoefler, V. B. (1989). The student teacher who wouldn't go away: Learning from failure. *Journal of Experiential Education, 12*(2), 14-21.

Knowles, J. G., & Holt-Reynolds, D. (1991). Shaping pedagogies through personal histories in preservice teacher education. *Teachers College Record, 93,* 87-113.

Koerner, J. (1963). *The miseducation of American teachers.* Boston: Houghton Mifflin.

Kohl, H. R. (1986). *On teaching.* New York: Schocken Books.

Kohl, H. R. (1988). *Growing minds: On becoming a teacher.* New York: Harper & Row.

Kozol, J. (1991). *Savage inequalities.* New York: Crown.

Kramer, R. (1991). *Ed school follies: The miseducation of America's teachers.* New York: Free Press.

Labaree, D. F. (1988). *The making of an American high school: The credentials market and Central High School of Philadelphia, 1938-1939.* New Haven, CT: Yale University Press.

Labaree, D. F. (1990). From comprehensive high school to community college: Politics, markets, and the evolution of educational opportunity. In R. G. Corwin (Ed.), *Research in sociology of education and socialization,* (Vol. 9, pp. 203-240). Greenwich, CT: Jai Press.

Labaree, D. F. (1991, October). *Limiting a generous vision: Thoughts on the evolution of American teacher education.* Paper presented at the conference on "Continuity and Change in Teacher Education," Faculty of Education, University of Western Ontario, London, ON, Canada.

Labaree, D. F. (1992a). Doing good, doing science: The Holmes Group reports and the rhetorics of educational reform. *Teachers College Record, 93,* 628-640.

Labaree, D. F. (1992b). Power, knowledge, and the rationalization of teaching: A genealogy of the movement to professionalize teachers. *Harvard Educational Review, 62,* 123-154.

Lakoff, G., & Johnson, M. (1980). *Metaphors we live by.* Chicago: University of Chicago Press.

Lampert, M., & Clark, C. M. (1990). Expert knowledge and expert thinking in teaching: A response to Floden and Klinzing. *Educational Researcher, 19*(5), 21-23.

Lanier, J. E., & Little, J. W. (1986). Research in teacher education. In M. Wittrock (Ed.), *Handbook of research on teaching* (pp. 527-568). New York: Macmillan.

Leinhardt, G. (1990). Capturing craft knowledge in teaching. *Educational Researcher, 19*(2), 18-25.

Leinhardt, G., & Smith, D. (1985). Expertise in mathematics instruction: Subject matter knowledge. *Journal of Educational Psychology, 77*, 241-247.

Levinson, D. J. (1979). *The seasons of a man's life.* New York: Ballantine Books.

Lieberman, A. (Ed.). (1984). *Rethinking school improvement: Research, craft, and concept.* New York: Teachers College Press.

Lieberman, A. (1986). Collaborative research: Working with, not working on. *Educational Leadership, 43*, 28-32.

Liston, D. P., & Zeichner, K. (1991). *Teacher education and the social conditions of schooling.* New York: Routledge.

Little, J. W. (1990). The persistence of privacy: Autonomy and initiative in teachers' professional relations. *Teachers College Record, 91*, 509-536.

Lortie, D. C. (1977). *Schoolteacher: A sociological study.* Chicago: University of Chicago Press.

Louden, W. (1991). *Understanding teaching: Continuity and change in teachers' knowledge.* New York: Teachers College Press.

Lucas, P. (1988). An approach to research-based teacher education through collaborative inquiry. *Journal of Education for Teaching 14*(1), 55-73.

Lynd, A. (1953). *Quackery in the public schools.* Boston: Little Brown.

Maas, J. (1991). Writing and reflection in teacher education. In B. R. Tabachnick, & K. Zeichner (Eds.), *Issues and practices in inquiry-oriented teacher education* (pp. 211-225). Philadelphia: Falmer Press.

Macdonald, H. I. (1985). *Report on the Royal Commission on the financing of elementary and secondary education in Ontario.* Toronto: The Commission.

MacKinnon, A. M., & Grunau, H. (1991, April). *Teacher development through redirection, community, and discourse.* Paper presented at the meeting of the American Educational Research Association, Chicago.

Maher, F. (1991). Gender, reflexivity, and teacher education. In B. R. Tabachnick, & K. Zeichner (Eds.), *Issues & practices in inquiry-oriented teacher education* (pp. 22-34). Philadelphia: Falmer Press.

Majhanovich, S. (1990). Challenge for the 90s: The problem of finding qualified staff for French core and immersion programs. *The Canadian Modern Language Review, 46*, 452-468.

Majhanovich, S., & Fish, S. (1988). Training French immersion teachers for the primary grades. An experimental course at the University of Western Ontario. *Foreign Language Annals, 21*, 311-320.

Marland, P. W. (1977). *A study of teachers' interactive thoughts.* Unpublished doctoral dissertation, University of Alberta, Edmonton, AB, Canada.

Marshall, H. H. (Ed.). (1990). Metaphors we learn by [Special issue]. *Theory into Practice, 29*, 70.

Martin, J. R. (1987). Reforming teacher education: Rethinking liberal education. *Teachers College Record, 88*, 406-410.

Marx, R. W., & Peterson, P. L. (1981). The nature of teacher decision making. In B. R. Joyce, C. C. Brown, & L. Peck (Eds.), *Flexibility in teaching: An excursion into the nature of teaching and training* (pp. 236-255). New York: Longman.

Massey, M. (1980). Teacher training in Canada: The state of the art. *The Canadian Modern Language Review, 37*(1), 25-29.

McKay, D. A., & Marland, P. W. (1978). *Thought processes of teachers.* Paper presented at the Meeting of the American Educational Research Association, Toronto, ON, Canada.

McLaren, P. (1986). *Schooling as a ritual performance.* London: Routledge and Kegan Paul.

Mian, C. (1984). A 'first' for a Toronto high school. In *Language and Society*, Vol. 12. Special Issue: *The Immersion Phenomenon* (pp. 11-14). Ottawa, ON: Office of the Commissioner of Official Languages.

Mills, C. Wright. (1979). *Power, politics and people.* New York: Oxford University Press.

Mitchell, L. S. (1931). Cooperative schools for student teachers. *Progressive Education, 8*, 251-255.

Mitchell, R. (1981). *The graves of academe.* Boston: Little, Brown.

Moeller, P. (1989). French student-teachers: Who knows how good they really are? *The Canadian Modern Language Review, 45*, 445-456.

Mohr, M. M., & MacLean, M. S. (1987). *Working together: A guide for teacher-researchers.* Urbana, IL: National Council of Teachers of English.

Morgan, G., & Smircich, L. (1980). The case for qualitative research. *Academy of Management Review, 5*, 491-500.

Munby, H. (1986). Metaphor in the thinking of teachers: An exploratory study. *Journal of Curriculum Studies, 18*, 197-209.

Munby, H. (1987). *Metaphors, puzzles, and teachers' professional knowledge.* Paper presented at the meeting of the American Educational Research Association, Washington, DC.

Munby, H., & Russell, T. (1989). *Metaphor in the study of teachers' professional knowledge.* Paper presented at the meeting of the American Educational Research Association, San Francisco, CA.

National Institute of Education. (Ed.). (1975). *Teaching as clinical information processing* (Panel 6 Report). Washington, DC: Author.

Neill, A. S. (1960). *Summerhill.* New York: Hart.

Nelson, M. (1992). Using oral histories to reconstruct the experiences of women teachers in Vermont, 1900-1950. In I. F. Goodson (Ed.), *Studying teachers' lives* (pp. 167-186). London: Routledge.

New College. (1936). *Teachers College Record, 38* (1), 1-73.

Nias, J., Southworth, G., & Yeomans, R. (1989). *Staff relationships in the primary school.* London: Cassell.

Noddings, N. (1986). Fidelity in teaching, teacher education, and research for teaching. *Harvard Educational Review, 56*, 496-510.

Noddings, N. (1992). *The challenge to care in schools*. New York: Teachers College Press.

Noffke, S. (1990). *Action research and the work of teachers*. Paper presented at the meeting of the American Educational Research Association, Boston.

Noffke, S., & Brennan, M. (1991). Action research and reflective student teaching at the University of Wisconsin-Madison. In B.R. Tabachnick, & K. Zeichner (Eds.), *Issues & practices in inquiry-oriented teacher education* (pp. 186-201). London: Falmer Press.

Obadia, A. (1984). Le professeur d'immersion, le pivot du nouveau bilinguisme au Canada. *The Canadian Modern Language Review, 41*, 376-387.

Obadia, A. (1985). La formation du professeur d'immersion français au Canada: Une conception philosophique et pédagogique en devenir ou à la recherche d'une troisième voie. *Canadian Journal of Education, 10*, 415-426.

Oberg, A., & McCutcheon, G. (Eds.). (1990). Teacher as researcher [Special Issue]. *Theory into Practice, 29*, 142.

Oja, S., & Smulyan, L. (1989). *Collaborative action research: A developmental approach*. Philadelphia: Falmer Press.

Ontario, Department of Education Regulation 352.s.35 (1965).

Ontario, Legislative Assembly. (1988). *First report of the Select Committee on Education*. Toronto, ON: Author.

Ontario, Legislative Assembly. (1989). *Second report of the Select Committee on Education*. Toronto, ON: Author.

Ontario, Legislative Assembly. (1990a). *Third report of the Select Committee on Education*. Toronto, ON: Author.

Ontario, Legislative Assembly. (1990b). *Fourth report of the Select Committee on Education*. Toronto, ON: Author

Ontario, Ministry of Education. (1990). *Action plan 1990-94*. Toronto, ON: Author.

Ontario, Ministry of Education Regulation 262, 20(8)(c) (1978).

Ontario, Ministry of Education Regulation 262, 1(d), 20(9) (1980).

Ontario, Ministry of Education Regulation 269, 4(3) (1980).

Ontario, Ministry of Education Regulation 557/93, (1993).

Ontario, Royal Commission on Education in Ontario. (1950). *Final report*. Toronto, ON: King's Printer.

Ontario, Royal Commission on Learning. (1994). *For the love of learning: Report of the royal commission on learning*. Toronto, ON: Author.

Paley, V. G. (1981). *Wally's stories*. Cambridge, MA: Harvard University Press.

Paley, V. G. (1989). *White teacher*. Cambridge, MA: Harvard University Press.

Palonsky, S. V. (1986). *900 shows a year: A look at teaching from a teacher's side of the desk*. New York: McGraw-Hill.

Patterson, R. S. (1991). Teacher preparation in the normal school. In L. G. Katz, & J. D. Raths (Eds.), *Advances in teacher education* (Vol 4, pp. 20-36). Norwood, NJ: Ablex.

Perkins, D. N., & Salomon, G. (1989). Are cognitive skills context-bound? *Educational Researcher, 18*(1), 16-25.

Perl, S., & Wilson, N. (1986). *Through teachers' eyes: Portraits of writing teachers at work.* Portsmouth, NH: Heinemann.

Perrone, V. (Ed.). (1989). *Working papers: Reflections on teachers, schools, and communities.* New York: Teachers College Press.

Perrone, V. (1989). Teacher education and progressivism: A historical perspective. In V. Perrone (Ed.), *Working Papers: Reflections on teachers, schools & communities* (pp. 123-136). New York: Teachers College Press.

Perrone, V. (1991). *A letter to teachers: Reflections on schooling and the art of teaching.* San Francisco: Jossey-Bass.

Peterson, P. L. (1988). Teachers' and students' cognitional knowledge for classroom teaching and learning. *Educational Researcher, 17*(5), 5-14.

Peterson, P. L., & Clark, C. M. (1978). Teachers' reports of their cognitive processes during teaching. *American Educational Research Journal, 15*, 555-565.

Peterson, P. L., & Comeaux, M. A. (1987). Teachers' schemata for classroom events: The mental scaffolding of teachers' thinking during classroom instruction. *Teaching and Teacher Education, 3*, 319-331.

Platt, J. J., & Spivack, G. (1975). *Manual for the means-ends problem-solving procedure (MEPS): A measure of interpersonal cognitive problem-solving skill.* Philadelphia: Hahnemann Community Mental Health/Mental Retardation Center.

Pollard, A., & Tann, S. (1987). *Reflective teaching in the primary school.* London: Cassell.

Ponsart, G. (1991, July). *Response to "Dead Poets' Society".* Unpublished manuscript, Simon Fraser University, Burnaby, BC.

Popkewitz, T. S., & Wehlage, G. G. (1973). Accountability: Critique and alternative perspective. *Interchange, 4*(2), 48-62.

Radwanski, G. (1987). *Ontario study of the relevance of education and the issue of dropouts.* Toronto, ON: Ontario Ministry of Education.

Reason, P., & Rowan, J. (Eds.). (1981). *Human inquiry: A sourcebook of new paradigm research.* Chichester, England: Wiley.

Resnick, L. (1991). *Situations for learning and thinking.* Paper presented at the meeting of the American Educational Research Association, Chicago.

Rosenholtz, S. (1987). Workplace conditions of teacher quality and commitment: Implications for the design of teacher induction programs. In G. A. Griffin, & S. Millies (Eds.), *The first years of teaching: Background papers and a proposal* (pp. 15-34). Chicago: Illinois State Board of Education.

Ross, D., & Krogh, S. (1988). From paper to program: A story from elementary PROTEACH. *Peabody Journal of Education, 65*(2), 19-34.

Rudduck, J. (1987). Partnership supervision as a basis for the professional development of new and experienced teachers. In M. F. Wideen, & I. Andrews (Eds.), *Staff development for school improvement* (pp. 129-141). Philadelphia: Falmer Press.

Russell, T., Munby, H., Spafford, C., & Johnston, P. (1988). Learning the professional knowledge of teaching: Metaphors, puzzles, and the theory-practice relationship. In P. P. Grimmett, & G. L. Erickson (Eds.), *Reflection in teacher education* (67-90). New York: Teachers College Press.

Ryle, G. (1949). *The concept of mind.* London: Hutchinson

Sandefur, W. S., & Nicklas, W. L. (1981). Competency-based teacher education. In AACTE institutions: An update. *Phi Delta Kappan, 62,* 747-748.

Saphier, J. (1982). The knowledge base in teaching: It's here, now! In T. M. Amabile, & M. L. Stubbs (Eds.), *Psychological research in the classroom* (pp. 76-95). Toronto, ON: Pergamon.

Sarason, S. (1990). *The predictable failure of educational reform.* San Francisco: Jossey-Bass.

Scheffler, I. (1960). *The language of education.* Springfield, IL: Charles Thomas.

Schneider, B. (1987). Tracing the provenance of teacher education. In T. Popkewitz (Ed.), *Critical studies in teacher education* (pp. 211-241). London: Falmer Press.

Schön, D. A. (1983). *The reflective practitioner: How professionals think in action.* New York: Basic Books.

Schön, D. A. (1987). *Educating the reflective practitioner: Toward a new design for teaching and learning in the professions.* San Francisco: Jossey-Bass.

Schön, D. A. (1988). Coaching reflective practice. In P. P. Grimmett, & G. Erickson (Eds.), *Reflection in teacher education* (pp. 19-29). New York: Teachers College Press.

Schön, D. A. (Ed.). (1991). *The reflective turn: Case studies in and on educational practice.* New York: Teachers College Press.

Schubert, W. H., & Ayers, W. C. (Eds.). (1992). *Teacher lore: Learning from our own experience.* White Plains, NY: Longman.

Schwab, J. J. (1978). The practical: A language for curriculum. In I. Westbury, & N. Wilkof (Eds.), *Science, curriculum and liberal education* (p. 287). Chicago: University of Chicago Press.

Shapiro, B. (1985). *The report of the commission on private schools in Ontario.* Toronto, ON: The Commission.

Shavelson, R. J. (1973). What is the basic teaching skill? *Journal of Teacher Education, 24*(2), 144-150.

Shavelson, R. J. (1976). Teachers' decision making. In N. L. Gage (Ed.), *The psychology of teaching methods,* Seventy-fifth Yearbook of the National Society for the Study of Education (Part I). Chicago: University of Chicago Press.

Shavelson, R. J., Atwood, N. K., & Borko, H. (1977). Experiments on some factors contributing to teachers' pedagogical decisions. *Cambridge Journal of Education, 7,* 51-70.

Shavelson, R. J., & Stern, P. (1981). Research on teachers' pedagogical thoughts, judgements, decisions, and behaviour. *Review of Educational Research, 51,* 455-498.

Sheehy, G. (1976). *Passages: Predictable crises of adult life*. New York: Dutton.

Sheehy, G. (1981). *Pathfinders*. London: Sidgwich & Jackson.

Shulman, L. S. (1987a). Knowledge and teaching: Foundations of the new reform. *Harvard Educational Review, 57*, 1-22.

Shulman, L. S. (1987b). The wisdom of practice: Managing complexity in medicine and teaching. In D. C. Berliner, & B. V. Rosenshine (Eds.), *Talks to teachers* (pp. 369-386). New York: Random House.

Shulman, L. S., & Elstein, A. S. (1975). Problem solving, judgement, and decision making: Implications for educational research. In F.N. Karlinger (Ed.), *Review of research in education* (Vol. 3, pp. 3-42). Itasca, IL: Peacock.

Sikes, P., Measor, L., & Woods, P. (1985). *Teachers careers*. Philadelphia: Falmer Press.

Sikula, J. (1990). National commission reports of the 1980s. In R. Houston (Ed.), *Handbook of research on teacher education* (pp. 62-71). New York: Macmillan.

Simon, A., & Boyer, E. G. (Eds.). (1970). *Mirrors for behavior: An anthology of classroom observation instruments*. Philadelphia: Research for Better Schools.

Sirotnik, K. (1990). Society, schooling, teaching and preparing to teach. In J. Goodlad, R. Soder, & K. Sirotnik (Eds.), *The moral dimensions of teaching* (pp. 296-328). San Francisco: Jossey Bass.

Smith, J. (1983). Quantitative versus qualitative research: An attempt to clarify the issues. *Educational Researcher, 12*(3), 6-13.

Stanley, W. B. (1985). Social reconstructionism for today's social education. *Social Education, 49*, 384-389.

Stern, H. H. (1983). *Fundamental concepts of language teaching*. London: Oxford University Press.

Stones, E. (Ed.). (1990). *A new agenda for teacher education*. Birmingham, England: Carfax.

Strang, H. R., Badt, K., & Kauffman, J. (1987). Micro computer-based simulations for training fundamental teaching skills. *Journal of Teacher Education, 38*, (1), 20-26.

Strevens, P. (1981). Training the teacher of foreign languages: New responsibilities require new patterns of training. *The Canadian Modern Language Review, 37*, 526-534.

Swanson, H. L., O'Connor, J. E., & Cooney, J. B. (1990). An information processing analysis of expert and novice teachers' problem solving. *American Educational Research Journal, 27*, 532-556.

Sykes, G. (1984). Teacher education and the predicament of reform. In C.E. Finn, D. Ravitch, & R. Fancher (Eds.), *Against mediocrity* (pp. 172-194). New York: Holmes & Meier.

Tardiff, C. (1984). La formation des enseignants en situation d'immersion. *The Canadian Modern Language Review, 41*, 365-375.

Taylor, D., & Dorsey-Gaines, C. (1988). *Growing up literate: Learning from inner-city families*. Portsmouth, NH: Heinemann.

Teacher Education Review Steering Committee. (1988). *Final report.* Toronto: Ontario Ministry of Education and Ministry of Colleges and Universities.

Teaching Profession Act, British Columbia Statutes. (1987)

Thiessen, D. (1991a). Living collaboratively in action research. In I. F. Goodson, & J. M. Mangan, (Eds.), *Qualitative educational research studies: Methodologies in transition,* RUCCUS Occasional Papers (Vol. 1, pp. 171-180). London, ON: University of Western Ontario.

Thiessen, D. (1991b). *Influence of student-teacher interactions on the emerging professional identity of a beginning teacher.* Paper presented at the meeting of the American Educational Research Association, Chicago.

Thiessen, D., et. al. (1991). *A review of recent literature on innovations in teacher education.* Toronto, ON: Ontario, Ministry of Education.

Tikunoff, W. J., & Ward, B. A. (1983). Collaborative research on teaching. *The Elementary School Journal, 83,* 455-468.

Tom, A. R. (1980). Teaching as a moral craft: A metaphor for teaching and teacher education. *Curriculum Inquiry, 10,* 317-323.

Tom, A. R. (1984). *Teaching as a moral craft.* New York: Longman.

Tom, A. R. (1991). Whither the professional curriculum for teachers? *Contemporary Education, 14,* 21-30.

Tom, A. R., & Valli, L. (1990). Professional knowledge for teachers. In W. R. Houston (Ed.), *Handbook of research in teacher education* (pp. 373-392). Washington, D.C.: Macmillan.

Traugh, C., Kanevsky, R., Martin, A., Seletsky, A., Woolf, K., & Strieb, L. (1986). *Speaking out: Teachers and teaching.* Grand Forks, ND: North Dakota Study Group on Evaluation.

Travers, R. M. W. (1973). *Second handbook of research on teaching.* Chicago: Rand McNally.

Turner, J. (1990). Teacher education under threat. In E. Stones (Ed.), *A new agenda for teacher education* (pp. 5-10). Birmingham, UK: Carfax.

Uhler, S. (1987). *Alternative paths to entry: New Jersey and elsewhere.* Paper presented at the meeting of the American Educational Research Association, Washington, DC.

Ungerleider, C. (1991). *Power, politics and professionalism: The impact of change in British Columbia on the status of teachers and their professional conduct.* Paper presented at the "Teacher Development: Key to Educational Change" Conference, Vancouver, BC.

van Manen, M. (1977). Linking ways of knowing with ways of being practical. *Curriculum Inquiry 6,* 205-228.

Veblen, T. (1918/1962). *The higher learning in America.* New York: Hill & Wang.

Voss, J. F., Green, T. R., Post, T. A., & Penner, B. C. (1983). Problem solving skill in the social sciences. In G. Gower (Ed.), *The psychology of learning and motivation* (Vol. 17, pp. 165-213). New York: Academic Press.

Ward, B., & Tikunoff, J. (1977, February). *Collaborative research.* Paper presented at the NIE "Implications of Research on Teaching for Practice" Conference, Washington, D.C.

Watkins, C. E. (1990). The separation-individuation process in psychotherapy supervision. *Psychotherapy, 27,* 202-209.

Weade, R., & Ernst, G. (1989). *Through the camera's lens: Pictures of classroom life and the search for metaphors to frame them.* Paper presented at the meeting of the American Educational Research Association, San Francisco.

Whitehead, A. N. (1957). *The aims of education: And other essays.* New York: Macmillan.

Wigginton, E. (1985). *Sometimes a shining moment: The Foxfire experience.* Garden City, NY: Doubleday.

Wigginton, E. (1989). Foxfire grows up. *Harvard Educational Review, 59,* 24-49.

Wigginton, E. (1991). *The Foxfire approach: Perspectives and core practices.* Rabun Gap, GA: The Foxfire Fund, Inc.

Winnicott, D. W. (1965). *The maturational processes and the facilitating environment.* London: Hogarth Press.

Wittgenstein, L. (1958). *Philosophical investigations* (2nd Ed.). Oxford, England: Basil Blackwell.

Wittrock, M. C. (Ed.). (1986). *Handbook of research on teaching* (3rd. Edition). New York: Macmillan

Yinger, R. (1987). Learning the language of practice. *Curriculum Inquiry, 17,* 293-318.

Zeichner, K. (1983). Alternative paradigms of teacher education. *Journal of Teacher Education, 34*(3), 3-9.

Zeichner, K. (1988). *Understanding the character and quality of the academic and professional components of teacher education* (Research Rep. No. 88-1). East Lansing, MI: Michigan State University, National Center for Research on Teacher Education.

Zeichner, K. (1990). Contradictions and tensions in the professionalization of teaching and the democratization of schools. *Teachers College Record, 92,* 363-379.

Zeichner, K. (1991). *Teacher education for social responsibility.* Paper presented at the meeting of the American Educational Research Association, Chicago.

Zeichner, K. (1992, June). *Educating teachers for cultural diversity.* East Lansing, MI: Michigan State University, National Centre for Research on Teacher Education.

Zeichner, K., & Liston, D. (1987). Teaching student teachers to reflect. *Harvard Educational Review, 57,* 1-22.

Zeichner, K., & Tabachnick, B. R. (1991). Reflections on reflective teaching. In B.R. Tabachnick, & K. Zeichner (Eds.), *Issues and practices in inquiry-oriented teacher education* (pp. 1-21). London: Falmer Press.

Zeichner, K., Tabachnick, B. R., & Densmore, K. (1987). Individual, institutional, and cultural influences on the development of teachers' craft knowledge. In

J. Calderhead (Ed.), *Exploring teachers' thinking* (pp. 21-59). London: Cassell.

Zinn, H. (1980). *A people's history of the United States.* New York: Harper & Row.

Zumwalt, K. (1982). Research on teaching: Policy implications for teacher education. In A. Lieberman, & M. McLaughlin (Eds.), *Policy making in education* (pp. 215-248). Chicago: University of Chicago Press.